HEALING WOUNDED HEARTS

Healing Wounded Hearts. (cover)
Eagle. Rainbow Light. Sun Rise. Flowers in Bloom. all give a Vision.
Renewal. Hope.Possibility. help us Heal our Wounded Hearts.
feel Joy and Love in our Lives.
commissioned Beadwork by Maryann Whitefish
(Cree Artist from Northern Saskatchewan).

HEALING WOUNDED HEARTS

FYRE JEAN GRAVELINE

Fernwood Publishing • *Halifax, Nova Scotia*

Editing: Brenda Conroy
Cover image: Beadwork by Maryann Whitefish
Printed and bound in Canada by: Hignell Printing Limited

What Part of No Don't You Understand—revised version appears in American Indian Quarterly, 27(1&2), 2004.
I Dreamed this Job—revised version appears in Carl James (ed.) Experiencing Difference. Fernwood. 2000.
Imagine My Surprise—revised version appears in Canadian Journal of Native Education, 25(1), 2001.
Recovery from Chronic Neutral.itis—revised version appears in International Journal of Qualitative Studies in Education,13(4), 2000.
In Defens'ive Truth—revised version appears in Atlantis. 24(1), 1999.

A publication of:
Fernwood Publishing
32 Oceanvista Lane, Site 2A, Box 5,
Black Point, Nova Scotia, B0J 1B0
and 324 Clare Avenue
Winnipeg, Manitoba, R3L 1S3
www.fernwoodbooks.ca

Fernwood Publishing Company Limited gratefully acknowledges the financial support of the Department of Canadian Heritage, the Manitoba Arts Council, and the Canada Council for the Arts for our publishing program.

Library and Archives Canada Cataloguing in Publication

Graveline, Fyre Jean
Healing wounded hearts / by Fyre Jean Graveline.

Includes bibliographical references.
ISBN 1-55266-142-3

1. Graveline, Fyre Jean. 2. Métis women—Biography. 3. Authors, Canadian (English)—21st century—Biography. I. Title.

PS8613.R377H42 2004   C818'.609   C2004-903471-5

how Love grows

elaborately we place
a bouquet of wax Flowers
on brown bare Soil
our Tears fall like Rainwater
we envision
green tendrils
bursting through Eternity

Words to Know to Read Me

MÉTIS.MITCHIF. are MyPeople.
We are a "people between two worlds."
a mix of Cree. French. and Orkadian Ancestors.
Originally from Red River area.
Now. redistributed around North America.
MITCHIF is a language spoken by Métis people.
Some Métis peoples now prefer.
to refer to themselves as Mitchif peoples.
Sources on Métis.Mitchif culture and history include:
Sealey. Cambell. Barkwell.
on language. see Fleury.
on our infamous leader Louis Riel. see Siggins.
on Gabriel Dumont. see Dumont or Woodcock.
on Anne Marie Lagimodiere. see MacEwan.
on other strong MétisWomen. see Carpenter. Boyd. or Brown.

NEHIYÂW'AK is a word with Mitchif.Cree roots.
I am re-creating it here. to include any Indigenous person.peoples.
those who want to include themselves are welcome to.
I intend to simultaneously culturally locate myself.
and to be inclusive of. and replace. terms previously used.
like Indian. Native. Aboriginal. First Nations. and Métis.
these terms may appear when using quotes of others.
or when Tribal. Historic. or Politically specific terminology is required.

MOONIYÂS also has its roots in NorthernBush.Mitchif.
I am re-creating it here to refer to White peoples. and cultures.
Literally. it can mean People who Talk with Money.
Janice Acoose names WECCP (WhiteEuroCanadianChristianPatriarchal).
Eurocentrism. is also used to refer. to a mindset. or World.View.
"a product of the development of European culture.
People are not genetically encoded to hold this outlook;
they are acculturated to hold it"
says Russell Means. American Indian Movement Activist.
Be Aware. If. You are Uncomfortable.
when White. Mooniyâs. WECCP. Eurocentrism. is mentioned.
You are Not alone.

see Graveline. Jay. McIntosh. Razak.
some say WhiteMan is Trickster. see Keeshig-Tobias.

WISAKECAHK is Trickster's BushCree Name. see Cuthand.
TRICKSTER is a backwards teacher.
She.He. shows us what is Right. by doing what is Wrong.
Trickster is present in literatures of Africa. Thailand. South America.
China. West Indies. New Zealand. Mexico.
and all across North America.
COYOTE is one form Trickster likes to take in Stories. see Bright.
WOLF is Coyote's Cousin. my SpiritGuide.
MAHÊ'KUN is her Cree Name.

INDIGENOUS CREATIVE NON-FICTION
is what you are about to Experience.
I am not only giving. theoretical. information.
I am sharing personal. painful. spiritual discoveries.
telling factual Stories. in a fictional way.
I use original research. reflective journaling.
creative use of Languages. Dialogue.
I Story to make People. Places. Times. Events. Beings. come alive.
I blend Personal and Political. Academic and Poetic.
Humour and Tragedy.
Modern and Traditional. Anger and Forgiveness.
this is a collection of Stories. Narratives. Poetry. Art.
Transitional and Experimental. SocioPolitical yet Playful.
Opinionated and Provocative.
see *Crisp Blue Edges*. Marsden 2000.
for other Indigenous Creative Non-fiction.

my Words. build on Contemporary. Compelling. Brave.
WarriorWomen. WordSmiths. Sisters. like:
Maria Campbell. Beth Brant. Paula Gunn Allen. Jeanette Armstrong.
Lee Maracle. Chrystos. Beatrice Culleton. Ruby Slipperjack.
Louise Erdrich. Linda Hogan. Patricia Monture-Angus. Janice Acoose.
Rita Dion Buffalo. Isabelle Knockwood. Emma LaRocque. bell hooks.
Trin Minh-ha. Clarissa Pinkola Estes. dian marino. Dori Laub.
Seema Kalia. Ester Supernault. Chandra Mohanty, Sherene Razak.
Phyllis Chesler.

Brothers like:

Russell Means. Vine Deloria, Jr. Gregory Cajete. Ben Carniol.
Paulo Freire. Carl James.

and Dazzling. Daring. anthologies like:

Gathering of Spirit. Writing the Circle. Colour of Resistance.
Reinventing the Enemy's Language. Kelusultiek, Into the Moon.
Living the Spirit. All my Relations. Indigena.

GETTING STARTED. ON DIS HEALING.JOURNEY.

Dis Journey.
Travel with me. like Mahe'kun tracking Wapoos (Rabbit). in Snow.Storm.
sometimes Trail will be hard to See. maybe lose Tracks. of where we are goin'.

StoryTelling.
   Nehiyâw'ak Teaching.Healing. tool.
   a Medicine.
         Strengthening. Connecting.
               Individual and Community.
               we understand Power of Language.
                     to Heal. Regenerate. Create.
               Words give Life.
               we open ourselves to others with Words.
               we make Questions. Ponder. Meditate. Dream.
                     Communicate powerful Truths.
                     Enrich our Imaginations.
                     Deepen our Desires to Live.
StoryTellers are Seed Bearers.
   Plant images in our consciousness that take Root and Flower.
      Stories Grow out of our Lives. like Roots grow a Tree.
      Stories grow us. Grow us into who we are.
            these MedicineStories are Twinned. Twisted. Braided.
            are Shaping. Shifting themselves and me.
            are images of possible histories.
                           present realities.
                           unfolding futures.
      Stories contain Incoherencies. are Trickster tales.
      Wisakecahk is with me. side by side. as Witness.
            when I land flat on my Face.
            Be Aware.
                  Falling Down is a very efficient way to learn.
                  Accept me. Share my Fallibility.Vulnerability.
                  Free me to be Wrong. Foolish. Weak.
                     to be Whatever. Whomever I am.
                     this Freedom allows me more Self Respect.
                           more Self Love.
                           less Shame.
Our Ancestors Teach.Heal. with MedicineStories.
   show us Right. and Wrong. ways to Live.
   weave together Mundane and Arcane.
                  Everyday and Supernatural.
   compel linear thought processes. to Chase. Bite. their own Tails.
                  like Coyote. or Mahê'kun.
   Transform from one Place. Condition. Reality.
                  to another.
Healing is enabled through MedicineStories.
                  by amount of Self that I am willing to Sacrifice. put into it.
"There must be a little spilled blood on every Story if it is to carry the medicine."

teaches venerate StoryTeller Clarissa Pinkola Estes.
MedicineStories must be worked with.
Watered with Blood. Sweat. Tears.
Sprinkled with Laughter.
when my Stories Bloom.
I myself burst into Bloom.
Look. See what Medicines. Stories make.
Learn where and when to apply Them.
that is work. my work. This Work.
these MedicineStories happened.
are happening in my Life.
some in educational institutions.
they are accounts of actual interchanges
I am choosing to illustrate. How. When. Where. Why.
Personal growth. Systemic metamorphosis
was. is. will be required.
I give my Breath. Voice.
Blood. Sweat. Tears. Laughter.
in these Stories.
some are about my Healing.
some are about my Teaching.
All I use to Heal. and Teach.
to plant Seed-Thoughts.
to shoot Light Arrows.
this collection is my Speaking Place.
my re-memoried Experiences.
woven with TraditionalTeachings of my Elders.
my Stories are Not Traditional.
it is not my place to decide.
When. Where. by Whom. Whether.
TraditionalTales belong in public realms.
my Stories are Traditional.
they are a statement of Cultural Identity.
my memory continuously Adapts received Traditions.
in present circumstances.
I am re-inventing My.Our. capacities to Survive.
I teach what I know. learn.
careening down dusty. bumpy. curvy. Road. GoodPath.
my Healing.Teaching. Journey.
I know. Live. Difference. between Nehiyâw'ak.
Indian. Bush.
Communal. We Consciousness.
and
Mooniyâs.

White. Cowboy.
Industrial. University. I Consciousness.
I Live. savour Life every Day. in intersecting. parallel. planes of reality.
fifteen years in Recovery. through Ceremony.
twenty-five years in educational institutions. of Higher Learning.
thirty years in WomenCircles. getting my consciousness raised.
almost fifty years of my Life.
through three generations of my MétisAncestors.
I know both Worlds. I know each of them.
how they Collide. Blend together.
I am Weaving. Spinning. fragments of Memory.
into a Coherent. Circular. Cosmic whole.
All details. a full Story.
I believe Stories are Sacred.
meant to be Spoken. to be said Out Loud.
when honouring Oral Tradition.
I choose each word carefully.
aware of Significance. Truth. Beauty.
I re-create Dialogue. Meaning. Events.
for relevance in Telling. Now. in this immediate moment.
I empathize with Dori Laub. as She struggles to craft her Story of Incest.
"There are never enough words or the right words,
there is never enough time or the right time,
and never enough listening or the right listening
to articulate a Story that cannot be fully captured
in thought, memory and speech."
Stories always change. Each telling is Different.
Teller. Audience. Occasion. Time. All creatively combine.
as my Daughter insightfully accuses.
"You change your Story each time you tell it!"
Each audience demands a New version.
Each a True version. as true as Truth can be.
Writing MedicineStories
can drive a Wedge.
between experience as I Live it. as I verbally express it.
can establish distance. between mySelves. my Experiences.
my Community of listeners.
as I struggle to Externalize an Internal understanding.
of a SociallyConstructed reality.
to capture a moment. in Words to last Eternity.
in this One and Only telling.
Storying holds. enfolds. a multiplicity of experiences.
casts Reflections. Connects across Time. Place. Space.
Word Images carved in Stone are solid.

no longer Fluid. Transparent. Flowing.
Shifting as sands of Time slip.
Writing can move me further.
further away from Heart. Soul.
Writing requires Re-inventing. EnemyLanguage.
as I re-place Words on page in these ways.
Expected. Assumed. thought flow. is Interrupted.
I draw on an innate sense of Artistic. Dramatic playfulness.
Spacing. Punctuation. Capitalization. Grammatical Incorrectness.
become Tools to foreground questions.
of Authority. Power. Privilege.
carefully craft Words. Lines. to Create different perspectives.
to Transform. to Surprise. your consciousness.
into new ways of Seeing. Believing.
Linear text flattens out Reality.
my Words paint pictures. my Art talks.
describes. makes sense. re-presents experiences.
Wounded. Healing. Hearts.
as I tell Stories of my Person. my Lives.
I blend Political. Social. Cultural. Spiritual dimensions.
I create Reality. I use accurate details.
Settings. People. Events.
and I don't.
I fictionalize as much as possible. whenever possible.
bend everything. In. and Out. of shape.
can be seen as creative Misinterpretation.
I locate MySelf. my Words. within contemporary Nehiyâw'ak dialogues.
I face. Voicelessness. Stereotypes. Appropriation. Ghettoization.
Linguistic. Cultural. Sexual. and Colonial Cages.
surround my Experience. my Self-Expression.
in concert with my Sisters. I am called to address my Womaness.
Birthing. Mothering. Nurturing. Vulnerability.
Fear of Violence. Sexual Assault. Sexism.
Tensions between Male-defined Traditions and Women's Power.
Loss of Innocence. Hypocrisy. Betrayal.
I Story times I face Black. Cavernous holes. Depression.
Devastation. Death. Discrimination.
BurnOut. Backlash.
I Story how Ceremony. Dreams. Ancestors. StrongWomen.
help me Survive. Thrive. Heal.
to Live another Day.
to tell another Story.
this collection of MedicineStories.
sets out different kinds of information.

Intellectual. Spiritual. Emotional. Material.
Diverse. Disparate sensations are described.
Seen. Heard. Smelled. Tasted. and Touched.
Historical. Contemporary. Futuristic are combined.
Local. National. International. Supernatural.
following examples of Traditional Tellers.
Patterns. Boundaries. Connections. are not sharp or distinct.
barely discernible to some for long stretches.
may be Invisible to you.
use your Nose. to sniff out faint Trails.
in Grasses. Forests. left by small Creatures.
Be. like Wolf. tracking Rabbit through Snow.Storm
Communicating these ways.
is closer to how I experience realities.
Multifaceted. Mobile.
Moving. through many layers. Simultaneously.
this Text. is a Balancing act.
I want to reWeave. Learning with Living.
Cultural contexts with Political realities.
Personal Lives with Societal structures.
Humans with AllBeings.
in Ordinary and NonOrdinary Worlds.
some Beings are friendly towards Humans
who adventure among Them.
many are Unfriendly. Hostile. Dangerous.
my Spiritual Growth evolves by Need.
to court positive helpers.
to avoid or protect against others.
I want to reConnect Heads. Spirits. Hearts. Hands.
Critical. Creative. Art. Academia.
I Resist. Challenge.
prevailing patterns of Alienation. Fragmentation.
that Confine. Define. Shape me.
I make Time to Connect. Words. Images. History.
when words Create. Thoughts are Embraced. Shared.
Connections all happen at once.
HealingWoundedHearts is a process. a flow.
MedicineStories chart movement.
towards Wholeness. Love. Truth. Forgiveness.
taught Not to fight back. turn another Cheek.
too many times. in too many ways.
I know. Now. Truthful words are Medicine.
I choose to carry as WarriorWoman.
Language can be an EnemyWeapon.

used to perpetuate Racism. and Hate.
I must bend and shape language to make Truth.
recreate new ways. to Wordsmith. to Heal. Grow. Love.
Healing does Not occur when I try to Be. what I am Not.
happens when I Live. more of Who I Am.
Ripples move though Water. once Stone is tossed.
when I am Whole. my Heart Voiced.
Healing Ripples. into Ocean of All human experience.
Healing is Inevitable. Vast. Iridescent.
I toss this Stone. deliberately crafted with LovingCare. Conviction.
to open Doorways. create Pathways.
Ripple from centre to periphery. to Heal.
Deep Scars. Stories. Water. Sky. Fire. Earth.
Desire. for a deeper Life. a fuller Life. a saner Life.
All are Doorways. Pathways. to Healing.
Stepping through Doorways takes Courage.
I reach for my WarriorWoman within. to stand beside me.
as I renegotiate old Wounds. Scars from Traumas.
Free myself from a painful past.
Stand up to Tyrants. Abusers.
Internal and External.
Individual and Collective.
be Accountable. Self-disciplined.
willing to serve a Cause bigger than myself.
willing to do whatever it takes to Grow.
willing to Change myself.
my Words. my Worlds.
through MedicineStories I teach and I learn.
I heal and I am healed.
I tell and I listen.
both Teller and Listener are necessary to Story.
both Telling and Listening are Intense. Intentional.
Giving. Receiving. Giving.
complete Circles of Nehiyâw'ak Truth.
Be. Aware. Listen and Learn.
what can you be Surprised into Seeing? Believing?
Watch Out! Land mines are strewn across StoryTelling Paths.
Pay Attention. to how you Hear.
how you take up Stories of my Life.
will you be an innocent bystander to my painful recollections?
will you judge my Life too chaotic? too dysfunctional?
or will you awaken to see yourself. your process?
reflected like Rainbow Light through a prism.
Multifaceted. Beautiful.

where does my.your. Voice come from?
whose Histories. Political realities. forms of Consciousness.
                                    frame my. your. LifeNarratives?
how do multiple realities Shape. Transform.
        Perceptions. Practices. of Teaching.Healing.
                in multiple contexts. Worlds. Global pillage.
                        we find ourselves. immersed in. Today.

We. AllBeings. are Interconnected in Great Web of Life.
    tell me…
        what is our Community? our Unity? what is our Diversity?
        Listen up.
        Learn Me. Learn You.
        Heal Me. Heal You.
            Watch. GrandMother Spider.
                Weave. your Story. within my Stories.
                        your Lives. amidst my Lives.
                as She Weaves. we'll make Fire.
                        and Sing again. ReNewed.
            Welcome to my World. Sit Down. have some Tea.
                don't get too Comfortable.
                        I haven't been.
                this Book. is Not about Happy Endings. or Resolutions.
                    it is about ongoing Struggle.
                    I will not wrap things up.
                        in a tidy package. with a shiny bow.
                            contribute to your Denial.
                                it would be a falsehood. a Lie.
these Stories. are my Voice. my Truth.
    I've told them True to me. True to what I know.
    what my Ancestors knew. what they told me. tell through me.
                                        a Truth.

WARNING!!!

WHILE THESE STORIES
ARE BASED ON MY TRUE LIFE STORY.
SOME CHARACTERS.
A NUMBER OF INCIDENTS.
HAVE BEEN COMPOSITED.
INVENTED.
FICTIONALIZED.
AND ALL NAMES CHANGED.
INCLUDING YOURS.

I begin ...
    I grew up in NorthernBush country.
        Harsh. Untamed. Isolated lands.
  when Rebellions. Resistance Movements. of 1800s were squashed.
    by hanging of Louis Riel. in 1885.
      MyPeople were scattered. South to States. North to Shield.
Métis are a Nation in diaspora.
    as are Acadians of Eastern seaboard.
      Blacks of African continent.
located throughout Prairies. there remain. pockets of Métis culture.
    role models of Resistance. as a Survival Strategy. as a Culture.
MétisCulture is continuously under Creation.
    shaped by Environmental pressures. Survival demands.
      Remembered. Retold. Reshaped.
        through Stories of Riel. Dumont.
        Strong MétisWomen. my Relations. Elders.
we Live through great Stories. of Culture. Race. Place.
nurture for telling Stories. comes from Those who have gone before.
Telling. Hearing Stories. draws Power from Ancestors.
      joins one to another. across Time and Space.
        like Trin Minh-ha. I wish to acknowledge.
          "My Story, no doubt is me,
           but it is also, no doubt, older than me."

A TRIBUTE TO ENDURANCE

to my Auntie Eva. to my Mother. may I Honour you in this Telling. Today.

GentleToothSmile
feeds HungryOnes.
Re.envisioning.
in wake of
colonial Destruction.
Violence.
orphaned Children.
abandoned Women.
fend for ourSelves.
takes Strength.
Determination.
Endurance.
to Survive.
Starvation.

this Story was told many times. by my Mother. GrandMother. Aunties. Cousins. it is a Story told to All Women. Men. and Children. but. it is a Women'sStory. this is TheWay of MyPeople. we view our past Ancestors as Guides. seek Their help. to Survive Life's problems. many times. when my Life is difficult. I am counselled—Remember Eva.

my Auntie Eva. now in Spirit World. is a Woman of Courage and Determination. Her Story is often told. when times are Rough. as a Tribute to Endurance. to let us know. just when you think. you have given. All you can give. you have to give a little bit more. just a little bit more.

when Auntie is very young. She marries a Trapper. they Live in Bush. in a Shack. this is a common Lifestyle. for Nehiyâw'ak people in general. and Métis in specific. Then. AtTheTime. they have no running Water. only Wood heat. Subsist. on what they catch. can harvest. can pack in. when supplies are brought.

Well. it is early fifties. they are "making do." Eva. little teeny four-foot-five-inch Eva. and Arvey. and their twelve Children. it is Winter. Eva is pregnant with her thirteenth Child. this is Not extraordinary. Not considered a large number of Children.

Anyways. Eva is pregnant with her thirteenth Child. when tragedy strikes. Tragedy Struck. Arvey goes off into Bush. does not return. Did

Not Return. maybe He is killed by Bear. maybe He is killed by Gun. NoOne knows. so NoOne tells Story.

what does get talked about is my Auntie Eva. LittleEva. and twelve Babies being left stranded. in Winter. up in northern Bush country. it is cold. so Cold. She has to heat with Wood. Wood is running out. Running Out. Children scavenge. and so does Eva.

they put on all Clothes they have. huddle Together. under all Blankets and Furs they have. especially at Night. especially when NorthWind blows big blizzards. Big Blizzards so white. you can't see hand in front of your face. can you believe it? couldn't See Hand in Front of Your Face. you have to tunnel out. to get outside house.

Winter conditions are nothing new to Eva. She is born to it. but. lack of Wood. No Wood! it is so cold! and No Arvey. No Arvey to go out and get Wood. is a Real Problem. She keeps hoping. Hoping that he will return. or SomeOne. AnyOne. will answer Messages. She sends out to GrandMothers in her need.

"GrandMothers please." She prays as she puts Tobacco down. but. Not only then. She prays at all Times. and in all Places. She prays with her BlackBeads too. She prays to EveryOne. and AnyOne.

it is cold. Really Cold. but. that isn't Eva's only problem. they are also running out of Food. Running Out of Food. they are getting hungrier. and Hungrier. Eva goes to MeatShack each day. cuts a Strip. hacking with SharpKnife. on frozen MeatBone.

whenever I hear Story. as a Girl. I always want to know. "how did you reach It. Auntie? how did you reach so high Auntie?" I know. how high Moose stand is. to keep out of Dogs reach. I know. how tall Auntie is. I have to know. "how did you reach It?" but. I am told. "Hush up. leastwise till She's done." Till She's Done Story. never do find out. or figure it out. one of Life's Mysteries.

Anyways. Eva cooks what little they have. melting Snow and Ice to cook MooseBoneSoup. what you cook when all Meat that can come off is stripped. Soup smell drives them all wild. even Eva. but. She does without. Eva Did Without. She gave what little they have to feed Children. to feed hungry Children. Twelve Hungry Children. Imagine. She Did Without.

That is. until she feels movement quicken. in her Belly. in Her Belly. and she knows. She Knew. She must feed herself. Her inside self.

but. this is nothing new to Eva. who Lived harsh Bush Life of subsistence for many years. She's been hungry many times. felt many Babies quicken in her Belly. delivered Them in her cabin. many times already by herself. by Herself and with Arvey. but. now. it is Different. She trudges out each day to try to hunt. She shoots some small Birds. Partridge. Spruce Grouse. "they taste just like their name." She tells it. Eva traps Rabbits. watches carefully for Trails they leave. She strips Willows. and other Plants. whatever She can find. in places Snow is not too deep.

Eva knows. Animals. Plants. give up their Lives. in order for people to Survive. Life in Bush requires an intimate survival relationship with Natural World. Sight. Smell. Sound. Taste. Touch. are all of equal importance. participating Together with Mother Earth. Bush consciousness. Eva knows Trees and Clouds. Snows and LightningStorms. Berries and Bark. Rabbits and Moose. and Bears.

but. Eva is growing weaker. and her Belly is growing larger. and her Children are growing hungrier. and still no Arvey. Still No Arvey. She doesn't know what to do. She Didn't Know What To Do. She lays huddled with her Children. All of them. in one pile. under all Blankets. and Furs. and Clothes they have.

She sings soothing Chant. to keep them safe over long cold Nights. Sacred Songs send a message for help. "GrandMothers help me. what to do? send me a Message. a Sign. GrandMothers." She prays. She Prayed Real Hard. Real Hard She Prayed.

She dozes. She Dozed. and she Dreams. She Dreamed and she knows. She Knew what she must do. She arises before Dawn. packs what little Food is left. ties a Bundle of what they have. What Little They Had! Although. it is not near as much as what they will Need.

at first Light. of BrightRoseDawn. She awakens Children. Bundles Them in all Clothes. Blankets. and Furs. Children drowsy with sleep are Bundled. packs YoungOnes in sled. Long sled. one for hauling Moose. "I want Moose.Steak so bad." She says when she tells it. She Really Wanted It Bad!

She walks and makes OlderOnes walk. and they walk. and walk. and Walked and Walked. they pull sled. and they walk. and walk. and Walked and Walked. their Feet crunch on hard Snow. for Days and for Nights … crunch … crunch … crunch.

they can't rest. they might freeze. They Might Freeze. "don't fall asleep. you might freeze." we are all told. regularly. they sleep a little by Day. but. Never by Night. Never By Night. and Eva never sleeps herself at all. No. Eva Never Slept. Not At All.

they walk and they walk. and They Walk. Eva and her twelve Children. and One in her Belly. Hungry and cold and tired. Hungry! Cold and Tired. Eva is weakening. All Children. but One. are in Sled. She feels she can Not go on. Can Not Go On. No! "maybe we goin' Wrong Direction. maybe we makin' Wrong Decision." Her Fears speak loudly. "maybe we will All Die."

Finally. Eva sits down. Tears freeze to her Cheeks. as they spill down her blue. white. red. patchy. frost bitten Face. She buries her self in her Fur. "Go Away. I have to sleep." She growls to her Son. as he tries to keep her Awake. is all lost?

Suddenly. Eva hears a BeautifulSong. Bright and Lively. She looks around to see who might be singing. "it is like an Angel on High." She tells it to her Christian friends. "it's like a beautiful sweet. long. Bird call. many of them. all at once. over and Over again." She tells us. "I wonder. maybe I died and crossed over."

Eva jumps up. No. All is as it had been. All Children are still in Sled. looking real cold. Real Cold. Eva is Energized. from SweetSongs of IceFairies. She is able to trudge on. Refreshed. Tired still. but. willing to go on. to Live on.

after a long while. they finally arrive. Arrive at Road. Road to TheTown. they wait and wait. and wait. Waited and Waited. Cold. Hungry. and Tired. along comes a Truck. a Ride to TheTown. Yeah!! a Ride to TheTown. they are Happy for a ride to TheTown. crouching in Back. Wind sailing over their bowed Heads. they happily speed to TheTown.

to TheTown. our Family welcomes them. Welcomed Them All. LittleEva and her twelve Children. "my 'ow Children 'ad all grown. an' OneMore in Belly. Bien! Wonderful! come in. Come In! Welcome All." Feasted. Bathed. Warm. and Rested. Eva tells her Story.

Now. Story didn't quite end here. because. part I like best. is yet to come. Soon. after Auntie Eva comes to TheTown. one in Belly. Cousin KooKoo. is kicking to be born. my Auntie already birthed twelve Babies in Bush. She doesn't want to go into no Hospital to have her last one. "No Way!" She says. but. She is living in TheTown. Now. so They say. "She has to." They Said She Had To.

Well. my Ma is just about to have her first Baby. being she is a Nurse in TheHospital. and familiar with Procedures on maternity ward. She offers. "I'll go in wit you. Eva. to get you settled. an' help you out. seein' as yer so nervous."

they do end up going in Together. but. it doesn't work out quite as they talked about. No sireee. it isn't Ma helping my Auntie. She already knows what she is doing. She Knew. What She Was Doing. it is my Auntie helping my Ma. KooKoo is already long outta there by time little JoJo is born.

"Fun-nee." Ma tells it. "how sometimes we set out to tink. we're goin' to be Teacher. or Helper. an' it ends up bein' another way around." Fun-nee. it's work of Wisakecahk to teach us Reversals. UpsideDown. InsideOut lessons. to make sure we don't take ourselves too serious. Don't Take Yourself So Serious. don't make yourself to be more important than you are. "don' tink yer King of Turd Island. when yer only Fart da Messenger." Ma would warn us. if she ever thought we were getting "too big for our britches."

just to put this Story in historical perspective. I am still an Egg. I was born five years later. in mid-fifties. almost fifty years ago. my people were BushPeople. today. some still are.

I begin with Eva's Story. to Honour my Ancestors. my first responsibility in speaking. Eva. Ma. and other Women in my Life teach me important lessons. a WarriorWoman has to give long and hard. before she takes even a small bit. even a little bite. for herself. what she takes she uses. through HardWork and real Sacrifice. to further and nurture Life. Nurture Lives. that she is Responsible for. including her own.

OPENING CLOSED DOORS.
I AM CAGED. ARE YOU?

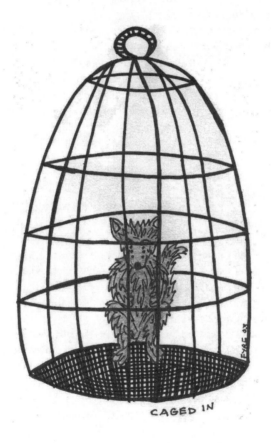

CAGED IN

I am Caged. are You?
Mahe'kun unwittingly finds herself Caged. by Social and Cultural expectations.
hard to See. beyond Tears.Fears.

I Story my Life to Resist.
Reveal insidious nature of "coercive liberalism."[1]
to De-colonize Minds. Hearts. Bodies. Spirits.
Establish Nehiyâhw'ak Presence. Space. Everywhere.
to Reclaim. Restore. Renew relationships.
within OurSelves. Our Families.
Our Communities. Our Earth Mother.
to Stimulate Imaginations.
Inspire Creativity.
to Strengthen our Hearts and Hands.
to work for united. but. Not uniform.Nations.
Teaching.Healing. Resistance.
can bring Discomfort. Messiness. Disruption.
becoming disruptively Connected.
ultimately leads to opening more Doorways.
let's Heal.Learn. together.
my MedicineStories. are about Oppression. Resistance. Recovery.
as Nehiyâw'ak people. we have been Historically.
are Currently. Oppressed.
Pressed. Moulded. Flattened.
Reduced in bulk. Caged In.
Caught between or among forces.
Restrained. Restricted.
Prevented from Moving. Penalized.[2]
Life is experienced as a set of DoubleBinds.
Options reduced. to very few. seems None.
All Choices. bring Penalty.
We do what needs to be done. to Overcome Oppression.
We can function. or not function.
with.in. Enforced Adaptation.Assimilation.
for you.me. I Story. Cage-ness of my existence.
Métis.Woman. Mother. Traditionalist. Artist. Activist. Academic.
Alive today. in Heterosexist. Patriarchal. Eurocentric Worlds.
Working for wages. in Hierarchical.Bureaucratic. institutions in Canada.
I enter into educational Systems. Seeking. a better Life. Empowerment.
I experience Marginalization. I am Ignored. Abused. Streamed.
Tokenized. Assimilated. Patronized.
"For My Own Good."
I am a Carrier of multiple. Systemic. Burdens.
External. Internal judgements.
about roles of Nehiyâw'akWomen in Families. Societies.
Ceremonial commitments. Community obligations.
Political conundrums. ongoing Battles.
with bureaucratized Colonialism. RedTape.

If. I do Not School. Work with.in. CanadianNation.
    I Live Dependent on TheState. another set of Oppressive tensions.
        each and every Choice. I am Privileged to make.
           Places me in a DoubleBind. every day. in every way.
Painful. Debilitating. potentially Paralyzing. parameters.
as I Story my Journey.
    Victimization. Self-Blame. Politicization. Empowerment.
     I wonder. what do you. as Readers. Need to know?
       to appreciate how SocioPolitical. Cultural. Historical.
           Contexts. Patterns. and Processes.
              Shape. Mangle. CageIn. My.Our. Lives?
don't be too Surprised. to find you don't See. beyond Personal. "Problems."
        if Structural Bars. have been Invisible. to You.
    since Europeans Spacially. Politically. Culturally.
       Dominate our Territories.
    Some are raised with Material. Cultural privileges.
       named WhitePrivilege.^{2} Mooniyâs. Eurocentrism. WECCP.
Naming is Necessary to Clarify. Disrupt Silent Dominance.
    when Names.Labels. used. to designate Race. Gender.
are attached to All speakers and All issues. It. is a Political Act.
SomeTimes you have to Position yourself someWhere.
        in order to say someThing.anyThing. at all.
OurCommunities have many Labels. attached to Us.
    White is TheUnspeakable. Invisible. Hegemonic.
      Assumed. Anonymous. Category.
I hope you realize. We. are on a Journey.
    to Transform Hegemonic Eurocentric Patriarchal consciousness.
    to See how it Envelops. Binds. All members.
      Creates. Sustains. Internal. External. Obstacles for Change.
    it is Overpresent. Overwhelms current "Multicultural." 'Inclusive'.
    Political. Educational. Spiritual realms.
Hegemony obscures Power relations.
    CommonSense allows. acceptance of Structural Inequality.$_{3}$
    as Accidental. as a by-product of larger political systems.
revealing hegemonic Inequality.
    definitely produces Reactions.
      from those privileged to be in Denial.
        Denial of our shared history.
          of our current responsibilities.
            to create equitable environments.
Hegemony blinds Dominators. Dominated.
    allows Distance. from historical Abuses.
    blocks Responsibility. for role in Change processes.
            Personal or Political.

when Some assign Problem. Responsibility for Isms.
to those of us Hurt. by Them.
They can ignore Benefits. They Gain from it.
Eurocentrism. Mooniyâs.
a way of Knowing. Being. Seeing. Understanding TheWorld.
a form of Consciousness. an Ideology.
Hidden. Expressed.
reinforces Past. Present. Superiority.
Domination of Europeans over all Others.
"you people."
Nehiyâw'ak.
re-produces Dominant. MonoCultural World.View.
Humanism. Rationalism. "Scientism." Materialism.[4]
Capitalism—analytic. quantitative. consciousness.
sustains concrete Social. Economic. and Political agendas.
WECCP: White Euro Canadian Christian Patriarchal interests.
Denial of Indigenous Title. and Guardianship. of Lands.
Bestowing European place names. exemplifies Appropriation. Possession.
"myth of emptiness." central to European approach to Space.
McMaster and Martin ask.
"Why would colonists assume these lands were unclaimed and unnamed?"
Dehumanization. Relocation. Reeducation. Redefinition.
Falsification. of Reality. Voice. History.
Colonialism rewrites Histories. of all Oppressed groups.
Distorts. Disfigures. and Destroys It. Them. Us.
Cultural misunderstandings re-occur.
expressed by Mooniyâs-Minds as
"the past is the past. over and concluded."
Nehiyâw'ak know. Past continues into Present.
how I. We. formulate or represent Past.
shapes my. our. understanding of Present.
Denial. allows Mooniyâs to morally Justify.
Conquest. Conversion. Cumulation. Control.
Denial. continues to be supremely Profitable. for some.
Impoverishing for others.
"Indigenous peoples exist in conditions of imposed internal
exile, economic prisoners of a system beyond their
comprehension, and in conditions that are beyond their
control." reports Geohring.[5]
Profit. Wealth. was. is achieved through Resource Extraction.
Rape of Earth Mother.
by most efficient and profitable methods.
supported by a linear-future Commodification of Time.
Change and Development are actively sought.

Progress is Desired. Expected. Reinforced.
in modern Urban Life. Clocks. Calendars. History. Books.
everyone's Time. must be productively put to Use.
Spent. Consumed. Marketed.
Individualism. Competition. Struggle with other persons.
for material Wealth. re-produces Tyranny.
needs of Mooniyâs globally prioritized.
over wellbeing of all Beings.
Communities of People are divided.
through multiple Hierarchies.
Sexism. Racism. Classism. Heterosexism. Ableism.
MyStories. are riddled with these Isms.
Individualist supremacist ideologies make possible.
Genocidal. Ethnocidal. methods used to Colonize. Subdue.
Nehiyâw'ak Lands. Peoples. Realities.
continue to Cage. Subdue me. Today.
Murder. Scalping. Disease.
Ninety Million Nehiyâw'ak Lives. lost in Americas. from 1492 to 1550.
Military slaughter of Buffalo. Millions of rotting carcasses. littered Plains.
Elders. MedicinePeople. GrandMothers.
Devilized. Heathenized. Persecuted.
Theft. Desecration. Destruction of Sacreds.
Imprisonment of Ceremonial Leaders. Participants.
tactics of Conversion and Control. legislated from 1884 to 1951.
Confiscation. Appropriation. Collection of SacredBundles.
now a Norm. Hobby. Business.
Legally obtained from Collectors. Galleries. Pow-wows. Shops.
Illegally removed from Sacred Burial Sites.
Spiritual Freedom remains Illusory.
SacredBundles. Pipes. EagleFeathers.
still Confiscated at Border crossings.
still held in Museums.
like Thousands. in British Museum in London.
Help Us. Free Them. Please.
SacredLands fenced off.
continuous Clashes to halt Economic Development.
from Nation to Nation. around Indigenous worlds.
No Rights. to practise Nehiyâw'ak forms. of religious expression.
within Prisons. Educational. Medical Systems.
No Respect. Shown. for what Nehiyâw'ak holds Sacred.
No Redress. for Historical. Ongoing actions.
to Demonize. Repress. Cage.
Enforced ResidentialSchooling. assured attendance.
Regulation of all aspects of Life. Dress. Language. Behaviour.

Rules strictly enforced. through all forms of Violence.
Physical. Sexual. Emotional. Mental. Spiritual. Abuses.
are Daily occurances.
followed by SixtiesScoop.
widespread Apprehension of Nehiyâw'ak children.
further contributes to dissolution of Identity.
continues to erode Family. Clan. CommunalCare structures.
Mooniyâs. still legislate. "the best interests of the child."
with many Tragedies to show for it.
Thinking with Head. Cognition.
Separable from Heart. Feelings.
is still Expected. continuously Reinforced. through Required curriculum.
Rationalism keeps us locked in our Cages.
Elevating Reason. Disregarding other human Powers.
can lead me.us. to Pessimism.
feelings of Helplessness. Hopelessness. Fatalism.
can keep me.us. from Social Action.
Schooling. Past. Present.
acts to replace Nehiyâw'ak languages. with English.
Oral Tradition. with written word.
Sacred MedicineStories have been Appropriated. Translated. Distorted.
Retold by EuroExperts.
in Anthropology. Art. Literature.
History. Politics. IndianStudies.
Nehiyâw'ak writers' manuscripts Returned.
"too Indian" or "not Indian enough."
Coercive powers. of Dominant. Dominating. institutions
make us Speak it Right. Speak White.
refuse to publish our texts.
or shape them through editorial processes
to fit Expected conventions.
Why should we continue to sustain status quo?
Stop reifying EuroExpert voices as Truth.
Stop suppressing Nehiyâw'akPeople's own Truths.
Live. Tell. Read. Teach. Learn. from First Voice.
from my.our. Truths.
I Story. to dispel Lies.
current conditions caging Nehiyâw'akPeoples
context for my MedicineStories.
did Not happen simply through Bad Choices.
Not because of some cultural defects.
Denial of OurStory. OurOppression. Colonization.
will lead you to Minimize. Monsterize. MyStory.
I Story. to retell acts of Resistance.

Bend Wires. Slip Between Bars. Open Doorways.
necessary for my.our. Escape.
Survival.
Recovery.

BLACK AND BLUE

to my LittleGirl "jenni-fire." who survived to tell Story.

Black and Blue.
as a young Girl.
in MissionSchool.
my Hands were
made black 'n
blue.
by an angry Nun.
many suffered
fates much
worse than
mine.
Scars remain for
all.

I First Know. Racism. Cultural Oppression. experience a Cage. when I go to MissionSchool. I go to DaySchool. better than ResidentialSchool. I.We. Live at Home. have help from Family and Community to Survive experiences. but. Not much better. Same Nuns and Priests run both Schools. use Same methods to exact Obedience. Many have gone before me. to tell how ResidentialSchooling. damages our Core. Reverberates beyond all other colonial mechanisms. all fashioned to Subjugate. Assimilate. Annihilate.

what I now know. understand. label as Oppression. Colonization. Acculturation. Assimilation. Racism. Ethnocide. does not adequately Name. or Describe. my.our. Experiences. All what I know. all common sense Assumptions. Values. ProperConduct. what to expect. from me and from Others. especially Adults towards me. are fundamentally challenged. my.our. Experience. History. Voice. Spirit. is Devalued. Denigrated. subject to Abuse. on a daily basis.

I'll tell you Story from this Time. my First Time.

on FirstDay of School. and every day for a Long Time. We are shown FlipCharts on Hell. fully illustrated. Glossy. with lots of Devils. Scary faces. and Fire. lots of Fire.

We are told. "You will go here. If you Disobey." If. we Disobey. Nuns or Rules. in Any Way. We are Not told Rules. We are Punished. Punished for disobeying. Them.

FirstWeek of School. I am strapped. Strapped with a thick black belt. Thick Black Belt. on TheBack. TheBack of MyHands. They puff up Blue. Blue and black. Black and Blue. Imagine.

I take off. I run Home. I am Six. I run five miles up IslandRoad. When I am Six. I run five miles home. Imagine. Home. I have to get Home. I can't stay at School. No way. I am Humiliated. I have Never been hit before. Never been Hit before. Not like That. No. Not Like. That. First Time.

I do Not know where to turn. I am Strapped with a Thick Black Belt. by TheNun. By TheNun. So. that means. I Must have Disobeyed Nuns. and that means. I am going to Hell. and if I am going to Hell. than I am going to Hide. Hide. I will Hide at Home.

Anyways. Here I am. Hiding. Hiding under MyBed. Hiding Under MyBed. and waiting. Waiting. Waiting for Devils. and all Horrible Creatures. from FlipCharts on Hell. to come. to Come and find me. Find me under my Bed. and take me. Take me from my Home. and my Family. Take me to Hell. "Oh what am I going to do?" What Was I Going To Do? I already knew. lots of Children disappear. Now. I realize. where They go. I am Terrified.

Then. I hear my Name being called. "Jenni? Jenni-fire? where are you? Ou et t'il?" I remain very quiet. only answer when Papere comes right into Room. calls my Name. softly right under MyBed. my bottom bunk.

They are Worried. "where 'ave you Been? come an' 'ave some food. Mange." pulls me. tightly. into his StrongBrownArms. "dry dose Tears. Bebe. it can' be dat bad. it can' be Dat Bad." He croons. "Pauvre Petite."

"Oh but it is! Papere!" I cry. Tears Stream. down my upturned face. "it's worse dan Dat Bad. it's Worser. Worses'! I'm goin' to 'Ell for sure now. Dey'll be 'ere Any Minute!" I glance around. FearFull.

He holds me. strokes my Hair. gently kisses MyHands. MyBlueBlackHands. Tears fill his ObsidianBrownEyes. We sit in Silence. He finally says. in a small gruff voice. "I don' really believe in 'Ell. anywuss. mebbe. Mebbe somebuddy jis made it up."

"mebbe somebuddy jis made it up." "Jis Made It Up???" I shriek. my GreenEyes open Real Wide. "Really??" I can hardly believe my Ears. "Yeah." He says. "Really!!" He motions his finger across his pointed lips. opens eyes wide. eyebrows arched. "Ferme la bush. Listen Up. don' never tell Granmere I said so."

once I Calm down. Cuddled up. Tears dried. I tell Papere Story. after I am done. I tell him. "I'm never. Never. No! Never Ever. goin' back to School again. an' you better jis' get used of it. I'll stay wit' you. Dat's how it'll be. Okay?" I look up. Idolizing my Papere.

He laughs and says. "Life isn' always so easy. Bebe." He kisses me. on top of my Head. "oh how I wish it was. I Wish. it is up to me." my GreenEyes start to fill with Tears. "we'll see. com'on. let's eat. 'ave some bapbas."[6]

but. I didn't have to go back. Back to School just yet. I didn't go back to School. until I had to. Until. I Had to. Until. They Came. and Got me.

my First Week. one excruciatingly long week. of MissionSchool. Discipline. Christian Domination. Violence. Abuse. God. Priests. Nuns have Power. PowerOver me. Me. and my Family. and our Community. Religious Oppression. Creates. and Mirrors Mooniyâs rules. Seeds of Oppression. are Deeply implanted in my Psyche. I am Changed. my Spirit now knows. a Cage.

this abusive situation. my Reaction to it. my Father's Reaction to my Reaction. becomes a consciousness-raising experience. for All. me. my Family. and Community. AtThatTime. it seems. my Parents are quietly Assimilating. to certain forces that come through MissionSchool. like Not speaking Mitchif. at Home. because OlderOnes are Humiliated in School. when I go to School. I speak more English. less Mitchif. YoungerOnes don't Speak at all. Not at all. as a Family. We attend Church. in our "Sunday-best" clothes. Pray on our Knees. with BlackBeads. Heads bowed. Hands clasped. Money in collection plate every week.

along with many others. We also keep up with Traditional activities. Papere. is a Healer. of Animals and People. WaterWitcher. WiseMan. Him and Ma know numbers and letters. a skill in short supply. lots come by our House. for help. We travel to other Communities. when his services are asked for. He always brings me along. when he can. I love to go. I always especially enjoy missing School. and HonouringFeasts. I still love Feasts…. mmmmm … Feasts.

Not Granmere. Family matriarch. carries Embodied message. of ResidentialSchool. from her era. "Obey. Don't Fight The Nuns." Ma went to Convent at DuckLake. She knew. TheRules. taught through

Abuse. Rote learning. Obey. Strapped. time and time again. Obey. follow TheRules. of colonizers. or be Disciplined. Beaten. "For Your Own Good."

my Parents. Grandparents. Knew. Teach your Children. You.They. Need a New Mind-set. to Survive. We. Have to. Painfully learn. Summarize. Memorize. Lists of details. GreenCoveredCatechismBook. Memorize It. Cover to cover. in Grade one. All of It. All of Us. Recite on our Knees. Hard bony Knees. on HardWood floor. "Now. Recite. after me." Pointer poised ready. Ready for Attack.

Many. Many times. We are told. "just memorize it. Just Memorize It!" harsh Voices. utter Threats. Threats followed quickly by actual Assaults. Blows to Head. and Hands. Flying objects. Sharp pointers across Backs. Thick Black Belt. Always visible. Discipline. "For Your Own Good."

OurParents. try to Assimilate. desire to be treated Humanly. Strongly Desire. better Lives for us. their Children. want us to Enjoy our Lives. experience Less Pain. than they did. avoid Pain. Learn. teach us. to Pass. some Resist. continue to Fight. Domination. They got Hit. Hurt. "For Your Own Good."

Anyways. after BlackBlueHands came Home. Papere begins to Talk Back. He tells my Story. to Others in OurCommunity. to Priest. to Nun. to Principal of MissionSchool. also a Nun. goes to local SchoolBoard. Threatens. to Pull me. Pull me. and All of his Children. out of School. Asks. other members of OurCommunity. to Pull All Their Children Out too. If. Abuse continues.

this Activism. on his part. and many others. eventually leads to MissionSchool closing. Him sitting on SchoolBoard as a Trustee. a beginning. part of an ongoing Struggle. to change practices of Schools. towards Nehiyâw'ak children. that were needed. still are needed. Still Are Needed.

even more crucial. to My consciousness. AtThatTime. is that I got to stay Home. for Days. I got to stay Home. Home is Safe. Safe Place to be. but. I am still Afraid. I am going to go to Hell. a Fear firmly Implanted. by those glossy full colour FlipCharts on Hell. very Graphic. very Real. very Believable. to us as children. especially before Television. before Television even came North. when we See it. we believe it. We Believed It! Seeing is Believing.

I am eternally grateful. to Papere. for teaching me. through Words and Actions. Nuns are Wrong to hit me. I Know. Nuns Are Wrong. Nuns Can Be Wrong. Wow! what a LifeSaver! Oppressive Authority is Wrong. what a lesson. Saved my Life. or at least my Spirit of Resistance. it's pretty hard to fight back. when you think. you are going to Hell. Immediately. I didn't understand the Death part. Yet.

through this Incident. and many others like it. I become conscious. of Difference. once Nuns quit physically assaulting me. I can pay more Attention. I notice. Violence. Nuns acting out on Others. Darker ones. Darker Ones. Ones with No Parents to stick up for Them. especially Foster Kids. They get it worse. They Got It Worse. and we all know it. We All Knew It. We are Glad it isn't us. Glad It Was Not Us.

Indelibly marking Difference. and Privilege. Marking what Privilege I do have. I Had my Father. my Parents. my Community. and my lighter skin. especially my Lighter Skin. although I learn since. there is a painful side. to light skin colour. to Passing.[7]

Anyways. I see a lot more. take a lot more Abuse. in MissionSchool. than I care to Story for you. right now. Do Not believe those who Minimize. Deny racist pain. Deny benefits of privilege. Elders say. "Don' talk about what ya don' know."

these lessons take me a LifeTime. so far. to Untangle. one Spring. FastFire. reveals to me. deep Healing insight. as I stare. Wide-eyed. Startled. Heart Beating fast. Fear Raging. I stare into Glowing. Flickering. Embers. and Flames. I see shapes. Shifting. pictures. Emerging. FlipChart creatures. first frightful Entities. Dark gaps. Mouths red. like Blood. BlackEyes shooting Flames. Devils. Dragons. Winged. and Horned. Hoofed Creatures abound.

as I hunch. Frozen in place. Immersed in painful memories. hours speed by. Fire Winks. and Blinks. Shifts Shapes. Frown to Smile. Leer to Twinkle. what I am taught to Fear. becomes Loveable. Transforms itself. teaches me. profoundly. Spirit is Love. Not Fear. I can leave my Fears. Hell. Punishment. Guilt. Domination. in FastFire.

I Story. for all who Struggle. to Heal your Spirits. Wounded in name of Christ. there is no Hell to Fear. only tortured Spirits. Humans. who have not been Transformed. by Love. like Petitot. who remained a Priest and practising pedophile. in TheNorth. for eighteen years. until he developed raging dementia. Oblates finally removed him. Finally.

1997. Canadian government apologizes. for their role in ResidentialSchools. Indian Affairs establishes HealingFund. 350 million dollars. 1,200 former pupils file lawsuits by 1998. mistrust of Police. confrontational court proceedings. followed by relatively light sentences handed to perpetrators. leads many to look for other routes.

2002. Five years later. notice given. Aboriginal Healing Fund is soon

FastFire.
many deeply
Frightening.
Funny. Messages.
about Devils.
Religion.
Spirituality.
how Fire
transforms
Spirits.
are Gifted
on FastNight.

Broke. Researchers. Lawyers. Healers. barely scratch surface.[8] of deeply submerged Iceberg. Healing. and Justice. still Denied. while many Die of broken Hearts and Homes.

Notes

1. thanks. to an inspired talk from Ian Baptiste 2000. this is his concept.
2. thanks. to Marilyn Frye (1985). for her early feminist work. helped me understand oppression.
3. White hegemony. includes "white privilege" (McIntosh 1990), eurocentrism (Blaut 1993), Merchant 1989, WECCP (Acoose 1995). Some others that help us understand. Mooniyâs worldviews include. *Indigena* by McMaster and Martin 1992, Kearney 1984, Said 1993, Thompson 1991.
4. my work on Hegemony. in this text. conspires with writing by marino 1997. She quotes Gitlin's definition: Hegemony "names a process of social-political control.... Those who rule the dominant institutions secure their power in large measure directly and *indirectly*, by impressing their definitions of the situation upon those they rule and ... significantly limiting what is thought throughout the society" (Gitlin 1980: 10). term was originally used. by Italian Marxist and activist. Antonio Gramsci.
5. I smith these words. a critique of certain tendencies. within the Mooniyâs worldview. to establish hierarchies. elevate certain things over others. Humanism.Humans over all other life forms. Rationalism.Rational thinking. over all other ways of understanding. Scientism.Scientific methods over all other ways of knowing. Materialism.Ownership.Hoarding of material goods. over all other forms of sharing wealth or being rich.
6. Many authors document painful historical factors. that combine to produce

an equally painful true reality today. like Goehring 1993. Paul 2000. O'Brian 1989. some focus on spiritual desecration including Gunn Allen 1986. Irwin 1997. Mihesuah 1996. Pettipas 1994. some document Schooling as an abusive tool of colonialization. like Barman, Hebert and McCaskill 1986. Haig Brown 1988. English–Currie 1990. Fiske 1991. Knockwood 1992. Grant 1996. Miller 1996. Milloy 1999. and other violent methods of child removal. like Fournier and Crey 1997. Kline 1992. Teichroeb 1997. Obomsawin 1986. Theft of our Ancestors' Stories. is addressed by McMaster and Martin 1992. Godard 1992. and Lutz 1991.

7.   bapas is a slang Mitchif word for something good to eat.

8.   my lighter skin. produces asking many possible versions of. "What are you?" I feel like some kind of alien. a misplaced person. as James tells it, "In addition to being rude, jarring and out of place, the question, repeated often, scars the soul, injures the psyche, and ignites feelings of inadequacy and alienation" (James 2000: 17).

9.   not only are Generations of First Nations families affected by these Schools. thousands of Métis survivors victimized in "convents." or "mission schools." have mostly been ignored. one local project funded through the Aboriginal Healing Foundation. through Manitoba Métis Federation. is a research project entitled. Lost Generations.

FEARS ARE A DOORWAY.
SHEDDING BLOOD. ON CAGE BARS

Shedding Blood. on Cage Bars.
CoverUps. Backlash. interLock with Denial. Defensiveness.
to sustain existing Privilege. Control of Money. Power.
Some shed Blood. Die. to maintain Others comfort.

I want to Transform Me.You.
        Tell You.Me.
            about Me.You.
  these MedicineStories. are an act of SelfDisclosure.
     I am revealing. core Truths about Me.You. Humanity.
        I hold a Mirror to my Life.
          to Reflect what has been done to all of us.
          by those that live Outside that Mirror.
     I want to oppose Oppression. Violence. Abuse.
        Racism. Sexism. Homophobia. Humanism.
           these Isms Hurt. Maim. Cripple.
               OurSelves. Soul Deep.
       I can become Angry. Lost. Despairing.
         Survive through Denial.
         Numb my Body.
         Rationalize my Feelings.
         Dissociate.
  SelfDisclosure means I engage less. in maintaining Denial.
         become PainFully aware.
             of Depth. Breadth. role Denial plays
             in Everyday Life. Everybody's Life.
             It.becomes Mind. Spirit boggling.
    I am Bearing witness.
        Refusing to bow. to outside pressures.
        to Revise. or Repress my experience.
      Making a decision. to embrace Conflict.
        rather than Conformity.
      Willing to endure. a Lifetime of Anger and Pain.
        rather than be seduced. into Revision. Repression. Denial.
I Story to Change.
   illustrate DoubleThink. an ever deepening Chasm.
        between how I am Told society operates.
          what I experience.
        how I am Expected to act to survive.
          how I am feeling.
        what I am being Guided to do.
          what others expect.
        I am soothed by Paula Gunn Allen's words.
        "To walk the medicine path is to Live and think in ways
        that are almost but not quite entirely unlike our usual
        ways of living and thinking...."
Surviving Daily Marginalization.
requires more than Revealing. multifaceted layers of a PainFul mirage.
requires engaging our Intuition. Imagination. our Creative abilities.

I Story to resist Eurocentric.Patriarchal practices.
    to manifest Nehiyâw'ak.Feminist alternatives.
    to prevent chronic Denial. social Amnesia.
I Story to recover.
    to take control over forces that would destroy me.us.
    to promote. inspire Healing.
    to transform mySelf.Others.
I present mySelf to transform Our Worlds.
    to move out of Separation and Fear.
                Terror and Discontent.
    to move towards Love.
"what's Love got to do with it?"
    I seek Love. yearn for Love.
    I am Healed. Wounded. by Lovers. Friends. Family.
    according to bell hooks.
    "wounded hearts turn away from love
    because they (and others around them)
    do not want to do the work of healing
    necessary to sustain and nurture love".
        "No one can rightfully claim to be loving
        when behaving abusively."
    my Heart is Wounded.
        See How I Am Still Loving.
Loving requires being willing to hear each other's Truths.
    affirming powers of TruthTelling.
    Healing takes Truth. to shatter Denial.
        Truth is a Release. from a "cyclone of pain."
    Cyclones. leave a Path. of Destruction. in their wake.
        Create room for new Growth. Rebirth.
            Be. Aware. Truth Hurts. and Heals.
            Teller. and Listener.

"SHE FOUGHT BACK"

to Helen Betty who died. all the "Girls" who still Live with the Legacy.
and all the "Girls" who are still dying. like Lisa Marie.[1]

Helen Betty was Found. Naked. Dead.
    by a TeenBoy. at our SacredBlueLake.
        thirty miles NorthWest of TheTown.
Her Face cracked in half. Her Teeth gouged out.
        fifty stab wounds pierce her Head. Face. Chest. Neck.

Fifty Stab Wounds.
maybe more.
Bloody screwdriver lay in Snow nearby.
Helen Betty. Nehiyâw'akWoman.
Abducted. from TheTown street.
She did Not submit. to Sexual Assault.
so She is Beaten.
Stabbed. Repeatedly.Viciously.
left to Die.
by four. maybe five. maybe more.
young MooniyâsMen.
GoodTownfolks.
my HomeTown.
Drunken? Yes.
aware enough
to seek legal advice. Soon after.
They are told. "Evidence is circumstantial.
Keep Quiet."
Some talk. while drinking.
One. brags.
"Do you know what it feels like to kill someone. It feels great."[2]
Witness later testifies.
One. confesses to TheLocalSheriff at TheLegion.
He keeps it to himself.
and warns Murderer.
"about the shit he could get me into because he was the sheriff."
Sixteen years later. three Men go to Trial.
ten Men. two Women. None Nehiyâw'ak. Decide.
One. goes to jail for Life.
Life is seven years. at most.
"Why did it take so long for her killer to meet Justice?"
Mooniyâs want to ask.
Will her Family ever meet Justice?
Nehiyâw'ak need to know.
Symptom of a corrupt JusticeSystem.
"Why take a case to court if you know you're going to lose?"
CrownAttorney asks.
Racist cover-up.
"Do you think people would have kept their mouths shut if a White Girl
had been raped and killed by Natives?" asks Chief Okimaw of Tribal Council.
"I think not"
He responds as collective consciousness of Nehiyâw'ak people.
Conspiracy of Silence.
writes Priest.

"Details are unimportant if you have no memory (because of alcohol abuse)."
DefenceAttorney argues successfully.
Sign of TheTimes.
Segregation of "Indians" and Whites is enforced in TheTown.
only six years before.
"Indian" and White students are only beginning to be Integrated.
in HighSchool. in 1970.
Seventy-five percent of TheTown residents admit their Racism.
in a 1965 poll.
Fights between two Races are common.
when Helen Betty's Rape.Murder. Happens.
TheTown is a racial gender WarZone.
it is presumed Girls.Women. Ask for it. Want it. Like it.
so Rape is not really Rape at all.
when Helen Betty's Rape.Murder. Happens.
Nehiyâw'ak Girls.Women. are Oppressed.
Restrained. Restricted.
Immobilized. Reduced.
Penalized for who we are.
experiences of Sexual. Physical. Intimidation. Violence.
an integral part of our Lives.
seen as Typical Male Behaviour.
Natural Rights of Men.
Not Prohibited. Regulated.
Fathers abuse Daughters.
Husbands abuse Wives.
Bosses their Employees.
Men unknown to Us.
can comment on.
Verbally Abuse.
Any Woman's Body.
AnyTime. AnyWhere.
All Men did not Choose. to exercise their Rights as Predators.
some are secured as Protectors.
but. This. is nearly Irrelevant.
Visible. Gendered. Power Differences.
are witnessed Hourly. Daily. Weekly. Yearly.
All Men have Power Over All Women.
If. you Live in TheTown.
or near TheTown.
and you are Female.
especially if you are Nehiyâw'ak.
even more if you looked Dark.
especially If You Look Dark.

You are Fair Game. a Target.
notice. a direct relationship.
between Race. and Gender.
between stereotypes. and violence.
Emma Laroque tells Aboriginal Justice Inquiry.
"Helen Betty Osborne was murdered... because these youths grew
up with twisted notions of 'Indian girls' as 'squaws'."
Helen Betty is not TheOnlyVictim.
was not TheOnlyVictim.
We are All Raped.
We were All Raped Regularly.
that's A.Story that Never gets told.
it's A.Story. Behind TheStory. that Never got Told.
Never Gets Told.
Lee Maracle knows.
"We have been the object of sexual release for white males whose
appetites are too gross for their own delicate women."
being Raped. is like being Squashed.
like a Bug. at high speed.
against a windshield. on highway.
We bleed inside and out.
Our insides pour out.
We hurt Spiritually. Emotionally.
Mentally. Physically.
when we swallow our Pain. we become Hollow.
Empty vessels. Need. to be refilled.
Rape is an act of Power.
Consciously.Unconsciously. Perpetrated.
Committed to cut Women off from our Power. Root. Sexuality.
SensualConnection to Self.
Others. Earth Mother.
We learn. learned. potent lessons.
Ignore It. Don't React.
Don't React. and especially Don't Fight Back.
Don't Fight Back.
Helen Betty didn't Die. Because. she is picked up.
and Sexually Assaulted by five guys.
lots of Girls had that happen.
Why do you think Murderers felt so Empowered.
Bragged about The RapeMurder
to so many people afterwards?
Why did GoodTownFolks cover it up?
Pandora's box can Not be opened.
could Not be Opened Up.

still can't.[3]

Helen Betty Died because. She Fights Back.
Because. She Fought Back.
and we all know it.
We All Knew It.
many of us Died trying to Forget.
some of us still know it today
some Still Know It Today.
Don't Fight Back.
Don't Fight Back.
We are Taught.
We were Taught.

Now. years later.
a monument sits.
erected at site of Helen Betty's RapeMurder.
far away from GoodTownFolk's eyes.
it Should say. "She Fought Back."
who wants to get Involved. to help protect Girls.Women.
from Men gone wild?
No One.

Doctors look away.
prescribe pills for Depression.
antibiotics for possible Infection.
morning after pill. "Just in Case."
"your fallopian tubes are so scarred."
I am told at age sixteen.
"you will Never have children."
Women.Girls of my generation
face a deathly Legacy.
STDs. Yeast Infections.
Immune Breakdowns.
Cervical Cancer.
Miscarriage. Infertility.

Police wear a Smirk.
Ignore Desperate 911 calls.
Advise Perpetrators
"You have a Right. read Duty. to remain Silent."
Cover up. close cases. Justice Denied.
GoodTownFolks. don't want to know
"what we don't know won't hurt us."
Blame Women.Girls.
what is She doing in TheTown. at Night?
She should be Home. read on Reserve.
Some notice. Her skirt is too short.

She is walking alone.
She should have a steady boyfriend.
my GranMere can't understand it.
"She was a GoodGirl.
why would it happen to her?"
I wonder. "does it happen to GoodGirls too?"
a glimmer of Hope.
If. I'm Good. maybe I won't get Raped.
at least Not as often.
So. when I am Raped regularly.
does that make me Bad?
Parents keep us in at Night.
inoculate us with Fear.
make us Responsible.
for avoiding victimization.
We are kept at Home.
our Freedom severed.
Rapists ran Wild.
Rapists were Brothers. Cousins.
Boyfriends. Uncles. SchoolChums.
Rapists are my Enemies.
WomenFolk teach us. "That's all Men want!"
All it takes to become a Rapist "is to see your body".
They try to protect us. by devaluing our WomanPower.
Hide my Strength. my Beauty.
Cut my Hair. Cover my Curves.
with many layers.
clothing. and fat.
Maybe. if I'm Ugly enough. I will pass Unnoticed.
when I am Thirteen. Helen Betty Died.
I steal a tensor bandage.
wrap it round and round.
confine my BuddingBreasts.
each Day. every Day. a Secret Ritual.
I am denied. Beauty of my budding Female self.
I try to hide. my Power. to stay safe.
it never does work. Never Did Work.
We learn Fear.
Never walk alone in TheTown.
or through woods at SacredBlueLake.
Fear. Men coming towards.
or walking up behind.
Fear. opening door to a knock.
or bathing in house alone.

Fear. dark back seat of cars.
Fear. Fear. Fear.
Hairs stand up on back of my Neck.
goose bumps raise on my Arms.
how did we. do we. Live?
Indoctrinated to Fear
half a HumanRace?
We take our Fear for granted.
Accept. Unpredictability. of Men's physical attraction.
Inevitability of Sexual Intimidation.
Sexual assault restricts Lifestyle. for All Women.[4]
We plan our Lives around it.
search for TheRightWay
to walk down a street.
to dress. to smoke a cigarette.
to drink from a glass. to laugh
to make. or avoid. eye contact.
We laugh as we share survival strategies.
for avoiding sexual come-ons. at parties.
at work. at school. at home.
find that none of them are foolproof.
Our instincts are injured by assault after assault.
these acts of Injustice. Destruction.
towards Us as Nehiyâw'akWomen.
become Normalized.
like those against our Ancestors.
our LovedOnes.
our Lands.
even our Gods.
it takes StrongWomen to Live in Fear.
Our Fear is a Survival skill.
teaches us to be like Wolf.
Strong and Wiley.
Safer. more powerfully protected.
one with ThePack.
my Mother taught me.
Courage is Not having No Fear.
it is knowing you are Afraid.
Living on. in spite of everyDay Dangers.
Speaking Truth is Healthy.
cultivates Courage.
strengthens us to Stand Up. for what we believe in.
encourages us to be Accountable. in Word and Deed.
releasing Rage. can reveal Woundedness.

I reconstruct Wounds of childhood.
by close inspection. of what I Lose my temper over. Now.
releasing Rage. also reveals Wellness.
Healthy instincts deeply React
to Disrespect. Threat. Injury.
Rage is a Messenger worth listening to.
tells me I am being Hurt.
my Rights are being violated.
my Boundaries crossed.
my Needs are not being met.
something is Not right.
Nehiyâw'ak.Women have Historical. Contemporary.
fuel to feed Fires. of our collective Anger.
Beth Brant tells it.
"We have a spirit of rage. We are angry women. Angry at
white men and their perversions. Their excessive greed and
abuse of the earth, sky, and water. Their techno-christian
approach to anything that Lives, including our children, our
people. We are angry at Indian men for their refusals of us. For
their limited vision of what constitutes a strong Nation. We
are angry at a so-called 'women's movement' that always
seems to forget we exist."
"My knee is wounded so badly that I limp constantly
Anger is my crutch I hold myself upright with it."
writes Chrystos.
swallowing rightful Rage. multi-generational Loss.
Chronic Silencing produces DisEase.
I have been Voiceless. experienced Tounglessness.
too many times. as a victimized Child.Youth.Woman.
in White.Patriarchal.Elite. Worlds.Institutions
Socially constructed realities.
contribute to collectively Silencing
articulate Nehiyâw'ak.Women.
unable. to understand our Experiences
or accept Truth of our perceptions.
some resort to psychologically Labelling.Blaming us.
I have been pathologized as Bitter.
branded as Biased.
my Anger exaggerated as "Militant."
by Family. Teachers. Students.
Colleagues. Administrators.
Union officials. Lawyers. Counsellors.
there is little Comprehension.
articulate Anger reflects an Awakening.

is a call to Liberation.
Not a psychological Problem
to be Recovered from.
quietly closeted
in Therapists' soundproof rooms.

"NO MORE"

to all Girls and Women of Courage. who have confronted abusers.
told them—"No More!"
and to all those who Wish they did. Wish they could.
still Want to. Will.

I stand at KitchenTable. up to my Elbows. Dishpan full of greasy Water.
finishing washing of CastIronPan. in He comes. full of mischif. snatches
up DishTowel. No. Not to help. to snap. Snap! Snap! Snap at my backside.
it is early Summer. my frayed cut-offs. sporting a peace-sign patch. on my
well-rounded butt. Snap! Snap! Snap! my patch a Target. Target of his
attention.

Ignore! I have been taught. Take it. Hope. he will go away. Don't
react. Remember. Don't fight back. Don't Fight Back. I boil inside. He
laughs in nasty glee. Anger oozes out my pores. Rage erupts. Repressed
emotions boil. Flood out. a long low wail erupts. from my once silenced
mouth. my HeavyStoneHeart beats faster. my well-tanned rosy cheeks
flush. Flame red.

my hard muscles flex. FarmGirl arms. Hands clench. Fist around
handle. CastIronPan rises. as if from its own will. out of brown soapy slush.
into Air. swinging a wide arc. droplets of GreasyWater. sail in every
direction. splatter on every wall. of SmallKitchen. Dampen old stained
woodfloor.

Heavy as Lead. CastIronPan. lands with ringing Crash. No. Not on
target. his Head. on offensive SnappingHand. Hand that holds down my
arms. in TheNight. Holds Down My Arms. as he Lays. his body on mine.
Lays His Body On Mine. trys to cover my mouth. Covers My Mouth.
with Alcohol infused kisses. Yeeeetch. I want to Gag. Still. Never Want
to Kiss. Never want to Kiss AlcoholBreath. No. Never Again.

CastIronPan. Smashes. SnappingHand. busting watch. GreenEyes
wide open. I stare. Stare. few seconds of horror. Horror at broken watch.
Horror at red blue black welt. RedBlueBlackWelt. quickly grows on his

No More!
Stop Violence.
JennyFire fights back.

Wrist.

I hear a Voice erupt. Erupt from my throat. my Throat. in a snarl deeper than. Deeper than I have ever known. I Snarl. "If you ever touch me. Again. I'll kill you. see this Knife." I flash. long wooden handled butcherKnife. from drain cloth. "it will be under my pillow. Waiting. Waiting for you to come. in TheNight."

"No More." I Hisssss. "No More." I glance up. meet his wide-open. white-ringed. Astonished BrownEyes.

I don't wait. for response. or reaction. I bound out Door. I run. Run as fast as I can. to TheTown. down five mile dirt road. to TheTown. I arrive. GirlFriend's house. Panting. out of Breath. collapse on BasementBed. break into a Fit. Hysterical laughter. Laughter! alternating with sobbing. Sobbing. Tears flow. Anguish streams. from my Lips. Eyes. Nose.

GirlFriend. sits quiet. holds my Hand. gives me hard one-ply toilet paper. to wipe my Tears. other fluids. when I become Calm. Terror takes over. I am afraid. I Am Afraid! Terrified. I begin to tremble. Tremble With Terror. what have I done? Assaulted apple of Ma's Eye. favoured GrandChild of my GranMere. a male twice my size and strength. Twice my Size and Strength. who still Lives under same roof as I. "what will he do to me. If. I go back home? He'll Kill me!" I wail. shake uncontrollably.

"He'll Kill Me!"

"I will have to move out." I conclude. Me move out? only a part-time job. in Grade 11. one year left. to complete HighSchool. Only One Year Left. "what will I do? to my Life? If. I don't go back Home? get a job at BusDepot?" my miserable short Life flashes. before my Tear-filled GreenEyes.

How could my Father die? leave me all alone. with no protector? How could Ma and GranMere. so obliviously. and strongly. Favour MeanBrother? Most Important. How could I do that? How Could I? How Stupid could I be? I Fought back! I have been taught. for so long. not to. Now. I am in real trouble. Real Big Trouble.

I fear Death. Fear Ma's fury. I know not All I Fear. I know. I Am Afraid. Then. like Magic. a flash of CrystalClear insight. a Magical Flash of Insight. Came. Came and is soon forgotten. or at least misplaced. for many years to come. I realize. I am no longer as afraid. I Was No Longer As Afraid. I looked Fear. in HisEyes. I Grabbed my chance. Grabbed My Chance. took my Survival. in my own Hands. my own Fist. I fight back. and Live. I Fought Back. And Lived.

I escape. Escaped. for a moment. Live to tell Story. I am here to tell. It. I eventually go Home. No word is mentioned. Not a Word. Except. "You sure left TheHouse in a mess." You Left TheHouse a Mess! One and only confirming fact. MyOlderSister says. many years later. when I tell her MyStory. "You sure left TheHouse in a mess."

That Day. Day of my Courageous Stand. ends MeanBrother's sexual abuse of me. Ended It! Does Not protect me. from Men. or by then. an ingrained belief. that Men had a Right. to MyBody. Men who appeared. all had same training. Uncles. Cousins. Neighbours. Bikers. TruckDrivers. Priests. Ministers. Counsellors. Bosses. Engineers. Doctors. Chiefs. MedicineMen. Patriarchy teaches All. same Script. different Lines. different Scenes. sometimes. different Endings. sometimes Not.

as I work to Heal. from Abuses. I re-examine all Guilt. Shame. Fear. I carry. LargeBurden. on my Back. Neck. Heart. Heavy. like a bag of Rocks. LargeBurden I carry. in my wire-meshed heavily armoured Heart. Heavily Armoured Heart. I know. Strong Lesson. Deeply held in MyBody. Hurts way. Way. Way. Inside. takes Body.Psyche.Heart. Healing to help. Heart Healing Helps.

this MedicineStory. Silently trapped. deeply held. in MyBody. Until. OneDay. freed by NarrativeTherapist. who wants me to "open space." "Search for exceptions to your problematic Story."[5] I am Told. Open Space. Search for Exceptions. Remember. when I challenge my abusers.

"Remember when you challenged Mean Brother." She tells me.

She has heard. More than she wants to know. More Than She Wants to Know. about MeanBrother tying me up. Wrists and Ankles rubbed Raw. too far from Home. NoOne to hear MyYells. MeanBrother throwing me through PictureWindow. shards of glass splinter. into MyHead. Hands. MyBlood blending. into flaming orange poppies. and more. Much More.

I am. like other victims of childhood abuse. "just sucked right into that tunnel where there was a thousand doors ... I couldn't stop talking about what was behind the doors that I did open."[6]

NarrativeTherapist tells me. "Don't book any more sessions. until you can share an exception Story." No More Sessions. She says. I leave Angry. Angry at Her. "How could she ask such a thing? How Could She! She's re-victimizing me." I complain loudly to Sisters.

after missing several sessions. I return with NoMore. Story to tell. took me thirty years. after hissing No More. Thirty Years. including twenty years as a feminist. to tell Story with pride. Pride of survival and resistance. Pride of recovery of self. my TeenWoman Self. I love her Spirit of Resistance.

Breaking Silence. does not mean. you will be Believed. or Loved. or Acknowledged. Denial is slippery slope. too Easy to fall into. One Time. in Recovery. from appendix attack. I am told. by Healer. "Release all Bitterness. and Resentment. Don't carry old Rage. a useless Burden. constant Anxiety. Wears on Mind.Heart.Body.Spirit."

Healer tells me. "Healing requires Forgiveness. of yourSelf. and Others. means Telling. Truths. Giving. others second chances. maybe many chances." I am wanting to be well. So. I send Brothers and Sisters. RecoveryLetter.[7] very carefully crafted. Hours Days Months of work. Hope to clear Resentment. Seek Acknowledgement. of NakedTruth. Help repair Relationships. Silence ensues.

months later. OneSister tells me. "I really can Not believe. that It ever happened. how could It?" I am a "vicious liar." my OtherBrother writes back. in his butI'mNotAngry Letter. my then eleven-year-old Daughter is told. by OneYoungerSister. "it takes two to have Trouble. in a relationship." No mention of PowerStrength differential. between a thirteen year old girl. and a sixteen year old boy.

AtThatTime. as my non-coincidental Life would have it. I am already enRaged. by FalseMemorySyndrome.[8] Tanya Lewis shares her.our. Story. "The reaction of my family of origin to the 'news' of my abuse soon taught me to tolerate multiple versions of truth in the same family. Either

MaMa defends her YoungOnes. Honors my Sister. Women. SheBears. all who rise up. and defend themselves. and their YoungOnes. against sexual exploitation.

that or accept the label of 'crazy' applied to those who speak the unwelcome truth."

Elders always teach. our ExtendedFamily. can be a great source of Strength. for each other. but. misplaced Family Loyalty. can cover up Alcoholism and Violence. MeanBrother continues to choose Silence. Denial. Can I pardon him without Admission of Guilt? without Acknowledgement of Hurt. or Acceptance of Responsibility?

"True Forgiveness requires that we understand the negative actions of another." teaches bell hooks. Can I learn. to feel Sorry for him. rather than Angry with him? Can I learn. to understand his Suffering. what drove him to offend. to begin with? Today. I struggle. like many others. to contextualize my Abuser. as an AngryYoungMan. he tried to take back his Power. by Victimizing his loved ones. as he was Victimized. MeanBrother was an AltarBoy.

Healing is ongoing. a Lifetime. Once abuse Ends. Once silence is Broken. Years later. I am able to help AnotherSister. stand Strong. Stop sexual exploitation. of Self. and Children. She knows. I Know. I speak my Truth. I Know. If. I stop talking. I'll stop Healing. so I Story. so I make Art. to help people Stop. Stop cycles of abuse. I give Loving support. I Believe It Actually Did. Does. Happen. Does Happen to Children. and Adults. Loving Truth Heals Relationships. ArtWork helps Heal. Supports ongoing Recovery.

Who Chooses?[9]

Who Chooses. to be a Victim?
  I want. No Need to know.
    as I sit in stunned silence. Mouth ajar.
    as I listen to those far too familiar.
      yet. still piercingly PainFul words.
      like a searing hot knife
      in an old cold infected Wound.
"I don't Choose to be a Victim." she says.
    in a somewhat smug. controlled. tight-lipped.
        Mooniyâs Voice of Authority.
I can't help feeling implicated.
I wrote. spoke my Wounded still bleeding Heart.
    just minutes before.
    poured out my carefully crafted dialogue of Despair.
    over never ending blatant institutionalized Violence.
    perpetrated regularly against me.
      as Nehiyâw'akWoman.
    against my Family. Friends. Students.
        CommunityMembers. Allies.
do you mean to say that I Do?
    that Women do?
    that Nehiyâw'ak. Black. Asian. Gay and Lesbians. Do.
    Do Choose. to be Victims.
      to be Raped. Exploited.
        Violated. Murdered. Marginalized.
I know from past experience
  that You will Deny culpability.
    Defend your Good Intentions.
      of course. You did not Intend. I am sure.
      to make such a sweeping racial gendered Slur.
      Supreme Court of Canada has ruled.
      Impact Not Intention.
      defines an Act of Racism.
I.We. are further victimized by insidious liberalist discourse.
        so called Choice.
Cuts across Race. Gender. lines.
  I was similarly slurred. not long ago.
  by a Nehiyâw'akWoman lawyer
    in whom I sought solace.
      when embattled in a decade long. Discrimination Dispute.
      "Why Choose to be a Victim?" she asks me.

I Want. No Need. You All to Know.
I did Not Choose to be a Victim Either.
We do Not Choose to be Victims. or to be reVictimized.
why do you Choose to be Perpetrators?

Notes

1. Lisa Marie Graveline, age 20, was murdered on Streets of Vancouver. in 2004. one of hundreds of Nehiyâw'akWomen "missing" in action. very scary.

2. direct quotes in this Story. are all taken from ThePas local Press. *TheOpasquiaTimes*, 1987. Published during Time of TheTrial. those eventually prosecuted for the rape and murder of Helen Betty: Volume 10. Number 73. November 27 (8) and Number 74. December 2 (1). another source is *Alberta Report*. January 11. 1988 (35). for a FullStory. by an outside media person. see *Conspiracy of Silence* by Lisa Priest 1989. for related Justice issues see *The Manitoba Justice Inquiry*. Volume II. 1991. by Hamilton and Sinclair.

3. I'll quickly tell. two short examples. ongoing Denial of this Reality.
   in 1989. I had returned to live in ThePas. I applied for a grant. to research personal. social. Sexual. Lives. Identities. of Girls.Women. of my age cohort. but. No "subjects." NoOne wanted to talk about It. no Funders wanted to support It.
   in 1995. I opened Take Back the Night March in Halifax. with "Ode to Helen Betty." from which this longer piece evolved. when I got to. "we were all raped regularly." CBC cameras. which were shining brilliant lights. into my Eyes. from beginning of my talk. suddenly went dark.

4. lots of Feminists. write about prevalence. and impacts. of Sexual Assault. a Manitoba version. done around same time of my research on Helen Betty. is Gunn and Minch 1988.

5. read Freedman and Combs 1996. on Narrative Therapy.

6. there are quite a few narratives. written by victims of Childhood Violence. like Lewis 1999. McNaron and Morgan 1982. But. this quote is from Nehiyâw'akMan. who was victimized by Priests. as a Boy. in Residential School. read more about his Story. Blakeborough in Fournier and Crey 1997.

7. my RecoveryProgram. is being guided by Kasl's work 1992. and StrongSisters in Women's Recovery Circles. AtThatTime. I was at Step Eight. of Sixteen Step Program. "We make a list of people we have harmed, and take steps to clear out negative energy by making amends and sharing our grievances in a respectful way."

8. I find literature on False Memory Syndrome horrible. and abusive. but. if you want to experience some of it first hand. read Bergun 1994. Wassil-Grimm 1995.

9. September 13, 2002. response to *Women and the Canadian Academic Tundra*. (Graveline 2002) book launch. Brandon University.

TEARS ARE A DOORWAY.
PLUMMETING THROUGH THEVOID

Plummetin'.
Mahê'kun hurtles though Black.Void. is it Despair? or darkSpace beyond Stars?
when It seems darkest. we must remember Dawn.

You. are experiencing MedicineStories.
arising from Cataclysmic Life experiences.
Events which have Taught me. Wounded me. Healed me.
Unbidden. Uncalled for Crises.
challenging. Life changing Transitions.
reveal Metaphysical. Mystic understandings.
Healing happens through Story.
when I recognize. I am like MotherEarth.
I am Strong and Fragile.
in my fragility. lies all possibilities of Growth.
in these MedicineStories I am communicating
through my Expressed Identity.
FirstVoice. Voice of Experience.
Spoken to Inform. Inspire.
to create Change
in Minds. Hearts. Lives.
I Story to know.
can my WoundedHeart ever heal?
like Beth Brant tells it.
"Our spirits hold loss, held in the centre, tightly.
We never have to remind ourselves of what has come down.
It is an instinct, like smelling autumn, or shaking pollen."
I work to remember. my Woundedness. is Not cause for Shame.
has been necessary. for my Spiritual Growth.
and Awakening.
Healing my WoundedHeart through Story.
requires actually being Heard. Validated.
Supported. Recognized.
within a like-minded Community.
Where is this Possible?
are you Listening?
can you Hear me?
Tell me. Where is a SafePlace?
to speak Truths about
Sexism. Racism. Classism. Homophobia.
Cultural Imperialism.
Pervading.Invading all our Lives?
Speaking Out. places me in a Vulnerable position.
Sharing my PainFull experiences.
can be Discomforting. Dangerous. a perilous Journey.
Wisakecahk asks.
how do I take Risks to Speak?
when I know not How.
or by Whom. my Words will be Taken?

how can I avoid. placing myself in too Vulnerable a position?
I am weary. wary. Aware of Listeners.
You may Project your Feelings. on Me.
Anger. Guilt. Fear.
Perceive me as Instigator of your Discomfort.
what about my Uncomfortable feelings?
targeted frequently. for Being who I am.
some ab-use Personal information
as Data. to Defend. their versions of Truth.
I Fear people's re-actions. Fear people's Fear.
Fear can Strip my Freedom. to Speak Truth.
Wisakecahk teaches. lessons Stronger than Words.
I am an Activist. I will continue to take Risks. to StoryTell. Teach.Heal.
to Resist. Disrupt. Dominant forms of Telling. Teaching.Healing.
to Challenge you to Examine. Change.
Systems which benefit Privileged.
my MedicineStories.
offer Learning.Healing. Opportunities. for us both.
like me. you must take Responsibility
for your Lessons.
for your Feelings.
my Life is a Journey.
an ebb and flow.
through Light and into Dark.
from Birth. we begin what we know of Life.
we Journey.
sometimes slow as molasses in January.
sometimes faster than falling Stars.
through Space and Time
to meet Death.
Here we Go.

DEATH OF AN ACTIVIST

to my dearest Papere. my Mentor. Heartfully appreciated. greatly Missed.

One Day. my GranMere says. "You work. You 'ave money. go upTown after School. buy yerself a BlackDress. You'll need one soon." I stare at her blankly. hung over. from my weekend basketball road trip. "What's she tryin' to say?" I think darkly to myself. I know better than to question her. I get up from table. I grab my books as I hear YellowBus honk out at roadside.

Driver always waits for me. He likes to look at round curves of my

Breasts. always wants to pretend it is Accidental. when his Hand touches me. I walk quickly by. and take my seat at back of YellowBus. All older Kids sit at back of YellowBus. Today. Driver puts his Hand out. grabs my arm. "'ow's yer Pa?" He wants to know. Everyone loves my Papere. Really. He always helps everyone. especially Underdog. "I don' know." I mumble. "Good. I guess." I just want to get by. and sit down. I don't like to be Touched.

Day drags on real Slow. my mind is blanking out. "How is Pa?" I try to think. I did talk to Ma on phone. She seems okay. "I'll go to Winnipeg on GreyBus. an' see Him." I think to myself. I make a serious mistake. I decide to go Home first.

GranMere tells me. "No. Don' go. Yer Ma doesn' need to be bothered wit you at a time like dis. stay Home. tend to yer chores." Chores. Chores. and more Chores. No Time to mySelf. No Time for myself. "No Time Left for you." I sing with TheGuessWho. in my mind. No one to Complain to. Keep it to myself.

ThatNight. I lay half awake in my Parents' bed. GranMere prefers mine. I Dream. I think it's a Dream. although I think I am awake. I DreamThink about my Father. my beloved Papere. Gentle. Loving. Kind. He comes to me. to say Goodbye. We have a good long talk.

He strokes my Hair. reMinds me. "I tol' you on your bed. OneDay. dat it was my time to go. dat I would'en survive da nex' trip. dat I would be taken out on a stretcher. an' not come back. You did'en wanna listen. an' tol' me it was'en true. but. it is true. mon Petite. c'est Vrai."

I can't believe it is True. I don't want to know. yet. I can't Deny it. I cry all Night. Curl up in a tight Ball. "Papere. 'ow can you leave me? leave us in dis 'arsh world?" I really want to know. but no answer comes. No Answer Comes.

I doze. and awake with a start to wailing of OlderSister. "Wake up. 'E's dead. Wake Up! Dad's Dead. Whaaaaahhhaaaaa." she wails. "like a Banshee." I think. I remember Shakespeare from School. I am calm. "I know." I say. "I talked to 'im. las' Night."

"Talked to 'Im Las' Night? Las' Night?" She stares in disbelief. Silent for a moment. I know she thinks me Crazy. Lodges Story in my Throat. Not to be told for many years to come. in that moment. I don't care. Neither does she. "Waaaahhhhh!!" she continues.

ThatDay. Granmere sends us to School. I am WalkingZombie. "How can she be so heartless?" I ask myself. my Anger percolates. slow brown black bubbles. Rising. Breaking smooth surface of my mind. I skip School. walk down to River.

my mind speeds. torrents of Questions. "Why me? Why Papere? what did I do to deserve dis? was I so bad?" Christian embedded Guilt rears its ugly head. Plummets me deeply into dark Void. of self-pity.

Now. I know. Papere died because of Cancer. like many veterans. a Victim of chemical warfare in WWII.[1] Now. I know. Cancer is not my fault. but. in that moment. I am convinced. like all Good Victims are. All Good Christians are. Bad happens to Bad people. Papere's Death. somehow. in some way. had to be because of Me. Had to Be Because of Me.

Elder recently teases me. when he hears me tell this Story. "You sure thought you had a lot of Power." I didn't think I had any Power. None at all. that terrible. Terrible Day. Frightfully cold Winter day. I am mittless and hatless. I stop by old MissionSchool. Now. shut down. Thanks to Papere. need to Hide. from bitter merciless February Winds.

OldPriest. friend to some family members spies me. calls my Name. invites me inside for Tea. and a Talk. I Need Tea. I don't need a sermon. I decide to go for Tea. know that I can close my Ears.

I keep wide open Eyes. always ready. to move away from roving Hands. my Legs crossing. uncrossing. wiggling in soft black leather chair. "softer dan a baby's bum." Ma would say.

OldPriest gently says to me. "so sorry about your fadder. 'E was a genuinely fine 'uman being. such a big 'eart. always gave to everyone. 'E will be missed." "yeah." I mumble Head down.

I concentrate completely on sipping. Sipping very hot. very sweet. very creamy liquid. We learned to drink Tea. like a meal. when offered. Cream … ummmm … such a luxury.

I am shivering myself warm. "do you want to Talk?" He asks. not waiting for an answer. "I'm a good listener." "No. thank you. Father." I say politely. I am still concentrating on my Tea. and keeping my guard up. one GreenEye on Door. other on OldPriest.

"I know it's 'ard to understand. why dese tings 'appen." He says. "I take comfort in my belief. Nothing 'appens witout a good Reason." OldPriest goes on. my mind begins to Whirl and Twirl.

"I always try to remember. what ever 'appens. it is God'sWill." He speaks in a comforting tone. reaches out to pat my Shoulder with grayish white gnarled Hand.

"God'sWill!" I burst out. Standing up. Dumping my Tea on rug. Burning my hand. Wetting my jeans. my only good seventeen dollar jeans. I wear them every day. "Merde!" I say under my Breath. trying to brush them for a millisecond. Then. I refocus.

"If. If. you're tellin' me dat YourGod wanted MyDad to die. I don' understand YourGod. He's Not MyGod anymore!" I shout. "Explain That!!" I shout even louder. "why would YourGod want MyDad dead? Why???"

I don't wait for an answer. I run out rectory door. up street. Tears Stream. down my Cheeks. Freeze. onto my Face. I don't care. I will die too. "Please God. dis is my las' Time. I'm talkin' to you. if yer really up dere. take me too. if you can will my Papere's death. will mine."

tires screeeech. BlueTruck slides to a stop. misses me by inches. Vince. my Father's friend. Jumps out. Grabs my arm. "what da 'Ell are ya doin'?" He yells in my face. Shakes me briskly. "Ya could be killed." He looks at my blue iced Face. and red Eyes. He says, "I jis 'eard. I am so so sorry."

He puts me in BlueTruck. drives me Home. just where I don't want to go. I slump deep into TruckSeat. Shut my Mouth. I will Not talk.

but. it's okay. Ma is home now. Granmere is gone to TheTown. We hug. I look at her sadly. She is Pale. Quiet. Her eyes are Hollow. I wonder if she knows about God's Will. I will wait to tell her AnotherDay. I see how her Spirit has left her. I get a glimpse. Now. We will be alone as Children. Olders raising Youngers. Life without Papere. a great Burden for her. for me.

I sit in front row. where I am put by Undertakers. I stare unblinking at a man's waxen face. Mouth pulled into a lopsided smirk. Gray. Thin. I hope. maybe it is Not Him. my Papere is Healthy. Brown. Weather-beaten. Strong. Not like this Pale. Wan. Lifeless. Spiritless. Corpse I see.

I hear YoungPriest's voice drone on. I wonder where OldPriest is. I hear later. He had a HeartAttack. shortly after. I fled rectory. and his well-intentioned talk. earlier that week.

I am startled back to unreality. I hear. "and on the fourth day Lazarus rose from the dead." Rose from theDead? can you believe it? I did. I see my Father's body rise from Coffin. Hang. suspended in Air.

I look around to see how everyone else is taking it. No reaction. I look back. He's back where he was. I am going Crazy. I know. I am still sane enough. to make sure I don't tell AnyOne.

not till more than twenty years later. after my Uncle's funeral. Auntie Eva and I seen my Uncle. Hovering in Air. over his Coffin. Laughing at us. only Then. I re-memoried this part of Story. Now. I Accept my Gift.

Anyways. in that moment in Time. I remain Calm. Cool. and Collected. a stoic mask that takes years to crack. jells in place on my Face. I cried my Tears in my Papere's Arms. four nights ago. when his Spirit came to visit. I cried enough.

I am indoctrinated to have Faith in God. I put out my last prayer. and nearly got an Answer. I am secure in my Faith. soon. I will find a way to join my Father. This Life. is Not for me. I am Not strong enough to cope.

months go by. my Body begins to wane. I drink and drug. I party with DangerousCrowd. I hitch-hike wherever I go. I ignore warnings of my Ma and GranMere. I hang with Bikers. become Donnie's girl. it's easy protection. after all. it's TheSeventies. in TheTown. MyHomeTown.

EveryOne Worries about Me. "what 'appen to GoodGirl? who goes to School. gets good grades. 'elps her Ma. takes care of 'er Brothers and Sisters. does chores?" GoodGirl fell. falls into a pool of Alcohol. I breathe It in. and feel Numb. I like that. Numb is Good. better than Guilt. Shame. Anger. Loss.

OneDay. SydMan comes to School. does a workshop for Youth. on Healing. He notices me. offers to give me some Time. I give Him a quick piercing gaze. I do Not want to be singled out of crowd. give Him a head shake. a quick curt. "No thanks." No Thanks. I say. tight little Smile. barely curling my upper Lip.

framed by Love.
Universally. Love has two dimensions. Love can Hurt. when Loss. Loneliness. Abandonment. Betrayal. Insecurity. Fears. take us over.

AfterSchool. Vince is outside with BlueTruck. wants me to go to his house for supper. I shrug. "Sure." anything not to have to go Home.

there He is. SydMan. Workshop guy. over for supper at Vince's. I eat quietly. Head down. Listen to them. chat about GoodOldDays. I do not realize. I am set up. until dinner is done. Until After Dinner Was Done. Vince quietly clears out with dishes.

"'Ere." SydMan says. "I'll sit 'ere. You sit dere. 'Ere's a chair for yer Pere. because 'e is still very much wit us. I see you clingin' on to 'im. it's makin' you both sick. 'E 'as to go. You 'ave to let 'im go. what do you want to say to yer Pere before 'e goes?"

my GreenEyes snap open. real wide. "is dis guy for Real?" I wonder to myself. I stare motionless. for a few long seconds. I realize he is serious. He actually means what he says.

He is brown. with black hair. His BlackBrownEyes crinkle. Twinkle. Glow warmly. like my Papere. "You Métis?" I ask. He says. "Oui. et-tu?" I say. "Oui."

all of a sudden. something hits me. Right in my Heart. like an Arrow flew from a Bow. I hang my head. and Cry. for FirstTime. since my Papere's LastVisit. Not loud racking sobs. just quiet hot Tears. Streaming down my Face. like two Rivers. burning lines in cold stone of my Cheeks.

I didn't know. Crying is good. I didn't know. Weeping creates a River. carries Canoe holding my SoulLife. how Tears lift my Canoe off Rocks. off dry ground. carries her downRiver to someplace New. to someplace Better.

AtThatTime. I feel Weak. Wimpy. and Embarrassed about it.

He sits and waits. waits quietly and calmly. He does not move. does not try to Comfort me. or Touch me. I am relieved. I start to Trust him more. a tiny little chink in my HeartArmour opens.

I tell him. "I'm mad at Pa for leavin' me." "tell 'im." He says. Points to EmptyChair with his Lips. I clam up. dart my Eyes between SydMan. and EmptyChair. slouch. try to bury myself in HardKitchenChair. He waits.

I tell EmptyChair. just slowly at first. feeling kind of Stupid. Then. all in a rush. All my Hurt. Anger. Guilt. my need to Die torrents out. I beg him to come back. to find a way to bring me with him. I am sobbing now.

He waits. offers Nothing. No kleenex. No pity. No conversation. No physical contact. I am further relieved. a little more Opening happens. I can feel a little twinge of pain. in my chest.

finally. raging rapids subside. when I'm done. He says. "Now. move. and change places wit yer Pere." He motions with his lips and chin. "sit in yer Pere's chair."

I stare at him. for a full minute. "I'm not doin' dis anymore." I think. I am surprised to find myself moving. against my Will. but Not. Not anything He is doing to me. at least. Nothing I can tell.

I find myself seated again. "Now. what does yer Pere 'ave to say?" He asks. "what does 'e want to say to you. about what you jis said?" I am confused at first. Then. Papere's Voice talks in my Head. Smooth. Deep. Sweet. like liquid Maple. collected and boiled in Spring.

my Mouth drops open in Surprise. Words start to tumble out. like a glistening Rainbow Waterfall over Rocks. "oh. Bebe. Chichi. Je't'aime. Pauvre Petite. I will always love you. You 'ave to go on. You're so Strong. Wise an' Beautiful. ma Cherie."

I feel Papere's love wash over me. Warm. Glowing. "You 'ave lots of work to do in da world. Remember. all I 'ave taught you. all dat we 'ave Shared. da work I 'ave started you will carry on. You mus' be Courageous. You mus' Survive. Weder you wan' to or not." in ThatMoment. I decide I want to. I Want To Survive. in ThatMoment that is.

my Mouth opens. and closes. Words jump out. in a Voice I recognize. it is Not mine.

"You always tooked everyting to 'eart. felt sorry for da hurt ones. Runt of da Litter. you're like me. We stan' up strong agains' injustice." River of Tears. are Streaming out of my Eyes. and Nose. giving my Canoe a good Ride. I wipe them on my sleeve. unselfconscious. Now.

"You're Not ready to come wit me. I will be wit you. I will 'elp you. when you need me. I'll be dere. when you're done your Life. I will see you 'ere in dis Beautiful place. where I am. Not before. Not Before. Life mus' be Live to 'is fulles'."

"You're Love by me. You will be Love by others. Remember. what I wrote in your autograph Book. "Love Many. Trus' Few. Always Paddle Yer Own Canoe."

Always Paddle MyOwnCanoe. "I'll really need dat now." I think. Later. "but. it isn't a message Just for me." I rationalize. He always wrote that in everyone's Book. We would run to get our Books when any Visitors came. I remember as LittleGirl. sitting on my Papere's lap. trying to correct his English. "These. Not Dese. Three. Not Treee. Com'mon you Can do it. Jis Try." I would say. He would Laugh. and try. for me.

when I am Done. No. I mean. when He's Done. Done talking through me. I mean. SydMan gets me to move again to my old place. "Now. respon'." He says. We go back and forth a few more times. I become more and more convinced. I am meant to Live on. I promise

Papere that I will survive. I am lighter and lighter each time.
HeavyHeartBurdens of Anger. Grief. Guilt and Shame. are being lifted.
I am more at peace. feel less like Cutting myself off. Cutting myself up.
at least for ThatMoment.

ThatNight. SydMan and I. and Papere. Work All Night. until pink
pearl Dawn creeps her way up over horizon. out of Darkness. I emerge.
GreenEyes blinking in growing Light. I will Survive this Loss. I will
mourn for many years. for my Lifetime. but. I know. I will Live to Love
others. from inside out. Ready or Not. I begin my HealingJourney.

Squeezing Life. between Small Spaces.

Truthfully. I Story to Learn. Help Tell.
how MedicineStorying can be part of Real. Deep. HeartFelt.
Personal.Political. Healing.
Stories from Therapy often end. like this one.
with some new small Triumph.
I can end Here.
as if. my struggles are Over.
as if. I have Arrived. somewhere.
my struggles are Not over that Day. or Day after that.
will Never be over.
shall I join millions of Humans in search of a single solution?
TheKey to HappilyEverAfter.
Grasping frantically at simple solutions for complex problems.
Social. Economic. Political. Cultural. Spiritual.
Swallowing pills to eradicate symptoms
enhances personal disconnection.
perpetuates victimizing.
serves domination.
where is TheMedicine that will cure me?
if I. move one more time.
learn to not get angry.
if I. eat right.
lose weight.
if I. get rich.
marry right. white.
will that take away my Pain?
like my Stories.
Life sometimes seems to go on and on.
Healing is a Journey.
like Life itself it has No Endings.

there is No Right Answer. One Truth.
No Magic Solution. Instant Cure.
No way to take away Pain.
No end to our HealingJourney.
in this Lifetime or next.
my view of this LifeTime. Worlds.
Male.Female. Nehiyâw'ak.Mooniyâs. Relations.
are shaped by my experiences.
during specific Historical times.
Sociopolitical. Cultural. Spiritual contexts.
my Life.Work. career pattern.
has been indelibly stamped with Themes.
working to end Violence against Women and Children.
fighting against Racism. Oppression. Eurocentrism.
with.in. and through.out. educational settings.
I Story to Heal effects.
Spirits of Ancestors. MedicineStories.
give me a Gift. Survival.
I know. in my Head.Heart.Spirit.
there is great Strength. Pride. in Surviving.
Surviving against great odds to continue to Fight.
in my early years.
I learn to see Life.World. through RapeColoured lens.
Live experiences of Domination.
I know. what it takes to Survive.
what it takes to Resist.
HelenBetty paid ultimate price of Resistance.
Death of my Father.
my most Beautiful. Cherished. Honoured Papere.
Poverty of a now Mother-headed family of seven.
events combined.
to make my HomeCommunity.
where I experienced Community.
SurvivalBushMétis Consciousness.
where I only know myself InRelation to Family. Community.
I have to leave.
Had To Leave
I know. I will die here. Die There.
as many Family. Friends have.
So. I leave.
use University as a way out. a Way Out!
a Métis bursary as a Reason.
little do I realize. what Path I am taking.
do I make a Rational choice?

do I have a choice?
Choose. Life or Death.
seems little Choice at all.
Little Choice At All
yet. is most profound one.
anyone ever makes.
much Later. when I return.
visit my Father's. Mother's. GrandMother's.
Uncles'. Aunts'. Cousins'. graves.
I wander about. Notice. many of my Peers. Dead.
Overdoses. Violent Deaths.
recently. I find out. an epidemic of BrainTumors. is taking my age cohort.
an experiment performed. on NorthernNehiyâw'ak peoples.
without anyone's knowledge or consent.
a double dose of polio vaccine.
Remember. pink sweet stuff on sugar cubes.
"Open up and down the hatch." StarchWhiteNurse would say.
my OlderSister. at fifty years old. already had brain surgery once.
I Choose to leave my HomeCommunity.
I Hope for Life.
but. who really knows when Death awaits?
UndergradArts at University.
more of Same. "You Don't Have to Understand. How It All Fits Together.
Just Memorize It." Just Memorize It.
Classroom relations resemble MissionSchool. without overt abuse.
No one mentions anything about Nehiyâw'ak people.
in any of my courses. All year.
I see no other Nehiyâw'ak students. that I know of.
have no Nehiyâw'ak teachers. this is Not new.
No Nehiyâw'ak anything.
I am TheOnlyOne. I am TheLonelyOne. OnlyLonelyOne.
I Live in a Box. Dorm. Single Room.
Bed. Desk. Chair. Closet.
I never had Room. to myself before. Never mind a Bed.
I cry. Cry and Cry.
I sleep in Lounge. Dangerous.
I sleep with Friends. whenever I can.
I phone my Mother. I cry on phone. We cry.
but. She can't Help.
I am so far away. So far. Far Away.
"and no. No. I don't want to go Home.
No. No. Not yet. I will wait. Just a little while longer.
Just. a Little While. Longer."
after all. I remember Auntie Eva.

my promise to Papere.
It isn't That Bad. Not as Bad as. as TheTown. MyHomeTown.
I persist. I know. I Have to. I Knew I Had To.
I can Not return. Not Return to TheTown.
MyHomeTown.
Poverty. Blatant Misogyny.
Death-producing Racial Hatred.
early. in my FirstYear. Arts.
I know. I will apply for SocialWork.
a person can get a Job. Get a Job back Home.
Back Home they said. They said.
"come back with a SocialWork degree."
I Dream of being a Teacher. Lawyer. Artist.
but. SocialWorker speaks to me.
"Help Poor People. Your People." so I do.
in my years of University Life.
I feel so different from other students.
most from Mooniyâs backgrounds.
mirror Professors. those who are my Teachers.
I wonder. "what can they Teach me?
when they know Nothing about my Reality?"
They Know Nothing of My Reality.
I'm Not prepared to tell Them.
I Never speak unless I Have to.
I often feel silenced. Silenced.
Again and Again. Silenced.
I listen to others. Speak of their issues.
on rare occasion. I speak my Truth.
I see disbelief in Their Eyes.
Hear it in Their Voices.
I Try to Lie.

BEING WHITE. AIN'T RIGHT.

One cold Winter's Day. my Mouth opens up. Words jump out. They are Not my own. a Voice speaks. "My Father was a banker." My Father Was A Banker! My Mouth says That? completely disconnects from my Brain. my Mind races. "Why did I say That?" I wonder wildly.

my Face flushes a deep crimson. NoOne notices. NoOne asks further probing questions. NoOne notices beads of Sweat. broken out on my upper Lip. NoOne can smell StressSweat Body is emitting. NoOne cares. conversation continues. I slip quietly into a silent retreat. for remainder of class. rest of term. my Mind Whirls. "I don't remember my Father going to Bank. He must have."

Why should anybody care? my Father TheBanker. fit in. with EveryOne's everyday reality. except mine. and my Father's. little did They know. HomeCommunity didn't even have a bank. my Father was a Carpenter. Farmer. WaterWitcher. Healer. Advocate. Trapper. Hunter. Mechanic. Engineer. worked with his Hands. Jack of all trades.

I am Ashamed. Ashamed of myself. I lied about my Father. wonderful Man that he was. Lied to fit in with Mooniyâs. at SocialWorkSchool. I go home that terrible terrible Day. Aching. Hating my oozing very WoundedRedHeart. feel it pound in my Chest. wish it wouldn't.

Later. I call Ma. "'ow's Life goin'?" I say. I want to tell her. Tell her what I said. I want to Laugh about it. to hear Her Laugh about it. turn it into a funny Story. be Amused. need LaughterMedicine for my Soul.

but. sumpPump is broken. No money for moccasins for TheKids. Cat had Kittens. on my MuskratCoat. "I'm going to sell GreyJeep. We need Money." She says. "Papere said GreyJeep was mine." I think this answer to myself. of course. She Will sell GreyJeep.

I find no Words. No right time. No time to bring It up. No time to Laugh Together. Story Arrow lodges in my Chest. Festering.

Later. Voice tells Story. brings Comfort to YoungMan. who tells his Story. He cut his Hair. to Pass as Mooniyâs. to get a Job. He knows. They won't hire Nehiyâw'ak. I tell him. how I Storied about my Pa. when I am trying. too Hard. to feel Comfortable. in a Mooniyâs crowd. Share how bad I feel. HeavyRedHeartBurden feels lighter.

Much Later. I make peace with Papere. through PipeCeremony. One Day. I pray him Story. make it into a funny one. Trickster tale. I can hear tinkling laughter. feel a warm glowing sensation. His flowing maple voice says. "You know. a Banker is da las' ting I would wan' to do. hangin' round wit all dat dead money. dos crush up Trees. what a Story. You must'ave bin havin' a real time of it. to make dat one up. You always love to tell a GoodOne."

my Papere. admired beings abilities. to Survive in many different circumstances. ShapeShift as necessary to do so. He understood. Rabbits and other Creatures turn White in Winter. Never had to ask Why. He Understood. BlackBear wanted to turn White. so bad he got cooked. in Wolverine's Lodge.[2] Never had to ask Why. Accept. No need to ask. Why?

Listen. and Learn. from our Experiences. many many people have to creatively Story tell. called Lying by some. Story to survive Racist. Alienating. situations. I'm Not alone. I'm not first or last. to try to Pass.

what about J. Edgar Hoover? read our Stories. find out. how we creatively cope. continue to thrive. even when our cultural identities are negatively internalized. Now. I question. why do we feel we have to disown our Selves. our Families. to be accepted. as one of TheGroup?

find out. how Nehiyâw'ak integrate into Mooniyâs society. without Losing ourSelves. Disowning our Families. George Longfish tells us. "The more we are able to own our religious, spiritual and survival information, and even language, the less we can be controlled ... to rid ourselves of these pictures and own who we are is to take control and not play the game by white rules."

Notes

1. Chemical warfare multiplied health costs. Russell documents. in 1936. a doctor thought lung cancer was "a rare disease that (they) might never see again." (Gunn Allen 1998: 107). Today. Cancers have risen to epidemic proportions. some blame Smoking. what about "the Bomb, nuclear testing, horrible proliferation of radioactive waste all over the country ... proliferation of electrical apparatus-power plants, power lines, electrification of every home ... seemingly endless variety of chemical toxins that have spread throughout the planetary biosphere...." (Gunn Allen 1998: 107).

2. Many tell Traditional Stories. most are Nehiyâw'ak. some write them down. most are Mooniyâs. One who wrote some down is Joseph Bruchac see "Wolverine and Bear." for example.

LOVE IS A DOORWAY.
LOVING ARMS. BREAK MY FALL.

Love Heals.
a fiery merging. of two Minds. Hearts. Bodies. Souls. is a Healing act of Self.Other. Love.

to my loving Sisters in Struggles. you know who you are.

OneTime. I am barely surviving.
Culture Shock. City Life. Loneliness. Lowliness.
when I stumble upon Women's movement. take up with AWARE.
Alberta. Women. Against. Rape. and Exploitation.
it is early Seventies.
early in HerStory of AntiRape movements in Canada.
I.We. are Waking up. to Male chauvinism. Patriarchy.
We are Angry. Angry Aware Women.
I can feel my Anger.
like a hard ball of granite. Hard Ball of Granite.
in the pit. in ThePit. of my Stomach.
Now. Only Now. Only Then. do I begin to realize.
how much Violence has been embedded in my Life. Story.
as a Métis.Girl. living Near. attending School.
in an Overtly WomanHating
Nehiyâw'akWomanHating Community.
I engage in ConsciousnessRaising. ConsciousnessRaising.
I am never ever. Never Ever TheSame.
Never Been TheSame since.
I begin to relearn language of Resistance.
Fight Back. They.We. said. Take self-defence.
Walk Tall. They.We. said.
Walk Strong. Tall and Strong.
Don't be a Victim. They.We. said. Don't take it.
I learn to See. and Name.
See. and Name. a societal structure.
contributing to my personal Problems. Inadequacies. Fears.
I learn a name for It. It is Patriarchy.
They tell me. "It Is Patriarchy!" I believe them.
"It is Patriarchy." I say to any. all who will listen.
and some who won't. "It Is Patriarchy!"
this begins a Healing process. for me.
for my WomanSelf.
I owe a debt of gratitude to Women. Sisters. who hear my Stories.
Listen without Disbelief. Love me.
I Saw. Felt. Love. Sisterhood. at that Time. Place.
StrongWomen. were. are my Family. Lifeline.
through some rough times. Rough Times.
reMembering. reLiving.
reTelling. our Histories of Abuse.
Raising our Consciousness. of our Selves.
as Victims.

as Survivors.
as Resistors.
Sharing our Anger. our Visions.
We cry. and cry.
Cried and Laugh.
Laughed and Love. Loved Together.
I am relearning. reMemory.ing.
how to Love myself. how to Love Women.
Strong Sisters in Struggle teach me.
Mighty WarriorWomen engage in battles unborn cannot fight.

MOTHER.DAUGHTER.SISTER. BLUES

while I am Journeying on in my Life. Healing. Reclaiming my WomanSelf. my Mother. Dear. Sweet. Strong. Independent Ma. is weakening. numbing her Loss and Pain through Alcohol. Life. No Death. in a Bottle.

several years have passed. since Papere's death. She is remarried now. to an alcoholic Man. Mister.

when my Birthday passes. "No call from Ma." I think. "this can't be. She would never Forget. Seven children She birthed. She would Not Forget one of us. Not on our Special Day." I call home. a little high from a few drinks after work at FavouriteBar. "Yer Ma's not home." GramMere says in her normally harsh tone. "She's in TheCity. in TheHospital."

"in TheHospital?" I shriek. "Why didn't someone call?" "Didn' wanna worry you." She says in her matter of fact tone. "What Hospital?" I ask. when I hear her say Name. I freeze. Papere died in ThatHospital. All people from up North die. in ThatHospital.

I call ThatHospital. find out her Room. call Plane and book a ticket to TheCity. Soon. I arrive. on steps of ThatHospital. Grey. Glass. Steel. Septic smell. Quiet hustling. Rustling starched shirts. Not a healing place. a death trap of old Germs. Drugs. Toxic cleansers. Disinfectants. Latex.

Soon. I see Ma. Mass of Tubes. Wires. Metal contraptions. my Heart stops a beat. how can this be? how can she lay so Lifeless? so Yellow? I want to Scream. Rage. Cry. Confess. Plead. instead I swallow hard. Clench my Jaw. and my Fists. cautiously approach her bed. Not entirely sure it is Her. Not wanting it to be True.

almost twenty years Later. Healer mentions to me. "something is deeply stored in your Jaw. Grief. maybe Anger. You Need to let it Go." Nothing comes to my mind. in that moment. as I rewrite this Story. I know. my Jaw never let go. maybe now it can. Healing stories I write for me. and for you.

Anyways. I call Ma back. back from FarAwayPlace. Her Spirit has taken her. maybe beyond Stars. where all is Blacker than darkest Nights. "Ma. I'm here to visit you. Wake up." Her eyes open. Whites first. Iris rolling with difficulty to focus.

She stares at me for a while. dry Tongue licks parched Lips. I grab a glass of IceWater with straw. place it in her Mouth. She sucks weakly. has a few small sips. struggles to sit up. I hold. No. Clutch. her now bird-like Hand.

I can hardly contain my Disbelief. it all happened so Fast. just last May. We had BigFamilyScene. pressure Ma to quit drinking. to go to AA. or Treatment. or something. Anything. after I saw her Doctor. heard she had four months to Live. Four Months to Live!

She quit drinking. She had quit. Youngers monitor her. as much as they can. They tell me. "Mister still mixes drinks. places them by her Hand. You know. beside her OldBrownRocker. in case Ma changes her mind. I guess."

"Can this really be True? is Ma really ending her Life? like This?" I think chaotically. I grab at thoughts. "How do I begin a conversation?" I try not to Stare. Stare at FrailYellowWoman. who has once been Strongest. Wisest. Toughest. Woman I know.

I remember. "I beat Boys at ice hockey. when I was at Convent." She brags. as she stick handles past us all on TheCrick. "She beat Boys up. for picking on Girls. even Girls she didn't like!" Ma's Girlfriends from Convent would giggle. She could Arm wrestle or Leg wrestle. wrestle any of us Kids down. even my Brothers. even MeanBrother.

my Mind flips back. roams over our Life Together. TheOneandOnly "fight" I ever had with her. was over HerCar. GreenMercury. She didn't want to lend it to me. one particular Night. because she heard. Heard I was drinking and driving. She says. "Forget it. if you're gonna be Reckless. I need MyCar. to go back and forth to work. to Town." I am Angry. "I already promised MyFriends!" I Shout at her. I raise my Hand.

next thing I know. Wham!! I am on WoodFloor. with her Foot on my Chest. "Don' you ever. No! Never! Raise yer 'and to me again. I'm Yer Mother!" she growls firmly. between her clenched Teeth. "I Am Yer Mother! an' Don' You Ever. Ever. Forget It!" Right now. I can Not forget it.

I am remembering her Strength. Right then. her Independence. Determination to carry on. Living on OurFarm. "for TheKids." after Pa died. "how can she? let this happen to her? how could she?" Judgement skips through my Brain. resting in my HeavyHeart.

I know. Now. how addictive a substance Alcohol is. how many. Many People. get into Alcohol's grip.[1] how alcoholism is hereditary. a physiological disease. Ma's Father. my GrandFather died young. an alcoholic. Alcoholism. a type of slow suicide. some people do Recover. Many. many people. do Not. Ma did Not. No.

AtThatTime. I know Nothing. I only know. this shell of a person is my Mother. I feel responsible. for choosing to Live my Life. when I Should have been rescuing her. from her Life. this unfinished business. follows me. throughout my Life. and my relationships. until. I finally lay rescuing to rest. just lately. I hope.

You know. You can Not Live anyone else's Life for Them. You can Not change anyone else. Only yourSelf. a Lesson I painfully learn. and relearn. am still learning.

Anyways. I sit here at Ma's deathbed. Numb with Guilt. and Grief. She squeezes my hand. "I love you." She hoarsely whispers. like she hasn't used her Voice in a long while. Tears spring to her.our. Eyes. "I love you too Ma." I whisper back. in a stuck in my throat kind of way.

"I'm glad you came." She says. a bit more clearly now. "I had to." I breathe. "I always regretted. I never saw Pa before he died. Granmere said. Said you wouldn't want me to come." She squeezes her Eyes shut. Tears drop out.

I feel Bad. Bad for bringing that old stuff up. at a time like this. I could've kicked myself. "Why can't I ever jis leave well enough alone." I silently berate myself. as she seems to doze off. HazelEyes close for a few minutes.

She drags open her Eyes again. Struggles to focus. "Ma was very hurt in her Life. You 'ave to forgive her. for her Bitterness. don't carry it on." dry Tongue darts over cracked Lips. "I would've liked you to come. Yer Pa wanted to see you Kids. but he couldn't." She looks so tired. Tired. Sad. and Yellow.

I want desperately to make it up to her. to make her Happy. "I could go and get TheKids. bring them here to see you." I say in a rush. All excited. finally. I latch on to something. Something. I think I can do to help. "No." She croaks hoarsely. "I don' 'ave Time. or Energy. I don' want dem to see me like dis. it'll give dem nightmares. I look bad. Don' I?"

I ignore her question. don't want to say. "but. what can I do? what can I do for You?" I cry. I want to be able to Do something. to Help. Do Something to fix TheSituation. in some way. She gave me Life. I feel I

Owe her Something.

I hang my Head. Tears Stream down my Face. "how can this be? first my Papere. Now. my Ma. what can I do? what did I do? do to Deserve this?" I allow myself luxury. feel very sorry. Very sorry for myself. for a few minutes at least. swallowed in a dark sea of self-pity.

I want to be able to Pray. I can't. God is Dead. He died with Papere. "God's Will. I am reminded. I never did tell Ma about OldPriest. "Now. is Not TheTime" I tell myself. I wonder for a minute. "is this God's idea of a bad joke?" "Forget God!" my inner Guide says. "Look at your Ma. see her Loss. her Grief. her Needs. Not your own."

I squeeze Ma's Hand. She opens her HazelEyes weakly. Struggles to focus. to Journey back from FarAwayPlace. her Mouth begins to move. I lean closer. hear soft scratchy words come out. "I'm going to die. You know." "No!" I say. I desperately want to deny Her reality. "No. You're going to get better." She is right. We both know it.

I stare at her blankly. Wait. for a time. in silence. finally. I croak. "what can I do for You?" She waves her hand limply towards Door. "Leave me. I'm okay. Go Home. take care of TheKids for me."

my Eyebrows arch in wonderment. "You're okay?" I think to myself. "just like my Ma." Independent. to very end of her Life. She reminds me. Her Strong. Self-sufficient self. after Papere died. She would rather struggle. with my help. to shovel LongDriveway. Knee deep Snow. it seemed every Day. in February. and March. rather than call any Uncles. or my Aunts for that matter. Would Not call Anyone to Help us. No One.

Then. She says. in a Voice. caught in both of our Throats. "I've Always loved All my Kids. You know." Hot Tears. brim over my Eyelids. spill down my already wet Cheeks. "I know. You've always been a GoodMother. to me. to all of us." I affirm. nod my Head. Tears flow. "I love you Ma." Ma moans. reaches to me. I reach to hold her. Her now thin and frail self. No barriers remain.

Soon. She closes her HazelEyes. nods off to sleep. I sit with her for several hours. Watch. as She rests. it is an Awakening for me. I realize. I never ever saw my Ma rest before. She was always busy with paid work. evening shift as an LPN. "LowestPaidNurse." She would joke with her nurse friends. over coffee and cigarettes. on her feet bustling. from bed to bed. with Comfort. kind Words. Medicines.

Subsistence Life on OurFarm made for lots of work. Cows to feed. Hay to stook. Manure to shovel. Garden to dig. Weeds to hoe. Pickles. Jams and Jellies to make. even with a small House. there always seems to be endless house work. Floors to scrub. Dishes to do. Laundry to hang and iron. Meals to cook.

of course. there is always MotherWork. seven Children to Feed. Clothe. Comfort. and DaughterWork. aging Mother. GranMere. to run errands for in TheTown. and CommunityWork. Bingos to work at. Bake-sales to cook for. Meetings to attend. People in need of help. Help for this and that.

Work took all Ma's time. "Rest In Peace." crosses by my Mind. many times that Long Night. I start to gain a small inkling. what that saying actually might mean.

at Dawn. I stiffly get up. I kiss her Cheeks. a kiss. a press with Cheek. first. one side. then another. Gently. Reverently. like my old Aunties did. when they hadn't seen me for a long while. hold her frailness close for a few minutes. seems like hours. Space and Time suspend. as her Body sleeps. her Spirit travels. preparing her Way. I Know. still Deny. it will be our Last Time.

SomeTime Later. I rise to go. "I will go Home. tell TheKids news. be there for Them." I think to myself. "it is what Ma wants." They are all Teens now. self-raised for last few years. while Ma drank. lots of Anger. Loss. Abandonment. Fears. Loneliness. I want to Love them. Nurture them. I Need to.

my Heart is heavy. HeavyHeart. burdened with Loss. Grief. Guilt. I leave her. I leave her room. Dazed and Confused. Confused about what to do. I take a Cab. catch next flight home. to "take care of TheKids." "Take Care of TheKids." I muse as I fly. "seems easy enough." how can I be so Wrong? Naiviety? Youthful optimism?

TheKids are excited. I am coming home. Home to OurFarm. I am Interesting. Fun. IdolizedOlderSister. take Time to talk with Them. do things with Them. when I am Home. how we Hug each other at Airport. They all come to greet me. want to know about Ma. Know I will be honest with Them.

We get Home to OurFarm. I want so much to be able to tell Them. "Ma's going to be all right." I am stopped. stabbed by a pain in my Back. sharp reminder of Anger. Betrayal. I feel at fifteen. when no one would tell me. Papere was dying. "You were too young to understand." I am told later. Shock and Disbelief. when he did die. and Anger. lots of Anger. at myself and others.

I face TheKids with facts of Ma's condition. offer. Against her wishes. to bring Them to visit her. They choose to Live through MyStories of her deathbed. They have for years. Lived through MyStories. of farm Life with Papere. of exciting worlds outside OurIslandHome.

We Live in an Uneasy state of Anticipation. anticipating Ma's Death. unable to do Anything. except pass Time. Try not to think about it. for a week. Life is uneventful. One Morning. after a hardy party Night before. I awaken. with an awful feeling. feeling of being Invaded. I glance around Room. All five were in Room with me. Not unusual. Usual for TheKids. sleeping with KnifeInDoor.

I creep downstairs. Mister is Home. "What can It mean?" I wonder. "is Ma gone?" Mister is Ma's husband of two years. an alcoholic man. with no love for Ma's Children. including me. He isn't shy to show us that.

Mister bore brunt. of my.our. collective Anger. Anger at Ma's condition. He opened up blurred Life of daily drinking to Ma. three years earlier. He knows. Alcohol is killing Ma. He already killed one Wife. with Alcohol. Reeks of Booze and BO. Refuses to seek help for himself. or Ma. Ignores her efforts at Sobriety. even if she has only four months to Live if she continues to drink. He is still alive. while she is dying. We Hate him for it.

and now he Returns. to our Sanctuary. OurFarm. OurHome. leaves Ma to lay. Dying alone. Lonely. without comfort. in white-walled prison of ThatHospital. for two days. We tiptoe around him. He stays. "to take care of some Business." He says in a nasty tone. when I mistakably ask. We are soon to find out. His Business is not in our best interests.

Ma hangs on for three weeks. We wait. without waiting. to pass Time we plan. "what are TheOrphanKids going to do?" NoOne talks about Ma's death. EveryOne creates OurFantasy. what we would all do next. set in a flurry of Fall. Canning. Haying goes on. as though waiting. as Though Waiting for Ma to come Home. Home from ThatHospital well.

until OneDay. Aunt and Uncle arrive at OurFarm. with OldestSister. waiting is over. Mister phoned them. He will be home with TheBody soon. Ma's words ring in my ears. "Take care of TheKids for me." Days following are a blur. Anger. Pain. and Grief. Public strength. and Private misery. Ma has groomed me well.

during her Funeral. I sit with YoungestSisters on either side. each takes a turn. Hysterical Crying. I have no time to mourn. No time for gaping hole. BlackHole in my HeavyHeart. I am stoic. Despair turned inward. I will Not cry again. No crying out of sadness. for a very long time. HeavyHeartBurden. feels like Lead. Weighed me down. for a very long time. Long time still. sometimes.

soon. parade of WellWishers. ColdTurkeySandwiches with crusts cut off. Dainties. is over. one last task remains. Reading of TheWill. We sit in silence. Mouths dropped to floor. Eyes pop open. to Hear so-called

FinalWishes of our Mother. We leave in Despair. and Disbelief.

No provisions have been made. No provisions made for her Children. TheKids. Us. OurFarm Gone. Farm of our Birth. Farm of our Labour. Labour of our Ma and Pa. left solely to Mister. Left Solely to Mister. we can't believe it.

We can Not. Do Not want to Believe it. "No. It can't be True." We exclaim. to Any and All who will listen. Not many will. or can. OurFantasy crashes. We can Not stay Together on OurFarm. We are Homeless. that is. Unless TheKids Live with Mister. They do Not want to. "Please don't make us." They say.

SomeThing has to be done. by SomeOne. Desperately. We begin to think up devious murder plans. If. he does not survive Ma. by thirty days. TheWill. will not be valid. and we will inherit OurFarm. which we feel. of course. is rightfully ours. We feel it is Ours. Not his. Not Mister's.

Legal advice is sought. "You can contest TheWill." We are told. "You can declare your Mother incompetent." "Incompetent!" NoOne wants to slur Ma. Tarnish or Belittle her memory. any more than her Alcoholism already has. NoOne can think Sane. NoOne can declare Ma Incompetent. Confused yes. Coerced yes. Her brain clouded. Pickled in Alcohol. Yes. but. NoOne can condemn her. Publically call her Incompetent. Not Ma.

Meanwhile. OurClan gathers. "Girls should go to BoardingSchool. to Convent at DuckLake. Boy can stay with Him. or live with Uncle and Aunt? or OurNeighbours? maybe He will move?"

All talk about us. rarely does AnyOne talk to us. NoOne knows what to do. many Arguments ensue. tear closely interwoven fabric of OurClan. OurCommunity. tear OurLife to shreds. Nothing makes sense. NoSense.

unspoken belief hangs in Air. I am influencing TheKids. against Mister. hangs heavy like sludge. in Dense. Tense. atmosphere. "Mebbe. if you leave. TheKids will settle down. wit' 'im on TheFarm." I am Told. Not very gently. by OneAunt. "after all. 'e was yer Ma's husband. 'e must'ave cared for 'er. for 'er Children. 'e married 'er." She assumes more than she knows. Her own steady drinking habit. blurs her sensibilities.

So. I leave. take oldest of TheKids. She is now eighteen. can say for Herself. She comes with me. one month passes. several hundred dollars later. in long distance phone bills. We return. We collect TheKids. grab a few belongings. leave Too Much behind. later all is Burned. by Mister. We didn't know. how Much we would Miss. Pictures. and Childhood Memorabilia.

We grab what we can pack quickly. a few bags stuffed. two Cats. and a Dog. move Together. to my two bedroom basement apartment. five hundred miles away. OurFantasy resumes. in a different location. We were Together. somehow in mist of it all. Together seemed Right. Together seemed best thing to do. AtThatTime. I remember. it was what Ma wanted. what Ma told me to do. what I understand I have to do. to make it Better. I would do it. for Ma.

We. Me and TheKids. Live Together. for nine months. Nine months seemed like Nine years. OurFantasy about living together is Shattered. replaced with Reality. OurLife is Hard. MyFantasy of living cooperatively. Everyone pitching in. becomes an administrative Nightmare. Imagine me. twenty-four years young. Trying. to organize a household. Trying. to Feed. Clothe. and Nurture TheKids. TheKids. struggling with Independence. Emotionally distraught. Blocked. Needy. Children. Not three semi-self-sufficient. almost Adult siblings.

my salary. more than enough for One. maybe even Two. stretched thinner than Mountain Air. No financial support from TheWill. or Family. matches my emotional reservoir. my Infallibility and Strength are Illusions. I am doing a high wire act. without a safety net. Never think I might fall off. I Never take my Self seriously. combine pressures of Work. and Home. Never miss grieving for my Ma. Never wonder how it will take its toll. Until. I Crash.

it's too Easy to Internalize. to be too Hard on mySelf.
I'm just not Strong enough. Talented enough.
Organized enough. Rich enough.
EveryDay. I learn. I am too Dark. or too Light. too Loud. or too Quiet.
too Smart. or too Dumb. too "Indian." or not "Indian" enough.
I must be Perfect. Body beautiful to media standards.
I am constantly backed. against BrickWalls.
Fear. Doubt. Ignorance.
Denial. Defensiveness. Despair
I am provoked. beyond a Reasonable doubt.
by behaviours deemed Acceptable.
in a Violent. Racist. Misogynist. Homophobic world.
Assaulted. Harassed. Insulted.
Evaluated based on Propaganda.
filtered through Distortions. Gossip. and Rumours.
it is Difficult. Dangerous to say: No! too Easy to get Exploited.
when finally. I have taken too much. too much taken from me.
Too Much. Loss. Objectification. blatant Injustice.
Irritation. Frustration. Anger. red pulsing Rage.
I want to Boil over. erupt like hot molten magma.

Pele be my Guide.[2]
I am well conditioned. to Swallow my Anger.
I already know. Don't Fight Back.
Conflict is too Scary. I might get Hurt.
I am well conditioned. to Swallow my Grief.
I already know. be Strong. be Nice. if you want to Survive.
I fear letting go. I may not come back.
I may be Labelled. too Angry. Uncontrollable. Overemotional. Insane.
where is my Support? or Safe Place.

STRONG WOMEN GET TIRED. HAVE FEARS. TOO.

Strong Women have Fears. Too.
Courage is Not.Never.
being Afraid. but. Living on.
in spite of.
or with awareness of.
Fears.

OneTime. lots of Times. AtThatTime. I have TooMany responsibilities. TooMany to care for. I am counselling AtRiskYouth. and their Families. in BoomTown growing from ten to thirty thousand people. in three short years. I work all Times. Day and Night. deal with AtRiskYouth on Streets. irate Parents. Police. Hospital workers. and whoever else involved.

I am now. Sister-Mother. to Siblings. We just Lost. OurMother. to Alcohol. I have No Time. to Grieve. No Time. for Depression. Self-pity.

or even Regrets. for my Loss of Freedom. I have No Time to Be. only be Strong. Self-assured. Competent. Optimistic.

what happens when I work. and Work? Work and work? there is no end to it. No End. Not enough resources to go around. No. I feel Responsible. for those who Fall between WideCracks. Lots do. Not enough Supports. too much Pain. holding Hands of Teens in DTs. four AM rushes to Emergency. witness Stomach pumps. sponge cut Faces. bandage stitched Wrists. "where are Parents that Care?" I desperately Need to know.

I get.got. really tired. I don't have time to Rest. Others Need me. at Home. I Struggle too Hard. rushing just to stay in one place. Rushing. Swirling River pushing. carrying MyOwnCanoe. towards rocky steaming Falls. Too little money. Too little food. Too little support. Too many issues. Too much stress.

Bravely riding upon WhiteWater. MyOwnCanoe rocking. Not quite big enough for us All. tumbling over jagged Rocks. barely staying afloat. when fatal Blow strikes. speeds with ultimate accuracy. through Air. lands inside our Craft. with a Thud resounding. Echoes throughout our shellShocked. and wellRocked Lives.

Income Lost. Sexual Harassment. BossMan. finds me an AttractiveWoman. wants me. Wants me to find Him attractive. tries to Flirt with me. puts his Hand on my Knee. Stares longingly into my GreenEyes. I recognize ThatLook. "like a hungry Dog starin' at a Bone." Ma would say.

BossMan tells me. "look how Beautiful you are." asks me to come up to HisHotel. Wants me to stay overnight. I am Overwhelmed. with other Struggles. I am Not wanting him. Do Not Want Him. Sex is not on my agenda. my Heart starts to Pound. my Face starts to Flush. He starts to run his Hand. up my Leg. I Squirm. inside. Skin is crawling.

I smile. and I lie. "Thanks for the offer." I have learned to lie. convincingly. Lie to survive. "Not tonight." Not Tonight I say. HotRedFlush covering my Body. and Soul. "my children are at Home. Waiting for me." I leave. as quickly as I can. I feel ashamed. Ashamed and Relieved. Relieved and Confused. Confused and Worried. Worried and Angry. All at the same time. Head spinning as I rush Home. Home to Safety.

two weeks later. too soon. BossMan is back. for a Christmas gathering. with EveryOneElse. back at HisHotel. Dinner. Pool. and Sauna. in Sauna he moves right next to me. Right Next To Me. all Casual. Slides his Arm on ledge behind me. places his Almost Naked. Saggy. Grey white Body.

right next to Mine. I feel Afraid. Revulsed. Trapped. Body tenses like Rabbit. frozen Smile. I chat. Act Natural. with EveryOneElse. I Minimize. I Deny. I think. "Nothing's really happening. Yet."

Too Soon. EveryOneElse gets up to leave. I do too. BossMan grabs my Hand. pulls me down. twists my Arm. enough to Hurt. I am too Afraid. Do Not put up a fuss. "Don't Fight Back!" Once firmly wedged in my Psyche. Once again. rears its ugly head.

desperate GreenEyes watch. as EveryOneElse leaves. BossMan leans over. Kisses me. on MyLips. Kisses Me On MyLips. Yeetch! GagMe. I hold my Mouth stiff as a board. I do Not kiss him. No! He pulls back. Surprised at my lack of response.

small space is Created. I Leap. Fly from sauna. Flee Hotel. run out front door of HisHotel. out into Cold Night. in my bathing suit. in thirty below. can you imagine? leave my Keys. my Purse. my Clothes. my Coat. I run for it.

outside into Cold Night. I shiver. AnotherCounsellor. Lee. is just driving away. I wave frantically. She stops with a slide. I jump in. I am Shaking. Head to Toe. Sick Inside. I feel Dirty. Slimed. Teeth Chattering. Jaws Clamp Shut. I won't talk. Can't talk to Lee. or anyone. about It. I am afraid.

Lee doesn't push It. puts her coat around me. helps me Home. "Doctor Lee's orders. Brandy and Bed." is all she says. pours amber brown liquid in coffee cup on counter. looks long at me. Sad BrownBlackEyes brim with sympathy. NoWords are necessary.

do you Believe it? I turn BossMan down. I Actually Turned Him Down. I feel Guilty. Ashamed. for being in TheWrongPlace at TheWrongTime. I could have a brief Glimpse of Pride. feel proud of myself. I felt no! acted on my Gut. I did Not desire Him. I did Not let Him have me. I got Away. without Rape. Now. that's Revolution.

Anyways. I have No time to feel Good. Soon. my Life begins to Change. for TheWorst. I am confronted as incompetent. at Work. Then. SchoolAuthorities call about TheKids. I become increasingly Stressed. Depressed. I can't understand. "Why? Why are things going so Bad? so Fast? Why Me?" I cry to myself. don't know who to Trust. begin to isolate mySelf.

Now. I know. I rejected BossMan. Broke his Rules. didn't play HisGame. He is BossMan. RuleMaker. RuleBreaker. SexualPredator. I am expected to Submit. Submit to Sex. Sexual Harrassment. Sex to Advance. one of His Rules. I didn't Play. so I couldn't Win. I have to Lose. I Had to Lose. He has all Cards in HisGame.

BossMan. quickly finds SomeOneElse. willing to Play HisGame. older confidant for my SisterMother insecurities. SomeOneElse somehow reDecided. my Mothering becomes a Problem. calls ChildWelfareAuthorities on me.

"She's probably dealing Drugs." SomeOneElse says. "who knows all what goes on over there. just her and three teens. She's only a teen herself." almost. only twenty-four. SomeOneElse is thirty-four. Mature. much more Believable. I become Distrustful. don't know who my Real friends are. I am Paranoid. I self label.

Investigated. Spied upon. They find Nothing. I become increasingly Afraid. long standing Fears wake up. Fear of Authorities. awakens my Psyche. I know this Fear. Inherit it. a multigenerational reality. "It's in our Blood." I've since joked. in our Genes. in Eggs in Wombs. in Myths and Stories. We are Told. We Know. OurChildren Do Disappear.

Suddenly. I face Fear. Loss. Loss of income. Children I can lose to Authorities. Failure. my Health begins to fail. Heart palpitations. can't Eat. No Appetite. close to anorexia nervosa. can't Sleep.

MyOwnCanoe hits bottom. One sharp jagged Rock too many. Tips over. Swirling eddies all around. I go down once. then twice. I am drowning. I clutch for a Branch. "SomeOne. AnyOne. Please Help Us. Please." I try to Pray. even though I don't believe.

Phone rings. OurNeighbours back Home. arrange for TheKids to stay there. "Just. so I can have a break." I say lightly. "Sure. No Problem." my Ears want to Hear.

after journeying East. and back. I return Home. two months lost. I mean completely lost. in deep dark void. I barely remember. I am Shocked to learn. TheKids are Wards. Wards of TheCourt. OurNeighbours. once trusted FamilyFriends. want to be paid. Paid to Foster TheKids. business owning. two cars. swimming pool in yard. OurNeighbours Need. Need to be paid. to keep two Teens for two months. "Anything we can do to help" my Ears had heard. when Ma died.

I fall. back into a Deep. Dark. Hole. Bottomless. Sticky. Oozing. Stinking. Pit. Misery. Wallow around for two more months. seemingly endless. Pain. Anger. Guilt. Grief. Grief not allowed. Not free to feel or express. I acted For others. Not reacted for mySelf.

AtThisTime. I recall very little. Nightmares. Act out in my Sleep. Lash out Physically. Verbally. Wake drenched in Sweat. Tied in blankets. Bone achingly tired. Do not speak. for days. except occasional expressed Fear. "don't let them lock me up. Promise." Do not eat. can only sleep. Sleep. Sleep and Dream. Depression. bottom out emotionally. in every way. low as I have ever been.

Lost will to Live. Think daily about SelfDestruction. SelfMutilation. SelfAnnihilation. Incredible despair. No thoughts of recovery. or happiness. SelfEsteem badly shaken. Stupid. Incompetent. Ugly. Hopeless. Worthless. can't look at mySelf in Mirrors. can't love myself.

I failed. Failed to keep Ma alive. Failed to care for TheKids. Failed AtRiskYouth I had abandoned. I am a Failure. Lost my creativity. No energy. Deeply mistrust others. Isolate myself. become locked away in my miserable self. become a cynic. Look for TheWorst. Expect TheWorst. Find TheWorst. in People. in Life.

my Heart is deeply Wounded. capacity for intimate relationships changed. can't reach out to others in an openHearted way. become more Introverted. more Selective. Re-evaluate family relations. and friendships.

I fly with rushing currents. over Falls. hit sharp Rocks. Bloody gashes flow with Waters. swallow gallons of ice cold Water. gasp for Breath. first Flailing. then Not. finally. I Surrender. allow Waters to wash over me. through me. I am one with Waters. soon. All is Still. Calm. there is a StillPlace Inside. centre in midst of Turmoil. Eye of a Tornado does not Move.

huge Lessons for me. I am given a Gift. my Survival. my Life. is preserved. Delusions of Invincibility dashed. over-estimation of my capacity to change Worlds momentarily drowned. Only Momentarily. Vision. Breath regained. I still desire to change Self. Worlds. Confidence returns. Stronger. I Story to tell. I have Touched. Transformed people. Parts of Worlds.

on my Journey. I begin to learn. difficulties inherent in Womanhood. in Mothering. pain of Self-sacrifice. burden of Guilt. Soul searching for what is Right. necessity of Grieving. need for Self-nurturance. pleasure of Selfishness.

Later. I read Phyllis Chesler. I learn to ask. "who is a 'good enough mother'? who comes under scrutiny of Authorities?"[3] Ideals. Unrealistic images. Shoulds. Expectations. of our selves. and other Mothers. I know. Mothers. Women. have good reasons to Fear. I experience Fears. Vibrant. readily available. that means I am Caged in, are you?

MAHÊ'KUN GETS CAGED

to Mahê'kun, my WolfGuide. Cousin to Coyote. Wisakecahk. who helps me translate Uncomfortable. Threatening. Contradictory moments into lessons.

OneDay. Not to long ago. Not too far away. Mahê'kun wakes up with a start. She knows. something Big is going to happen today. She goes outside immediately. puts Tobacco down. in Crook in towering Birch. who lives next to Den she is sleeping in. She prays to GrandWolves for Strength. Wisdom to remain true to her Purpose.

Then. she busies herself. prepares for Circle that Morning. some AppleValley members. are coming to Circle today. their FirstTime. Mahê'kun is excited to include more Beings in Circle.

Anyways. it's a GoodDay for Circle. a few white fluffy Clouds prance across turquoise Sky. Mahê'kun glances overhead. catches a glimpse of her friend. Red-TailHawk. "Hrrrrr." She wonders. "why is he sweeping so low. wonder what Message he has for me." She thinks. a little worried. looking for a Sign.

Soon. Mahê'kun is at Clearing. Others are arriving. and chatting. a hush falls. when Mouse. and other LittleOnes. creep meekly to one end of Clearing. Mahê'kun quickly clears her Throat. intends to welcome them. a low growl comes out. scares Rabbit back into Woods. "Hrrrrrrr." growls Mahê'kun softly. "tougher than I thought. to create a Safe Place. for LittleOnes to join us Predators. in Circle." Mahê'kun begins to worry even more.

After awhile. EveryBeing is seated in Circle. SweetGrass is burned. SacredSongs are sung. Mahê'kun opens: "Today. we are talking about Community. what goes on here. in AppleValley. what each of us does. eats or doesn't eat. affects Others. Some take more than they need. Greedy. Some tease. Muscle LittleOnes. to get their Food. Bully. upsets Harmony. Balance. We want Equal Respect for all. in AppleValley community. a Good Life for All Beings."

Mahê'kun glances around Circle. as she speaks. Some look down. Some shuffle their Paws. Preen their Feathers. Glance side-to-side. as if trying to guess. who could Mahê'kun could be talking about? They wonder. Some are joking around. Show their Teeth to LittleOnes. "how can I teach a lesson in Respect. so all will understand?" Mahê'kun wonders to herself.

"let's play a Game." She howls. "let's have one or two. BiggerOnes in Middle. how about you Bear? or Wolverine? Now. let's have some others. Hold them in. form one of those wire things. like Humans use on Birds."

All Bird Nations. Immediately begin to flap their Wings. Waggle their Beaks. They Fly Up. Circle overhead. wait to see what will happen. from a safe distance. They all hear. They All Heard. They All Know. about Cages. don't want to Know. anything else.

"Mahê'kun and her crazy ideas!" Shrieks Bluejay. "OneTime. One of my Cousins. Crow. was Trapped in one of Those. We Never hear her Caw. ever again. Not something I will play with." "Me neither." chirps Canary. "lots of my Relatives. spend their whole Lives in one of Those."

Mouse and LittleOnes. scurry quickly to edge of Clearing. peer timidly through long Grass. nibble on a few Seeds. watch in wonderment. Others enthusiastically jump up. join in. at first. lots of Laughter. Then. Bear growls. "I don' like bein' Cage." Serious. neither does Wolverine.

Imagine! Bear and Wolverine. Caged Together. held by Relatives. like Skunk. Fox. Badger. Buffalo. and. of course. Coyote. EveryBeing in AppleValley knows. Bear is still Mad. at Wolverine. cooked his Brother in SweatLodge.

Fur starts to stand on end. Teeth are bared. growls are rumbly. real low in Throats. Mahê'kun decides. Enough is Enough. calls an end. to CageGame.

Mahê'kun calls EveryBeing. "back to Circle." She explains. "this Game teaches lessons. Think. what happens to Others. is it about Them? or about Us too? how do we behave? towards other Beings? We can sit on sidelines. be Afraid. Circle overhead watching. while others get Hurt. who likes to Live in a Cage? who Cages others? let's All Share." Mahê'kun growls in her nicest Teaching Voice. tries to calm EveryBeing.

HonouredGuest Mouse. Squeaks first. "Life is like that for us. as LittleOnes. often preyed upon. We Live Life in Fear. look over our Shoulders. Stories from our GrandMice. Great Great GrandMice. Life has been like this. for a very long time. Very long time Indeed. Not forever. LongTimeAgo. We All Lived in Peace. All of Us." Her round Ears. pointy Whiskers. tremble with Fright.

Mahê'kun can see lots of Surprise. Surprise at Mouse's squeaks. Fox says to Coyote. out of side of his Mouth. "I can't believe dat. can ya? OneTime. We didn't eat LittleOnes??" "Neva hearda it." Howls Coyote.

He winks one YellowEye. across Circle at Mouse.

Mahê'kun sends a piercing look. wants to silence their side-talking. sends thoughts. "it is still Mouse's turn. She still holds StoryStone. EveryOne else. Listen."

Mouse squeaks on. "lately. LittleOnesCouncil. We hear from Nests. Hungry. Crying. out of Food. We don't understand. why is this? OldOnes tell us. Mother Earth always provides for all. All of her Creatures. Big and Little."

She lowers her little Voice. "OurWarriors say. some FourLeggedOnes are eating. more than their share. They want to burrow Holes. trap FourLeggeds. make them Pay. Attention. many don't want. to see This happen. We just want Food. Share. only take what is Needed."

Deer. and Buffalo. glance at each other. exchange startled looks. "trap FourLeggedOnes!" Deer Mouths in surprise. BrownEyes. WideOpen. All FourLegged grass lovers shiver.

thoughts fly. "running along real fast. getting a Hoof stuck. in Hole. Broken Legs. mean Death. Scavengers ready to pounce." Hyena licks his Lips. enjoying thoughts. Moose hangs her Head. waggles her brown Beard. To and Fro. EveryBeing knows. Moose loves to eat. and eat. and eat. and Eat.

Mahê'kun feels bad. sends thoughts. "I should have been more careful. more clear about CircleRules. EachBeing talks. only about them Selves. Not to Judge. Blame. or Criticize Others." Later. Mahê'kun justifies. "Oh well. Mouse didn't know. it was her FirstTime. She didn't Intend. to Hurt anybeing's feelings."

Mole just shakes her Head. agrees with Mouse. Stone travels on. PrairieDog squeaks. "I agree with Mouse. things have to Change. If. we all starve to Death. what are Others going to Eat. Then." Mahê'kun nods her furry Head. Up and Down. She loves to eat Rabbit. and is already regretful about scaring Him. Remembers. He ran so quick into Woods.

Woodpecker. Eagle. Porcupine. and Raccoon speak. it is clear to Mahê'kun. CageGame had a strong impact on them. enhanced their feelings of Connection. to LittleOnes. that have come. Mahê'kun is beginning to feel real proud. Proud of herself.

Then. Fox speaks. all Disdainful. "I don' really believe in Greed. Bullyin'. Oppressin'. jis Mahê'kun. and 'er big Words. nuttin' todo wit me."

Mahê'kun is Stunned. things were going so well. She wants to cut Fox off. "Oh. he's so Rude." She thinks. "I just can't stand him". EveryBeing knows. "Fox loves to kill. Kills more than he needs." Mahê'kun whines to her Sister Timber. Later.

but. Mahê'kun is well taught by OldOnes. don't interrupt Circle. Her hurt feelings. is not reason enough to stop Circle. Not yet. Anyways.

Fox goes on. "I don' believe in so.called Equal.tee issues. Circle'll come over to my way of tinkin'. tings are da way tings are. for good reasons. I don' believe Mouse. it's always bin dis way. an' it always will. Bigger. Stronger. Faster. Braver. deserve More. what ever dey want."

Later. Mahê'kun howls. "can you Imagine? such a pre-Cambrian attitude?"

Fox passes Stone. Mahê'kun is very relieved. She can see Heads moving up. Up and Down. Agreement. Mink is next. He nods his little Head. Agreement. a grin on his Face. "Of course. Mink Would agree." says Timber. Later. "He's as bad as Fox. Killing more than he needs."

Mahê'kun begins to worry even more. chews bottom of her Lip. Coyote is next. "Everybein' should. lighten up." He yelps. "don' take everytin' so serious. game is a game. is a Game. it's a Game! Get It!" He howls. "it's depressin' to look round Circle. an' see so many serious Faces. don' take yerself so serious."

Mahê'kun thinks. "just like Coyote. make a mockery." Later. Timber says. "Coyote musta bin Uncomfortable. Hidin'. Silencin'. who wants to show Heart to 'im?"

Soon. Wolverine's turn. "I don't get it. Mouse gets eaten. I eat her." He shrugs. "fair is fair. She can run faster. or hide better. If. she wants to Live. I agree with my Brother." nods at Coyote. "it's a Joke. Respect LittleOnes as much as Us? Hah!"

Mahê'kun is thinking seriously. about stepping in. stopping Rock right there. "when I look back. maybe I Should have." Mahê'kun howls. Later. "HindSight is always best." consols an OldOne.

Stone comes to Hyena. He stands up. stretches his full six feet Spotted self. He points at Mahê'kun. accuses. "You're a Bully. Bully us into Game. You say one thing. do another." He says. "get over it. like our Cousin says. a game is a Game. jis for fun. don't act like. You know it all. can change EveryBeing. get a Life. We have a Life. and we're Happy."

Later. Mahê'kun howls with her Pack. "Hyena definitely attacked me". "He musta bin Hurt." suggests an OldOne. "I have No Time. to feel Hurt." Mahê'kun says. "I am beginning to Panic. Mouse and other LittleOnes. I gave them my Word. it would be Safe. Wolves are always true to their Word." All Pack howl. Agreement.

Anyways. after Hyena's outburst. Being after Being sit quietly. Stone moves. from one to another. till Coyote. large grin on Face. gives a

TailsUp signal. jumps up. runs into Woods. "Oh. that Coyote." thinks Mahê'kun. All Beings know. Sit. until Circle is Done.

Mahê'kun doesn't worry much. about Coyote. and his Disrespectful antics. Circle is going on. Skunk breaks down. Cries. Tears run down. pointy black and white Face. She sniffs. "I'm Disgusted. by what's been Said. I'm not going to share my Story. because of Stinking attitudes. We have Hungry Ones. We can't feed. We're picked on. Teased. because of who we are. how we Look. how we Smell. You don't Understand. You just don't Get It."

It is Grouse's turn. she puffs up Feathers. makes a whirring noise. with her Wings. keeps her Beak tightly shut. She will Not tell her Story either. finally. StoryStone moves back to Mahê'kun. who growls. to conclude Circle. turns to Mouse. and LittleOnes. and says. "I respect you. it took Courage to come here. tell your Story. to disbelieving predators."

Mahê'kun fears Violence. for her guests. closes Circle. EveryBeing quickly leaves Clearing. Later. Mouse tells Mahê'kun. She overheard Others talking. "They're making fun of Skunk. 'cause she Cried!" She squeaks. "and speaking Loud. AnyBeing could hear. Badger says. 'if She has a Problem. with Us. She should Not come to Circle'."

Mouse is shocked. Shocked that Others would talk. Talk in such a Disrespectful way. breaching Confidentiality like that. "I thought you told me. 'what is Said in Circle. stays in Circle'." small high-pitched Voice trembles. Mahê'kun shakes her Head. Side to Side. Sad. things seem to be going down. Bad to Worse.

it is a hard Lesson. "You can just Avoid. No direct Confrontation. You will be Happier. here." Elk counsels. Some Time Later. Mahê'kun howls to BlackBear. "NoBeing wants AnyBeing to talk about Sharing here. just keep Quiet. look Happy. if Predators are Angry at you. just Quietly take it. learn Not to get them Mad again."

She is still trying to figure it out. what she learned from this PainFull Time. "I guess you got Caged. by your own Game." Bear razes. Not one for Sympathy. when facing others' SelfPity.

Notes

1. Nehiyâw'ak levels of addiction. one-third of our population. says Brian Maracle. an epidemic. says Whitehead and Hayes 1998.
2. Pele. Streaming black lava Hair. Smouldering. Smoking. Fiery Eyes. She is Goddess. Creator. Protector. of the Islands of Hawaii.
3. Feminists. clearly articulate. struggles of Mothering. Motherwork. in a patriarchal society. like Chesler. Hall and Bucholtz. Fineman and Karpin. Ladd-Taylor and Umansky.

SCARS ARE A DOORWAY.
BRUISED SPIRITS. CLENCHED JAWS.
CAGES HURT.

here again.
Mahe'kun finds herself down that DarkHole. once more. Oooowwrrr.
NoBeing likes to return to a place of Fear.

as a Métis.Woman in Canada. my HomeLands.
I experienced Institutionalized Discrimination.
MedicineStories. tell about own Lifetime experiences of being Caged.
how I am Brutalized in MissionSchool.
watch Torture of other Children from my Community.
especially DarkerOnes.
how I. Girls.Women. of TheTown I grew up Near.
are Sexualized. Objectified. Raped. Murdered.
Now. I'll tell how I am Streamed into WorkEd. because of Where I am From.
Not what I Want. to Do in my Life.
how my Daughter. in her First School Experience. is called "Indian"
as if it is an Insult.
Later. I'll tell of Times I am Slurred and Belittled in classrooms.
as a university Student. and Professor.
Jobs I leave. because of Poisoned work environments.
HumanRights cases. School appeals.
Arbitrations. Legal situations.
I am Forced to learn. Witness. Advocate for myself and others.
my Elders teach. Insight comes from Anywhere.
Learn and Teach from your Experiences
especially PainFul Lessons.
I am here as a Guide.
familiar with processes of resisting. Sexism. Racism. Eurocentrism.
I am continuously Unlearning Assimilation.
learning to embrace a positive Cultural Identity.
I Story to raise awareness of Structural Forces.
which Impact. on soCalled "individual." Choices or Merits.
Let me tell you. Racism is not a fancy theory.
Racism is very real. an everyday part of our Lives.
Maracle knows. "The pain, the effect, the shame are all real."[1]
Racism hurts.
Blinds our Minds.
Deadens our Spirits.
Wounds our Hearts.
Attacks our Bodies.
Healing from Effects of Racist Trauma
requires a LifeTime.
a Holistic Approach.

Begin our Journey. heal Mind traps.

Racism is a Way of Thinking.
    a way of Life. a Power Structure.
    in a Racist Society. how we Think. is defined for Us. by Them.
    We Think. Live. Us and Them.
    "Facts" about Us. Nehiyâw'ak. Racially.Visible Others.
        have been. and are constructed.
        based on biased reports. written by Them.
    Colonial administrators. Missionaries. Anthropologists. Media.
Yes. OurAncestors have been Murdered.
    Denigrated. Acculturated. Problematized.
    let us always be aware of OurAncestors' Will to Survive and Thrive.
        despite many Masks of Racism.
    how we think. Whether we think. about Racism is defined for us.
    Racism is a concept. an English construction.
        Defines. Describes. Constitutes. Mooniyâs World.Views.
    Racism is a set of beliefs.
        some are acculturated to practise.
        act out on others Unlike themselves.
        Prejudice. RaceHatred. Bias. Ethnocentricity.
        Hidden. Blatant. Individual. Systemic.
    comes from so called RedNecks.
        and from Judges. Journalists. Doctors. Clerks.
        PoliceOfficers. Teachers. SocialWorkers.
        Psychiatrists. Politicians. Media.
Unicorn. an African.Canadian.Woman. tells it:
"I Breathe, Smell, Taste, Touch, Sleep and Live with/through Racist
experience/situations of my Own and Others Seven days a week and Twenty-four
hours a day. To constantly relive this is Emotionally and Physically Draining...."[2]
    If. We Live with Racial Overtones. Undertones. all around.
    it feels allConsuming. Confusing.
Racism can only be Eliminated when Women and Men.
    are willing to Challenge Publicly. Hidden.Overt.
        Costs of Racism.
        Benefits of WhitePrivilege.
    when I disrupt Silent Dominance. of Whiteness.
    Notice. Uncomfortable feelings arise.
    Guilt. Embarrassment. Anger. Fear. Responsibility.
embrace your feelings. a "starting point for cultural equality." says *Gela.*
    Gregory Jay warns. You may experience
        "pedagogy of disorientation" when White is named.
If. we can be Acculturated to hold Dominant views.
    Then. we can also be Unacculturated.

Spirit Heals Racist Scars.

being Silenced Hurts Our Spirits.
    Spiritual Healing requires Truth. Heartfully Spoken.
        Sharing our Truths can be Painful.
        Few places are Safe to disclose Stories of Racism.
        speaking about Racism can result in Denial.
            Minimizing. Incomprehension. more Overt Racism.
            when Painful Stories are heard. by ears open to Accusations.
                some wish our Continued Silence.
eliminating Racism requires cultural Pride.
    when we return to our Traditions.
        Our Cultural Gifts. Our Languages. Our Ceremonies. Our Elders.
            We can begin to enLiven Our Spirits.
Our Cultures. have been subjected. to influences of Domination.
            are also tools of Resistance.
Nehiyâw'ak Peoples. are rejecting assimilatory expectations.
        are returning to Powers of cultural ways.
in Circles. in Ceremonies.
    We find a Safe Place. to Live our Traditions.
        to Rekindle our ties to AncestralSpirits.
Our Spiritual Practices. have been Demonized.
    Our Leaders. Persecuted. Criminalized.
        Our SacredBundles. Burned. Museum-ized.
    Today. Mooniyâs aspire to Appropriate Traditions.
        Desire to become InstantShamans of TheNewAge.
    Wisakecahk teaches. Simplicity is an Illusion. Caution is Wise.
        You will get More than you bargain for.
        Reporters. No pictures or tapes please.

Heartfelt Sharing Heals Racist Hurts.

Racism Wounds Our Hearts.
    deep rooted feelings. must be Aired.
        Anger. Isolation. Discomfort. Desprited. Pressured to Conform.
    All are experienced Regularly.
        by Nehiyâw'ak. RaciallyVisible peoples. in all Settings.
        yet. infrequently Acknowledged.
Racism divides People. Families. Nations.
can make us Alienated. Isolated from and within our Communities.
reBuilding Community is an ongoing process. relies on Reciprocity
    Community is a feeling of Togetherness.
        an act of Resistance. a Survival strategy.

Healing our Hearts. recovering from RacistTrauma means.
strengthening of Individuals. inRelation to Communities.
strong RoleModels. Inspire others to Grow. and Change.
Visible. Lived Examples. of Strength. and Determination.
We will Not give up TheFight.
what Joy it is. to see. experience. Strong members of our Communities.
Truthfully Sharing Together.
Our Struggles. Resistance. Recovery.

Recover Health. to keep Resisting Racism.

Racism Attacks Our Bodies.
Racist Pain turned inward. becomes Disease.
High Blood Pressure. TMJ.[3] Diabetes. Cancers. Cardiac Failure.
sometimes Racism Erupts into Violence.
Suicide. Family Violence. Murder.
what about PoliceOfficers. who left Nehiyâw'ak.
to freeze to Death outside Saskatoon?
RCMP got convicted. six months in Jail. Six Months? Imagine?
what about Burnt Church?[4] YoungMan charged with throwing Rocks.
at RCMP. got three years in jail. Three Years! Imagine?
DFO officers charged with Attempted Murder.
for trying to drown Mi'kmaw Fishers.
got charges Dropped. Go Figure??
We must channel our Anger and Grief. into Change.
We All. Individually. Collectively.
can Challenge Racism daily.
reaffirm our Responsibility for Community well-being.
WE CAN DO IT!
even small Acts. have big personal Meanings.
each action is Valid. a step to further Activism.
SILENCE EQUALS COMPLIANCE.
Challenge others on verbalized Racism.
Challenge slurs. Stereotypes. in Social settings.
Workplaces. Schools. Media.
Speak Out. write about Racism. whenever we encounter it.
will create Uncomfortable feelings for Some.
ask yourself. "whose Comfort level. am I trying to Adapt to?"
Positive change strategies. Successes.
enacted by Individuals. Communities.
must be Supported. Reported. Storied. Shared.
COLLECTIVITY COUNTS.
Nadine asks. "I can't help but wonder what would happen to our society

if All the racially visible peoples and those discriminated against. Banded Together
to promote changes that would benefit them rather than having to Fight the larger
powers Solely?"
　　　how can we build Community between Nations?
　　　work Together to eliminate Racism?
　　　some People do Not notice. how Racism produces Daily Problems.
　　　　　　They are surrounded by White Privilege.
　　　　　"how can White people be expected to be seriously invested in
challenging White domination?" wonders Hattie.
　　　　Anti-Racist Actions. Big or Small. require taking Risks.

How Do We Sustain Struggling Force?

　　　keep focused on Politics. behind Personal attacks.
　　　remain Part of Struggle. Support others.
　　　Remember. Those who have gone Before.
　　　　　Others will come After us.
　　　Frederick Douglas. Civil Rights Activist. proclaimed in 1853.
　　　"Those who profess to savour freedom and yet depreciate agitation ...
want crops without ploughing up the ground. They want rain without thunder
and lightning. Power concedes nothing without a Demand. It never did and it
never will."
I Story to help Imagine.
　　　a World where Eurocentric domination is Not possible.
　　　　where all Voices and Cultures are Valued.

TODAY. I AM STREAMING MAD

to Verna Kirkness. a WarriorWoman. Role Model to me. and many Others.

Today. as my Throat closes
　　　and my GreenEyes well up.
　　　　　a strangled Voice erupts. Unlike my own.
　　　　　　　as I attempt. Not very successfully. to speak.
　　　　　　　　in a group of well polished Academics.
　　　　　　　　　　about MyReality. my educational History.
that's exactly my point.
　　　Today. it is not Just MyReality any longer.
　　　　　for years. I told StreamingStory. MyStory.
　　　　　　　how in Grade Nine I am placed in Work Ed (OEC).
　　　　　　　　how I struggle to get moved to Business Ed.

Then. finally to University Entrance (ue).
We all notice. We all got placed in oec that year.
EveryOne from across TheRiver.[5]
almost everyone from MissionSchool.
but Not my Friend Tee.
She is Mooniyâs. She is in ue.
so is my CousinJay. She Lives in TheTown. Passes.
Her Papere has a GoodJob.
"So. why am I not with Them?" I want to know.
it is like Pounding. my then fourteen-year-old body
against a Hard Brick Wall. Repeatedly.
Trying. Trying. Trying.
Trying to prove what?
"what do I have to do to Prove?"
Prove I am "good enough"?
Prove I am "smart enough"?
Prove I am "white enough"
to succeed?
"Who cares. what I want?" I Cry and Rage.
"I want to go to University."
and ue is TheOnlyRoute.
No mature entry. No ged. Then.
TheOnlyRoute is ue. and I am being Blocked.
I can Not understand Why?
my Parents. don't understand.
my older Siblings. don't have it happen to Them.
how can I change Systems. on my own?
Today. Literally. This Very Day. more than thirty years later.
as I sit listening to Verna's soft lilting Voice.
Cutting Humour. interspersed with Cold Hard Facts.
I find out Why. Why my Life. my future.
is Snatched from me. without Warning.
my feelings of Alienation. Anger. surface.
my Blood pulses. like a fresh. open. salted. Wound.
She quietly. and calmly. teaches us.
"Provincial governments. after White Paper of 1969. enforced assimilation
through integrated schools. When Native children were transferred in to public
schools a whole new classroom structure was created to accommodate them
known as oec. Aboriginal children were streamed there."
when she specifically cites TheTown. as an example.
Pain flashes Red. in front of my GreenEyes.
I am Streamed in 1970.
in 1970. my Mind races over this Fact.
a Fact. I now stumble. Tongue-Tied.

try to articulate to my Colleagues.
No wonder NoOne understood.
I am "pioneer-ized."
I am in first group of ExperimentalRats.
run through freshly created Maze.
a three-tier System.
created specifically to continue.
Residential. Mission. School. Legacy.
to continue to Train us.
to Service. Needs of Colonizer.
All these years. I know. write and read.
about White Paper. Chretien. Trudeau.
Manitoba Indian Brotherhood response.
All this Time. I know.
my educational historical narrative. my Life.
is Shaped. Twisted.
by Racist.Colonial Ideas.Practices.
but. in this moment. Today.
I glimpse a small Truth. about one very PainFull year of my Life.
how I am traumatized in that year. for years to come.
as a Survivor of Streaming.
as a Survivor of Institutional Racist Violence.
perpetrated on All Youth from my Community.
on All Nehiyâw'akYouth.
in that Time. and that Place.
across this entire Liberal. Equal.
not yet officially Multicultural Country.
Today. I remember Pain. Anguish. Isolation. Self-hatred.
Today. I Cry. Today. I Rage.
Today. I am Streaming Mad. I want to tell TheWorld about it.
I can say I am a Survivor. Today.
I have politicized. what is once internalized. RacistTrauma.
I have my Voice. University Degrees.
and my righteous Anger.
I give Gratitude for MyStory.
MedicineStory. I am Gifted to tell. Nehiyâw'akYouth.
"Don't let Them. put you Down.
Don't let Them. make you feel Dumb.
Fight their Categories. their Labels. You can do it!"
MedicineStory. I choke. trying to tell Mooniyâs Educators. Today.
in Grade Nine I was Streamed into Work Ed. OEC.
I was seen as Unlikely to Succeed. Academically.
I had to Fight for my Chance.
a Chance many receive. as a unrecognized Privilege.

Today. I have a PhD.
I run a University Program for Nehiyâw'ak People.
I experience SchoolSystems as Not Fair.
Never have Been. maybe Never will be.
Few of Us know. it is Possible to Succeed in spite of Them.
Help us Up. Don't put us Down.

"YOU'RE AN INDIAN"

to MoonTeen. may your Métis pride rekindle.

OneDay. Notlong ago. Not far away. YoungBoy calls across School cloak room. "You're an Indian." to MyDaughter. in a Nasty tone of Voice. MyDaughter. MoonChild. then six. already Wise and Wonderous. Ignores him. when she comes home. She does not mention TheIncident. to me.

NextDay. Saturday. She is out with Friends. Phone rings. YoungBoy. asks for MoonChild. I am Surprised. She usually hangs out with Girls.

Anyways. I say. "She's not Home. Right Now. do you want to leave a message?" I am curious. wonder what he wants. He says. AllInARush. "tell her I'm sorry. Sorry I called her an Indian. Sorry I caused her Trouble." "Oh." is all I can get out. At first. I am a bit taken aback. by his staccato. Rehearsed. speech. "You said what?' I ask. wonder at first if I heard right. I did.

I tell him. "I Am Sorry. I can't pass on a Message. like That. You'll have to callback. and talk to her yourself. or see her in School. on Monday. and tell her In Person." I don't want to let him off TheHook. that easy. I ask. "is your Mother home?" He hangs up.

when MoonChild returns. I give her a piece of paper. I wrote TheMessage. *Sorry I Called You An Indian.* I say. "YoungBoy called." She shrugs her shoulders. I ask "do you want to Talk? about It?" She says. "No. it's Nothing. He's Rude. trying to make fun. by calling me an Indian. I'm Not an Indian. I Am Métis. Métis are Not Indians. are we Ma?"

"Nooo." I say. "We are Native though. part Indian." "I know thaaaaT." MoonChild responds. in an exasperated tone. "He's Just Rude!" She says again. a little bit louder. trying to educate me. "He thinks. calling Indian is an Insult. but. it is Noooott!!" "Okaaay." I say.

I want to be relieved. want to think MyDaughter is secure. ForTheMoment. in her identity. She goes off to play. I am left questioning

TheIncident. Wondering. "what role should I take up?" Later. I later say to FriendBecca. "I Can Not Believe It! I can't Believe he just. called her an Indian. as if it was a Slur." We discuss together. long list of slurs. and stereotypes. we have been Called. or heard our Friends. Family members. Called.[6]

usually. Indian. is preceded by some nasty qualifier. or another hateful word is used. instead of Indian. to make It insulting. We both wondered. "is this better. or worse?" We agree. it is Better. MoonChild does not have to feel bad. or internalize a negative message. and Worse. Now. Indian itself is enough. to be insulting. without any qualifiers added.

my WoundedHeart
loud angry Words.
negative Slurs.
institutional Violence. are
Arrows. piercing my
already WoundedHeart.

YoungBoy never does Apologize. Never does Show Face. again. His parents move him. to another School. So. He never has to face Moonchild. or me. Imagine. moving your Child from their School. because they called a Slur! Never mind being on receiving end.

Weeks Later. I see FairMindedTeacher. at LocalGroceryStore. in Fruit and Vegetable section. I mention TheIncident to her. I express concern. question School race relations policies. or lack of them.

She gets on to topic of "Indians." She mentions her Son. in MoonChild's class. "MySon is absolutely Fascinated by Indians." She literally gushes as she speaks. "Oh yeah." I say. "that's not necessarily a positive thing."

I think to myself. of all people Fascinated by Those Colourful Indians. and other Exotic cultural groups. "I Hate it. when People say 'I find you so Fascinating'!" I tell Becca later. "Yeah." She shakes her head in agreement. "it's so positively Racist! did you Scream when she said it?" "Nooo." I laugh. "but. I should have. let out a blood curdling WarWhoop. and Danced around slapping my Mouth. Woowoowoowoo. could ya see it?" I act it out. "it would have fit right in. with our conversation." We laugh.

Anyways. FairMindedTeacher. stares at me. Blankly. obviously does Not understand. why I am Not Thrilled? with her Son's Fascination. She starts to squeeze Avocados. a little too roughly. I notice.

I Feel. like our conversation is Not over. Unfortunately. So. I ask. "what does your Son know. about Indigenous peoples? where is he getting his Information?" AtThatTime. I actually want to know. "ever since he was little." She drops Avocado. and goes on enthusiastically. "his FavouriteToy. is a plastic set of CowBoys and Indians."

I am instantly unable to Listen. "Hmmm." I interject. "that's definitely not a great source of information. especially in almost all Movies. TheCowBoys. end up killing off. All TheIndians." I say. quizzical expression on my Face.

I'm not sure. where my conversation. with FairMindedTeacher is leading. I am beginning to feel. quite Uncomfortable. breaking out in StressSweat. so is She. "Oh no!" Teacher says. in HorrorStruck Voice. "He's Not like that at all. MySon plays Equal. TheCowBoys. and TheIndians. All kill each other off." I am Stunned. for a moment. don't know what else to say.

Later. I process with Becca. "how can it be possible?" I say. "that FairMindedTeacher. a feminist. a so.called conscientious parent. can think a game Positive. that kills off All People. what kind of preparation for Life is that?" I ask. I intend a rhetorical question. "minimizin' Death." Becca says solemnly. "You only have to watch. NightlyNews. to see. what Kind of Society we Live in." We agree. reEnacting murderous wars. Wars between our two Races. is hardly evidence of Love for Indigenous peoples. even If. both Races are exterminated. Not Just TheIndians.

"I wonder. how she can possibly fail to notice. WhiteMale movie moguls construct us. Indians as BadGuys. Losers. to be killed. and CowBoys as GoodGuys. Winners. who Live. I know she is Totally Aware. of how media socializes Women. and Men. into our Proper Roles. do you believe. She can't apply same idea. to Indians. and Whites?"

"probably not." laughs Becca. "just hasn' thought about Racism. doesn' have to. Me. I grew up always wantin' to be John Wayne.[7] beggin' my Kohkum. for a set of toy guns. made my own. outta Wood." We laugh real hard over that one. as Becca butches it up. Her Hands suggestively poking. through. jean pockets.

"I Wish. I could have found my Voice. to tell her Off. AtTheTime." I ruefully say to Becca. I am self-critical. OneMoreTime. noticing. how my deeply held victim training. Tounglessness. continues to prevail. smiling fondly she says. "Yeah. ain't it always like that. in TheHeat of TheMoment. Racism. Sexism. Homophobia. You lose your Voice. Then. have to Kick yourself in the butt. Later. Here. Lean Over. I'll do it for you." I do. Laughing.

"maybe I'll get another chance." I say as I come up for Air. I Never Did. get to use my arguments. or my Voice. on her. I'll probably get another Chance. with someone else. some where else. Things being what they are. in ThisWorld. between Us and Them. Indians and CowGirls.

Be. Aware.
Media. a public forum. can Reproduce. or Challenge. Racist status quo.
　　like CowBoys and Indians. Media constructs.
　　　　Mythologized into Reality. through WhiteMaleCorporateElites.
　　like Letters to TheEditor.
often written by misinformed individuals. regularly perpetuate Myths.
　　　　like misconstruing Benefits. very few Nehiyâw'ak receive.
　　when income taxes are Not paid. when working on-Reserve.
　　They argue prevalence of ReverseDiscrimination.
　　　　like SoundOff. "It is time for our gutless government
　　　　　　to kill the aboriginal 'golden goose'."8
Editors make Choices everyday. about which Voices to Privilege.
Publicly declare their Right to edit. for "Good Taste."
　　　　disguise Racism under rhetoric. Freedom of Speech.
what is Tasteful. Freeing. about blatantly Misinformed. Racist. Opinions?
　　when Slurs. Stereotypes are Repeated. existing social order is Perpetuated.
　　Language is Political. usage is Not accidental.
　　　　part of an ongoing Power Struggle.
Media has power to Influence. Design. Dictate. Justify.
　　　　or Challenge. accepted Norms.
Publicly condoned Racism. simultaneously hurts Some. benefits Others.
　　feeds Denial. Denial of history.
　　　　Denial of current structural imbalances in our Worlds.
　　allows people to remain Blind. to Impoverished Third World Conditions

majority of Nehiyâw'ak exist in.
covers up Chronic overspending of taxpayers money.
like Burnt Church. who knows that millions a year are spent
in Military and DFO. to Stop Nehiyâw'ak from Fishing?
it is a wellDocumented Fact.
Mooniyâs experience Material. Political. Social. Personal. Benefits.
at Nehiyâw'ak Peoples' expense. Worldwide.
We are robbed of Lands. Resources. Labour. Lives.
Yet. We read "Nobody took anybody's land."
Denial is used to Repress Nehiyâw'ak. in our Quest.
for Independence. Equality.
like Pankiw's response. to Ahenakew Incident.
"Indian lobbyists and supporters of race-based rights and
privileges are nothing more than modern-day Klansmen."
how often do issues get Represented. from Nehiyâw'ak viewpoints. in Media?
OurVoices have been Locked out. Marginalized.
Discriminated against in public forums. including Media.
Voiceless. we are Invisible.
"When someone is invisible it is easy to pretend they don't exist."
says Mac.
Mooniyâs authors. continue to accrue Capital.
from Their edited versions of Our Lives.
most best-selling books. on Nehiyâw'ak issues.
continue to be written by Mooniyâs NewsReporters.
what about Appropriation. of Story.Voice?
Charlotte wonders. how can you deal with.
"such a deep old habit of control, tear apart, criticize, judge..."?
if you Lack proper attention to Context.
Lack acknowledgment of TheSource.
Gain profit from our Ancestors' Pain.
You are Appropriating. Our Stories.Voices.
enough Sensationalized Negative Headlines. and Editorials.
report Successes. seek Reliable. First Voice. Sources.

Notes

1. Nehiyâw'ak. AntiRacist authors. have gone before me. like Maracle. hooks. LaRocque. Todd. West. James and Shadd. Kelly. James. Razak. Fulani.
2. *Unicorn.* and several others in *italics.* are all participants in research done for my book. *Circle Works.*
3. TMJ. chronic soreness of Teeth.Mouth.Jaw. happens when you clench your Jaws too much.
4. see Christian Peacemaker Teams. 2001. for one version of Burnt Church Story.

5.	TheRiver is Saskatchewan River. creates a Boundary between TheTown. and Rez.

6.	materials on confronting Racism. in Canadian Schools. include Manitoba Indian Brotherhood. Schniedewind. Alladin. Canadian Race Relations Foundation.

7.	John Wayne is the King. of old shoot'em up Westerns. along with Clint Eastwood. Today. may be compared to Luke Skywalker. but. Killing off Indians.

8.	*italicized excerpts* are from *Brandon Sun*. First is from March 19, 2002: B5. Second from December 17, 2002: A5. Third is from March 13, 2002: A2. But. could be AnyTown. Canada.

9.	according to Stats Canada 2002. more than 1.1 million Nehiyâw'ak people live in Canada. 73% live outside FirstNationCommunities. 27% live on Reserve. you need to be employed to benefit. in Communities where

PUSHING DOORWAYS OPEN.
GLIMPSING LIGHT. NOTICING CRACKS.
SLIPPING BETWEEN BARS.

noticin' Cracks.
    Look. See. Cracks. Light openings in dark Cages of Oppression.
        Mahe'kun will slip through. will Not be Caged.

am I Helping you. to See.
   how I slip between Bars. Resist Cage of Oppression?
      to recognize. MindTraps set by Mooniyâs?
   do you Notice. any possible Hidden Cracks[1] in your Consent?
      ways to challenge. everyday PowerRelations?
   can I be Midwife to you? in a difficult but necessary Transition.
      from Consent to Resistance?
Be Aware. We are Not alone. on this Journey.
                    we follow a well worn Path. GoodPath.
Nehiyâw'akPeoples. develop many forms of Resistance.
   as varied as attempts to change our ways of Life.
Freire names Resistance as Universal.
   Colonial intervention.
      "provokes an incredible and dialectical counteraction."
I Story. to envision OurWorld. Free of Eurocentric Domination.
   a revolutionary utopian Dream.
   Now. OurVoices are becoming Heard. Ground is shifting.
      Decolonization. a protracted Political. Cultural.
         sometimes Military struggle.
         becoming more Adversarial. as Time goes on.[2]
many Resist actively. engage in Primary Resistance.
   like Métis Rebellion in Red River areas.
   like collective stands against continued military intervention.
      Oka. Davis Inlet. Clayquot Sound. Burnt Church.
      ninety of a hundred and twenty armed conflicts in World today.
         are between IndigneousPeoples and Centralized Governments.
            Nehiyâw'ak stand Strong against Genocide.
            All across Canada.[3] OurWorlds.[4]
Collectivity is a precondition for political Voice. in Democracy.
   some strategically Unite. as First Nations.
      in a nationWide self government movement.
   some as FirstPeoples. Indigenism. a Global Movement of Indigenous Peoples.
      we are developing parallel. Social. Economic.
                    Cultural. Political institutions.
            run by and for. to benefit Nehiyâw'akPeoples.[5]
I Story as a form of Resistance.
      to Embrace. Politicize. Traditional forms of Consciousness.
            Denied my Ancestors.
OurCulture is Not vanishing. Not only functional in ThePast.
Tradition forever Changes. to new demands of our Environments.
      Elders. Stories. Dreams. Traditions. still inform my Identity today.
            as I rewrite history. resurrect Stories.
      I remember Ancestral Gifts. contributions to OurWorld.
Foods. PlaceNames. Art. World.View. HealingMedicines. Democracy.[6]

remember Cultural Resistance of Ancestors.
Those who stand strong against Acculturation. Assimilation. Ethnocide.
   refuse to attend Schools. leads to enforced ResidentialSchools.
   refuse to learn Mooniyâs ways.
      use skills once learned. to Fight against Oppression.
   enact Spiritual Resistance.
      ignore Persecution. Criminalization.
         continue to practise OldWays. when told Not to.
      guard Ancestral secrets. Ceremonies.
         through Silence. Darkness of Night. Depth of Forest.
      Outward Agreement. and Inner Resistance.
         keeps many Alive. Ceremonies Survive. Spirits Thrive.[7]
my MedicineStories. tell how I Resist. Today.
   Redefine Self.
   Rid myself. of stereotypic negative Images.
   Tell and retell. my Resistance and Recovery.
   Challenge slurs and media portrayals.
   Use my Voice. to Challenge Hegemony.
      to Question. State's sanctioned version of Truth.
   Shift Blame.
      Recognize StructuralForces. that impact upon PersonalStories.
      Externalize. don't Internalize Racism.
         Sexism. Classism. Heterosexism. Eurocentrism.
   Take Time and Energy. to understand Nehiyâw'ak World.Views.
   less Time. Summarizing. and Reconfirming. Mooniyâs thought forms.
   Embrace Holistic World.Views.
   recognize interaction between Mental. Spiritual. Emotional. Physical.
         Dimensions. Gifts. Realities. Lessons.
      seek. Balanced Growth. in all aspects of Self.
         rely on teachings of Medicine Wheel.
            accompany Talk with Actions.
               Walk amplifies Talk.
               Walk your Talk.
   Acknowledge Spirit as vital.
      replace Rational. Mechanistic. Colonial. Mentality.
         with Spiritual. Holistic. Ecological. Knowing.
      revitalize Nehiyâw'ak Traditions.
         Storytelling. Metaphor. Myth. Ceremony. Art.
      restore Creative Energy. essential to reInvent. reCreate. Truth.
   Honour Elders. as Keepers. of Cultural and Philosophical Wisdom.
      combat idea that Degrees. are only avenue to knowledge.
      Listen. show Respect. practise Reciprocity.
   Reaffirm Powers of Nehiyâw'akWomen. LifeGivers.
      acknowledge Gift of our Children.

show Reverence for Sacredness of Earth Mother.
teach Respect for All Life to All people.[8]
Recognize Immanence. Balance. Interconnectedness.
Traditional philosophies. are Vital.
for empathic and imaginative Bridging.
of individual and cultural Differences.
Be a strong RoleModel.
Realize. Believe. Enact. One Person. can make a Difference.
Tell. and Retell. these MedicineStories.
Share Strategies. Recognize. and Resist Cages. and Traps.
Learn to Cope better. with current Struggles.
take some Responsibility. to Learn.
what you are able to Know. given your Path.
seek a GoodPath. Grow. and Share. with others.
We can Not be a Cure.
If. we are a part. of what is Diseased.

BITE HANDS THAT GRAB YOU. YOUR CHILDREN.

AtOneTime. I face a cavernous split. in my Lives. Nehiyâw'ak ways of living and knowing. are Alive in my HomeLife. Mooniyâs Bureaucratic Authority. is Central to my WorkLife. No Integration. Separation. is a Daily Lived Experience. I am Not conscious. or concerned. I accept. a Split in realities. I understand it to be how Life is. since I left Home. to go to MissionSchool. to go to University.

I go to work. each Day. drive miles of country roads. visit Nehiyâw'ak Wards. placed in Mooniyâs homes. sometimes temporarily. sometimes permanently. I become sadder. and sadder. Sadder and Sadder. long Faces. hollow brown-black Eyes. Lifeless slumped Bodies.

OneDay. I ask myself. "how can I keep working. in a SpiritDeadSystem. chewing up Nehiyâw'ak Kids. spitting them out. on TheStreets. to self-destruct. or kill each other?" I think. I See too much. I think. I Know too much. Really. I actually Understand. far too little. I do Not Know. Societal. Historical. Cultural. Racial. Economic contexts. of ChildWelfare work. with Nehiyâw'ak peoples. AtThatTime.

I am Sad. in Pain. burdened with Stories. Lives of Children. touch me personally. I can Not help it. I take their Pain. Home with me. I try to DoGood. DoGooder! is a Label I can easily wear. probably am called. I try. Try to right Wrongs. to educate IgnorantbutWillingMooniyâs Parents. build self-esteem of hopeless Nehiyâw'ak FosterKids. recruit

CulturallySensitive foster. and adoptive Homes.

I work with Joey. twelve years old. twenty-first FosterHome. tries to Hang himself. Regularly. reminds me of JoeyB. in MissionSchool. who used to Carve his Wrists. and Drum Johnny Cash. "I hear the Train a Comin." in perfect time. on his wooden desk top. with his stubby eraser-chewed-off pencil. JoeyB was a FosterKid too. He did Hang himself. Richard Cardinal was Not alone.[9]

I work with Angie. Stella. and Marie. adopted by Mooniyâs Parents. Now. AtRiskTeens. back in Care. They tell me OneDay. after a FamilyReconciliation meeting went Bad. their adoptive Dad. ProminentPsychiatrist. Sexually Assaults them. Regularly. and many others. who will believe them? or me? NoOne. Not in TheEighties.

what about Stephen. who Abuses Animals. and self-Mutilates. who has just been picked up off a Run. back to LockUp for him. I worry he won't Survive. much longer. or Lee. who runs away. after her adoptive Parents. Strip her. Lock her in her Room. for Days. why? advice given in FamilyTherapy session. where her Parents are told. by a well known Therapist. to "set firmer Boundaries."

I Grieve. for countless LittleOnes. who cry to visit their Parents. Kookohms. Siblings. Communities. those who are denied access. because their Parents can not "prove." to Mooniyâs workers. that they are "trustworthy." able to provide basic Food. Supervision to Mooniyâs standards. Love does Not count. Family. Community. Cultural ties. Do Not count.

1961. Provincial SocialWorkers. go into Nehiyâw'ak homes. On and Off Reserves. make Judgements about Parenting. Child-rearing. Proper Child care. according to WECCP values. widespread Poverty. results in many Children being Apprehended. from otherwise Caring Homes. No Services are offered. No Homemakers. No Preventive Family Counselling services. No funded Day-Care facilities. No Services. Mooniyâs Families in crisis may have received.[10]

by late 1970s. one quarter of Status Indian Children. can Expect. to be Separated from their Family. for all or part of Childhood. Imagine. thousands of First Nations Children that are Apprehended. taken. into Care. Stolen. Permanent Orders. placed in FosterCare. placed for Adoption.

until 1982. majority of those Apprehended. in Manitoba. are shipped out of Canada. by aggressive American Adoption agencies. No legal barriers. to out-of-province. or international Adoptions. Imagine. thousands. of mostly impoverished Nehiyâw'ak Children. Adopted out in

Mooniyâs Homes in U.S. many by my Employer. a WillRemainAnonymous ChildWelfareAgency. in just two decades.

what did these SocialWorkers know? about those Children. Families. Communities. wounded in TheSixtiesScoop? WECCP World.View clouds their Minds. their Judgements of TheNorm. their Theories. Code of Ethics. Beliefs.

SocialWorkers act like Puppets. promote a Destructive process. most WellIntentioned. No understanding. No asking. "is what we are doing Wrong?" when I Confront this practice in reality. it is a PainFull experience. I am Witness to ongoing Colonization. Soul Stripping.

AtThatTime. I know None of this. I am politically Naïve. despite a Progressive degree in SocialWork. I am still Numb. from my long descent into deep Depression. after Ma's Death.

AtThatTime. I am only Surviving. trying to do MyBest. Only Trying to do MyBest. Until. OneFatefulDay. I sit having supervision. in BossyOne's office. when my Ears hear him brag."Yeah. I take Great Pride. in My Work." He says smugly. arms crossed. pudgy well-fed Face cracks with Smile. "I single-handedly apprehended hundreds. Hundreds of those Indian Kids. in One Year. and got them GoodHomes." little did I know. AtThatTime. many SocialWorkers accepted financial Incentives. for finding Adoptable Children.

as usual. my Mind is wandering. I am mulling over plans. for a particular Child. His Words snap me back. Reality Check. "what? what did you say?" I ask "You got them GoodHomes?" I am like a Trained Parrot.

"Yep." BossyOne replies. with a twisted smirk. half a Smile. half a Grimace. "I don't know why ThosePeople. even have Kids. They don't Want to take Care of Them." I jump up. on my Feet. my Cheeks flaming. "Those people." I say as coldly as I can. "do take Care of their Children. You. You obviously know Nothing. how Hard Life is. for Native Families! or how Communities help raise Children. Not Just Parents!" I snap back.

"No need to get all Hot and Bothered." He says with a Smile. a full Teeth-bared Smile. Now. "I knew that would get a Rise out of you." He laughs. again. "Sit Down. and Cool your Heels. We'll finish our little Talk." Patronizing me. with his tone of Voice.

I can Not sit. I shift from one Foot to another. I say. "No! I'm outta Here. talk to your Self. You F...ing A...Hole! I don't care. what You have to Say!" I storm out. outside TheOffice building. walk a long way. down BackRoad.

"He's a Pig." I think. No. I correct myself. I will Not talk bad of Pigs. They are Good Friends to me. when I Need them. I always had very good relations with Pigs. on OurFarm. I would have Long Talks with them. They would Grunt back to me. in a very reassuring way. I Never eat Pork. "He is Not a Pig." I mentally note.

as I walk. I begin to realize. "I'm in a Mess. how can I face Him. again?" I ask myself. I kick dirt on BackRoad. drag real hard on DrumCigarette. I hastily hand-roll as I flee TheOffice. "how can I Return. EveryDay. to this Job? especially Now. Now. that I Know what I Know?" I Know. my Life is taking another turn for TheWorse. I am getting Dumped. Upside Down. on my Head. Again.

Later. that Night. some RezFriends drop over. Still. I can Not sit still. can Not visit over Tea. or play Cards. I am too Upset. with a little Teasing. a little Razzing. then Cajoling. I tell Story. I wonder. in my Mind. If. fighting with BossyOne is Confidential. I have sworn Oath.

RezFriends can't believe their Ears. when I tell them what Happened. what was Said. and worse. Much Worse. what has been Done. even More. They Can't Believe. I am worried. Worried I am going to lose my Job. "I don't know Why. you would wanna Work. for ThosePeople. Anyways." OneFriend says. as she Hugs me. going out Door.

It is such HotStory. They pass it On. to Others. around Nehiyâw'ak Country. Moccasin Telegraph. until some influential Chiefs hear. a few realize. They have found one missing piece. that fits their Puzzle. a Face and a Name. to attach to a larger act of Genocide. acts of Genocide. Now. well documented. but. AtThatTime. still Concealed. until I. unwittingly help. break it Open.

"A CHANGE IS AS GOOD AS A REST"

all interesting possibilities of Political Activism aside. I feel Hollow inside. my LittleFlickeringLight is dimming daily. in Traditional Societies. when I am Ill. or feeling Discomfort. I may be described as being "Indian sick." that means unknown Spiritual Forces are at work in my Life. to understand these Forces. I have to turn to Spiritual Teachers. Good People tell me. "You are getting Sick. and Tired. go see Elders."

raised to always follow that Advice when given. I do. I place my better Judgments. and my university Degrees. on a shelf. and I go in search of Elders. as is Customary. I did Not receive any advice. just Stories. Stories of ResidentialSchool. of Pain. Brutalization. and most importantly. of Survival.

Stories. of gaping holes gouged. in WoundedHearts. and Souls. Children wounded by Parents. Parents wounded by ResidentialSchool Abuses. Festering. Oozing pus. Now. a few generations deep. will to Live is Lost. when Children are Lost.

Stories of Children returning Home as Adults. from Schools. from Homes. Broken and in Pain. don't know who they are. looking for Family. that Died of BrokenHearts.[11] when Elders have No One. to Pass knowledge on to. takes away Hope for Future.

Much Later. Manitoba Judge Edwin Kimelman. called in to Investigate. concludes. "Cultural genocide has been taking place in a systematic routine manner."[12]

Then. OneDay. just when I feel I can't take any more. No. No More. a call comes. "come with us on Pow-wowTrail." AFriend says. "take some Time off work. and Come and travel with DrumGroup. it will do you Good."

I have to do it. I Had To. I know I am Sick. and Tired. I hear myself. telling anyone that will listen. "I am burnt out." I Was Burnt Out![13]

AtThatTime. many were telling me. "You need a Rest." OneElder says. "If. you're Tired. be like Bear. have a good long Rest." so Simple. so Profound. so Hard to Do. in fast-paced World we exist in. I Laugh. and say. "I need a Change. a Change is as good as a Rest." Flippant reply. I go for a Change. I go on a Journey. Changes my Life.

I learn Language of RedRoad. as I travel Pow-wowTrail. I walk Black Hills. site of AncientAncestralHealing Lodge. Centuries old. Power palpable. exudes out over Rocky Hills. out on Rocks. in a beautiful Circle of Mounds. Mounds of our precious Mother Earth. I find. mySelf. Visioning. for my Future. Visioning for my Future. out There. in all that Sand. in that hot. Hot. Hot Sun. after Days and Nights. Days and Nights of drumming. and dancing. and drumming. Drumming. Drumming. All Day. All night. All Day. All Night. Drumming.

suddenly. I see on horizon. thousands of Buffalo. BigBrownBuffalo. raising clouds of Dust. Sunflowers. big. yellow as Sun. fly in Air. as Buffalo frolic in field. Birds circle. over their Heads. enjoying Seeds and Bugs. Magpies call to each other. their blackblue Feathers glistening. in Sun. black Beaks pick Bugs. from Buffalo. picking Seeds from Ground. fresh GreenGrass. Food for Buffalo. Home for Bugs.

I see Circle of Life. Unity. and Interconnectedness. I Know. I have a Place. We All Do. Greatest to Smallest. All have an important part to play. Creation. I have my Ancestral Consciousness raised. Mystically. Psychically. Magically.

Returning Again.
like BuffaloNation.
Strength of our Spirits.
is returning again.
despite Generations.
of Persecution.
Confinement.

HeavyHeartBurden finally lifted. momentarily at least. I will now walk Lighter. on a different Path. I will see with different Eyes. I ask. "what will my LifeWork consist of? I know. I am Conscious of myself Spiraling. Spiraling to Centre of myself. and Out again. each Ending is a new Beginning. Ancestral Consciousness within. is Reborn.

Much Later. I learn to ask. Why. are so many Helpers. Healers. Sick themselves. from overWork. they can Not get well? Why. do professionals Deny. their own Problems? don't seek Help for themselves? Why. do we keep up Masks of well-being. while we Die inside? We call this BurnOut.

OneDay. I draw my Recovery. a RecoveryMetaphor. a GarbageCan. I am like TheCan. I start out. only my own Garbage. however much that is. I am Open. ready to take it all in. People throw their Trash in me. All their pain. problems. negative Life experiences. If. I take Time. for my own Healing. and Cleansing. I get rid of some Garbage. before it accumulates. If. I do not. Garbage keeps piling up. and Up. until. I am Oozing. Toxic Waste.

Then. when People try to give me their Garbage. I end up Spewing it. back at Them. after all. I begin to feel. their Neediness. is responsible for my Dis-ease. No. as Helpers. we are responsible. to keep our Cans clean. Agencies must help us to do this. by providing Garbage Collectors. Garbage Dumps. and a Recycling Depot. a supportive working Community.

FREE OURPEOPLE. ON A GOODPATH

after my descent. dark slippery Caves. of Loss. Despair. Death. Abuse. I begin to catch a Glimpse of a small flickering Light. illuminating a GoodPath. sometimes faintly Visible. often Not. brief moments of shadowy Clarity. bring a longing to Integrate my Life.

I look for a Message. Sign. something to show me a GoodPath. "GrandMothers. send me a Sign." I practise Praying. feel very self-consciousness. "send SomeThing.SomeOne. to Show me." I know. SomeThing. or SomeOne. can Appear. AnyTime. AnyWhere. Expect Unexpected.

Then. OneDay. I see it. I Saw It. I knew. an ad. Professors are being Hired. to develop and teach a SocialWork program. UpNorth. it is just right for me. Just Right For Me. I Am Hired! I will be Métis professor. in program UpNorth. I am Ecstatic!

I am going Home. Going Home. Home. but. Not Home. close geographically. but. Not right there. Not RightThere. don't want to be RightThere. Not back in TheTown.

UpNorth. we have few overseers. occasional fly-ins. from SouthernUrbanWhiteCampus. DownThere. few RoleModels. only what we have Seen. Experienced ourselves as Students. BankingMethod. Stand. and Deposit knowledge. in EmptyVessels. Students.[14]

OneDay. Rudy[15] asks. "do so-called Experts realize. talkin' down to People. is goin' against OurTeachins'?" "We learn from what we do. Observin' others. Tinkin' about what we Do. Feel an' See. or Stories. Teachins' of OlderOnes. makin' Mistakes. dats 'ow People Change. Not outta memorizin' a Book." Leticia adds.

I am Expected to implement TheCurriculum.[16] teach from texts. like Hepworth and Larsen.[17] discuss Competencies and Skills. as if they are Commonsense. Natural. Not culturally loaded. Not grounded in Scientific. Expert. Consciousness. Mooniyâs.

I learn to Question. Colleagues. "are you Aware? SocialWork theories. research and practices. are based on WhiteCulture?" few Mooniyâs realize it. Judith Katz tells it. "we cannot leave the trap until we know that we are in it."[18]

I PainFully witness. WhiteWorld.Views. taught by WhiteEducators. enacted by WhiteSocialWorkers. continue to Oppress. does Not Empower Nehiyâw'ak Peoples. AllGoodIntentions aside.

I wonder. "how can I teach. a concept like Empowerment. through Disempowering processes." Dena complains. "why do I 'ave to 'get it

right'? I should say 'get it White'." Lara exclaims. "what about what our
OldPeople Know? what about what we Know? this stuff is too Mooniyâs
for me! why do I Have to learn it?"

my Ears hear. too many Times. "I know it may Not seem Relevant.
but. it's TheCurriculum." I struggle Daily. to Not reproduce oppressive
ways of doing things.

I am PainFully aware. Schools can be like processing plants. like our
AnimalRelations are rendered into consumables. Students are conformed
to norms of Monniyas Corporate agendas. I want to be like Paulo Freire.
contribute to Freedom. Free OurPeople. Teach how to Recognize.
Resist. Change. Oppressive systems. not just Reproduce them.

AtThatTime. We do Not teach Students to critique CulturalBiases.
do Not include AntiRacist strategies. I am Expected to take a Neutral
position.[19] I want to take a Stand.[20] Transform SocialWork culture. make
Space for Nehiyâw'ak cultural realities. focus on Important social issues.

I try to Imagine. how will we ever meet Needs. of NorthernNative
Students? Empower them. meet expressed Needs. of NorthernNehiyâw'ak
Peoples. I feel these paradoxes keenly. EveryDay. Profs. are all Mooniyâs.
except MétisDirector and Me. They struggle to Adapt. Adapt to Our
CulturalEnvironment. demands. Resisting at Times. in Conflict at Times.
trying to understand how. They might FitIn with Us.

some manage by Ignoring difference. others add-on a few articles. or
guest speakers. Add-on. Add-On. without changing structure. take an
"additive approach." If. SomeOne puts Native art on walls. burns a braid
of SweetGrass. or holds a TalkingCircle. once in a while. when we're
upset about something. is that enough? or if most Students are Native. is
it like an Aboriginal program?" Trina wants to know.

some depend on Students to be CulturalInformants. to be well
informed about Culture. to provide Cultural content for themselves. and
others. They ignore multi-generational impacts. systemic assimilation
policies. stripped many of Cultural Roots. "I really felt bad when G.
turned to me. I really don't know. what my so-called Culture is. I never
grew up with it." Alex cries in my office. OneDay.

I received formal SocialWork education. in Mooniyâs institutions. I
am often as Unprepared as anyone. often as Unprepared as Anyone. to
fully realize alternatives. AtThatTime. mid-80s. I know only Campbell.
Manuel. Cardinal. Adams.[21] Angry outpouring of Injustice. is just a
beginning. I didn't know. how to Create Change. out of Desperation.

I.We. are still only Beginning. Only Beginning processes of re-
weaving Cultural Identity. re-establishing Nehiyâw'ak Ways of Walking

Life' s Paths. while working within Mooniyâs educational contexts.[22]

Education is Assimilation. places We are regularly Streamed. Demeaned. Chronically suffer Shame. Anger. Discomfort. Abuse. Fears. Fear of Failure. Fear of Authority. We feel Inadequate. Despirited. Isolated. Pressured to Conform. We. divided into Winners and Losers. learn to Memorize. more and more details. Regurgitate what professors want to hear. OneDay. Stan tells me. "You have PowerOver us. We do and say what TheProf wants. don't argue. or talk back. do what we are Told. even If. it is Meaningless."

I attempt to engage Learners. Engage Nehiyâw'ak Learners. work to Overcome extensive lessons in Passivity. They are prepared to Sit. and listen. Listen while I talk. while I Talk and Talk. but. I am not ready to be Elder. or Expert. I don't want to be OnlyTalker. I work at getting them Involved. and they did. and I Did. and they Did. They. We. Got Involved.

I use Humour. SacredMedicine.[23] We laugh long and hard. at ourselves. at Systems that Hurt us. Badly. Laughter is sometimes all we have. to Survive. Wisakecahk is always here. to help us see our Mistakes. to keep us Strong. and Sane.

OneDay. Rena comments to me. "I Love to sit in TheLibrary. when you are teaching Law class. EveryOne is Laughing so hard. Enjoying class so much. it makes me feel Good. to Listen. I can't Imagine. what is so Funny. about Law."

We Laugh. and we Cry. I Tease. *"this group has some of the best criers I have known."*[24] We Know. Crying is Healing. We Expect Tears to Flow. in Ceremonies. SharingCircles. Classrooms. whenever. wherever. Healing.Teaching happens. Releasing Pain. one catalyst for Change.

Laughter.Tears. intersperse with Anger. close to surface. Bubbling. ready to BoilOver. Anger. Righteous. MultiGenerational. Anger. Historical. Contemporary Injustices. now being Recognized. Theorized. All know wrath of Angry Students. determined to make an ImplantedProgram more Culturally.Relevant.

SelfNamed. Marxist.Phenomenologist.Colleague. is my greatest Teacher. how Enlightenment of Masses. getting them to Rise Up against Authority. can bring them Down On You. especially when your Voice is Authority. Colonizer. WhiteMan. with BigWords. one of those fingered. as Cause of our social conditions. ToDay. Embodied Wisakecahk. Thanks G.

often Mediator. I have many lessons in Education as Political. Learn to ask. Whose Consciousness? Whose History? Whose Voice? and Whose Experience? Who is acknowledged in University settings? even in

NorthernNehiyâw'ak locations?

    my past experiences. Feminist praxis.[25] combine to Push. Guide me. to Egalitarian models. a Spirit driven challenge. gives rise to Many Many lessons to Story. throughout my Time. in all academic Systems. I learn everyDay. efforts to Liberate. can reproduce relations of Domination. reinforce lessons received. in Silencing and PowerOver.[26]

    "I think SocialWorkers. must be trained to Oppress us. They are so Good at it." Rudy says. "who are they trying to kid? They can't help AnyBody. EveryOne knows their main purpose is Control!"

    I ask. "who has Power? how do they show it? use it? Ignorance is no excuse." We look at ChildWelfareSystems. a glaringly obvious illustration. No matter how Respectful I try to treat People. I represent Authority. TheAgency. I have PowerOver. Stressful. too easy to become Fatalistic. Systems reduce People. to Files. Investigate. Assess. Categorize. Classify. Plan for. Evaluate. Monitor. Review.[27] Disempowering. Spiralling into Apathy. reinforce Dependence on outside intervention.

    Redbird tells it. "You can't ask for help anywhere it seems, without some kind of reprimand … dealing with social workers and everybody like that, the whole thing has been nothing but a Nightmare!"

    when I See. Hear. Experience. Horrible treatment. what People have to go through. makes me want to Distance myself. from SocialWorkers. Paradox. I am educating Others. to be part of this System.

    I learn over and over again. Institutional.Red.Tape. Triggers backlash. of re-memoried. historical. colonial. Pain. Abreaction. Intergenerational abuse. was.is often perpetrated by same measures. Support. Advocacy. and Translation. is Necessary for Victims of Bureaucratic Colonialism.

    I listen. as Students find their Voices. to Question.

    Freida wonders: "why do all these Professors tell us. These are TheProblems in your Communities. These are TheThings YouPeople have to deal with. JustTheSameOldThing. IndianAffairsAgents Nurses SocialWorkers. always telling us what We need. what is Wrong with Our Families. I don't know. how much longer I can Listen!"

    "what about non-interference? like Elders teach. like GoodTracks talks about. why can't we make. our own Choices? our own Mistakes. witout outside pressures? who knows better dan we do. who we are? how we wanna be helped?" Archie debates hotly in class. OneDay.

    "why is mental health got to do with a Person's mind? with psychiatric diagnosis? why is OnePerson Treated. separated from their Families and Communities? what about our own Traditional Healers and Ceremonies?" Elsie wants to know.

much Later. I learn to ask. why are millions spent on Vaccinations? Now. linked to Diabetes. Brain Tumours. and more. while many MedicinePeople can barely afford to Eat?

Students Question. EveryDay. years of social service experience. decades of very rich Life experience. a Challenge to teach. learn to actively assert their Experiences. their Voices. their Knowledges. within SocialWork structures. They want More. More Nehiyâw'ak teachers. More Nehiyâw'ak content. Representation in curriculum. and classroom. Changes to format and climate.

Dedicated and Demanding Students. make very good Teachers. *"You had no hesitation in letting us know if you felt we were being biased—sexist, classist or racist, including Marxist or feminist."* I Tease them.

I am taught to teach. Taught to Teach by Students. by my Students. *"I honour each of you as my teachers and welcome you as a very powerful force, intelligent, political and possessing a keen respect for Native spiritual tradition. You will be leaders in Native politics and social work delivery in the very near future."* and They are.

I'M SICK 'N' TIRED. AGAIN.

I leave my Life. UpNorth. my Life. Work. where I learn. to Walk my Talk. I am Sick. Sick from emissions. from Smelter. IndustrialDisease. I have diarrhea Daily. Institution requires PaperTrail. call me to Account. for re-occurring absences. force me to see Doctors. Diagnosis. Crohn's Disease. offer Drugs. or maybe Operate.

"No. I don't want to." I have No investment in MedicalModel. not with my Life. and my Body. They have already Failed me. twice near Death. because of medical intervention. OneTime. too much Demerol. pumped too quickly. into my Body. Accidental Overdose. put into a Coma. awaken FourDays later. in TheHospital. Skin worn to Bone. on Wrists. Legs. Belly. from Restraints. Tied Down. so I won't injure myself. as I Thrash. Convulse.

Not just me. my Parents both Died. in TheHospital. my Daughter. PerfectHealthyBaby. Suddenly. Convulsions. Time after Time. Night-marish. Horrifying. High-speed trips. to TheHospital. No Help.

Later. I take her to SpringCeremonies. offer Tobacco and Cloth. Pray for her Life. Cleansing Sweat to prepare. MedicineMan takes his EagleBone. Sucks. Spits LargeBlackBeetles into container. quickly covered by his Scabio.[28] taken outside. into Woods to be Buried. "SomeOne put Bugs into her. don't let Them do it again." He solemnly tells me. "She will get Worse. then Better. it will Test your Faith."

I am Bewildered. "what does he Mean?" I wonder. at first Silently. then Questioningly. Story to Friends. until Time arrives. MoonBaby's next immunization. PublicHealthNurse begins to harass me. "bring Baby in for her Shot." Light Dawns. I know. The Devastating AlmostDeathProducing Bugs. SomeOne had put into her. Aiiieeeee. I know. Nightmare all started. with first Needle.

I refuse to immunize her. keep that Commitment. argue with several SchoolOfficials. PublicHealthNurses. and even Doctors. as necessary. to move within Systems.[29] NearDeath experiences. of Self. Daughter. Family members. close Friends. keeps me Committed. I do Not choose drugs or surgical intervention. in my Life.

but. when I am Sick. EveryDay. I begin to Wonder. "should I let Them treat me?" First. I go to see MedicineMan UpNorth. for Ceremonies. I want to know "what to do?" after we Pray. He says. "You have too much YellowPowder in you."

again. I am Confused. Not prepared to wait. to find Meaning. I am proactive. "Yellow Powder. Hmmmm." I notice Yellow ChalkDust on green boards. in classrooms. I stop board writing. who needs it? I am Not convinced I know. but. I am willing to try Anything.

early Fall. I scrape First Frost. off my windshield. in early Morning Light. "are my GreenEyes playing Tricks on me? No!" I know. in my Heart. it is True. Yellow Frost. Yellow Frost! can you imagine? I am Sick from Yellow Frost. Sulfur emissions from SmelterStack.

each Morning. I Notice. I begin to Pay Attention. Yellow fine sticky Powder. enough to scrape off my windshield. I research. I find emissions are eighty percent higher. than they are Supposed to be. Eighty Percent. Imagine. I am Shocked to Know. NoOne want to Listen. about my Body. or my Elder's diagnosis. NoOne hears when I complain. about EnvironmentalDisease? in Late Eighties.

I can see their Ears.Minds. close. NoOne wants to Hear.Know. about Pollution in a OneIndustryTown. Industrial Disease. "We don't want Them. to relocate TheSmelter. to some other Place." They say. "who's We? I do." I say. They Gasp.

I find it Unfair. when I need to take SickLeave. need to find a healthy place to Heal. I can get No Doctor. to write me Sick. unless I subscribe to Treatment. MedicineMan's Word is No Good. I can get No Administrators. to support me.

"If. you are not going to be Here. on Site. to do TheJob. No

Lead flows.
Healing from lead toxicity.
Environmental Disease. is manifest.
through an understanding of Flow.
Oneness. heat Heals.

contract." NewDirector decrees. "but. what about Fly-in Professors? They don't all Live Here?" I question. "that's different. You. must reside Here." "You Must Reside Here!" She asserts firmly. expressing her Authority. Authority to decide on my Health. my Life. Her Authority to decide on my Future well-being.

"but. I can't. I'm Sick." I say limply. feel like Battle is already lost. I feel Sick 'n' Tired. too Sick to care. too Tired to fight. "too Bad." I am told. I limp away to SacredBlueLake. retreat by her gorgeous clear icy cold Waters. I feel Battered. and Betrayed. Betrayed and Abused.

I am TheOnly Nehiyâw'ak faculty. in a Nehiyâw'ak program. I work hard for Program. I enjoy my work. feel Alive in my classrooms. I am living out my LifePurpose. I Know. I am on a GoodPath. contributing what I have learned. in my Life. to my Community. I am advocate for Students. liaison with Communities. program and policy Wordsmith. as Devolution of medical.social services. is being Negotiated. UpNorth.

"too Bad." NewDirector decrees. So. I have to Go. but. I don't Want to. I Do Not. I Did Not. Want To Go! I speak to Union. to upper level Administration. NoOne can Help me. NoOne. "too Late. You should have Lied. signed your contract. Then. gone on SickLeave. Your contract has expired. We can't help you. Now." too Late. too Bad. sooo Sad. should Have lied. Should Have Lied? that really makes me Sick.

Others do not want me to go either. I have support of Students and Chiefs across North. Students complain. Chiefs. other Nehiyâw'ak politicians find out. and They complain. Protest is happening. with my departure. Much Later. I hear. "this did Not work. in your favour. this is Proof. to NewDirector. that you are Trouble." TroubleMaker. One label I have learned to Wear. with Grace.

Meanwhile. I am Out of Touch. Meditating regularly. walking by SacredBlueLake. doing my work. off campus. trying to Heal. my Body.Spirit. I Laugh when I Hear Story. "at least it's Proof. SomeOne learned SomeThing. from my Activist teachings." I say. We are both Relieved. to find Humour in a very PainFull recollection.

Years Later. I run into Alice in TheMall. "I still remember when you left." She says. "it was such a Strong Lesson. in Fear. how much NewDirector Feared you. your Influence with Students. with Communities. it didn't make sense to AnyOne. what she Said or Did. She knew. You Should have been Director. You Should Have Been! She didn't last."

"No. I couldn't do it." I say. "Not AtThatTime. I was too Sick 'n' Tired." I was Sick and Tired. OverTired from Mental Pollution too. from Stress and Strain. always trying to lobby for This. and for That. Sick and Tired. always negotiating. Invisible.Distanced.Rational.White.Male. University. Way.Down.Urban.South. when Needs were Real. Felt. Visible. Immediate. for Nehiyâw'ak. UpNorth.

too Late. too Bad. sooo Sad. a short while Later. now Teaching. in White.Urban.Academia. I quickly learn to Mourn. Freedoms. I left behind.

Fires Rage. when I am leaving UpNorth. Fires. huge Fires. Orange.Red.Yellow.Blue. Fires. SmokyBlack Fires. burn up Forests of beautiful barren NorthLands. Bushes I Hunt. Trap. Herb.Berry pick. Wood harvest. Travel. with Parents. Aunties. Uncles. GranMere. as a Child. Bushes I fly over in small planes. Winter. Summer. as a community organizer in my Twenties. Bushes I Love to return to. as an educator in my Thirties. Now. I flee in my Forties.

Bush of my Consciousness. Bush of my Community. I cry and cry. Cried and Cried. BlackSmoke streaks. run like Rivers. down my ashen face. GreenEyes Water-filled. Glimpse of GoodPath blurs. as I drive Wildly. Narrowly escape. Barricades close as we leave. I am sure it is a Sign. Fire is always a Sign for Fyre Jean.

"GrandMothers." I pray. Now. somewhat more Comfortable with Prayer. I have been Forced. by Life circumstances. to seek Spiritual help. I Have received it. in my times of Need. I pray. "keep my Self. and my

Family. Safe. let me Glimpse Light. GoodPath. so I can Follow." and I have.

Notes

1. Thanks again to marino. for her readable work on hegemony. and resistance.
2. Edward Said's writing on imperialism and colonialism has greatly influenced my analysis.
3. for Stories about political resistance. read Richardson. Miller.
4. to learn about current.historical. struggles for HumanRights. by IndigenousPeoples globally. see Niezen. Goehring.
5. SelfGovernment readings include Hylton. Warry. Erasmus.
6. Weatherford. has a small book. packed with contributions. made by Nehiyâw'ak. to Canadian identity. Lifestyle. see Barreiro on RedRoots of democracy.
7. Stories of Nehiyâw'ak Ancestors' Resistance. to acculturation. are told by Beck and Walters. Fiske. Deloria, Jr.
8. Traditional values. are transmitted by Elders Stories. in written works. like Cruikshank. Meili. Kulchyski, McCaskill and Newhouse. St. Pierre and Long Soldier. (who interview Elders). and Acoose. Armstrong. Charnley. Gunn Allen. *Kelusultiek.* Maracle. Anderson. (who write for empowerment of Women).
9. Richard Cardinal's sad. sad. Story. is told in *Cardinal: Cry from a Diary of a Metis Child.* an NFB film by Alanis Obomsawin.
10. read about SixtiesScoop in Fournier and Crey. Howse and Stalwick. or Chartier. (on Métis).
11. as a B.C. Elder asked at a hearing in 1992. "Where are our artisans, our weavers, fishermen, medicine people, dancers, shamans, scuptors, and hunters? For thirty years, generations of our Children, the very future of our communities, have been taken away from us. Will they come home as our leaders knowing the power and tradition of their people? Or will they come home broken and in pain, not knowing who they are, looking for the family that died of a broken heart? (in Fournier and Crey 1998: 93).
12. quoted in Fournier and Crey 1997: 88.
13. some BurnOut sources include. Maslach. Jevne. Hudnall Stamm.
14. thanks to Paulo Freire. for inspiration. and terms like "pedagogy of the oppressed." "banking methods." and "the practice of freedom." Now. CodeWords used by many critical educators.
15. Rudy and others quoted. are paraphrased from actual discussions. *Redbird* is an actual quote. from thesis version of *Circle Works.*
16. this is mid-to-late eighties. June 6, 1998. Canadian Association of Schools of Social Work ruled. "the curriculum shall ensure that Students have an understanding of oppressions and healing of Aboriginal Peoples and implications for social policy and social work with Aboriginal Peoples in the

Canadian context." still a vision in progress. many programs still have no
Nehiyâw'ak faculty. most have only one half credit in CrossCulturalIssues.
to learn to "Help." All "Minorities."

17. I was using 1986 version. of Hepworth and Larson. been many new editions
since. basic philosophies remain firmly entrenched. require a BankingMethod
of teaching. "they promote a version of social work that uncritically
reproduced the rationalizing and technologizing effects of Western capitalism," says Rossiter 1995: 25.

18. Ferguson in Katz 1985: 615

19. content analysis of literature AtThatTime found that SocialWork is "naive
and superficial in its anti-racist practice" (McMahon and Allen-Meares
1992: 537).

20. Ben Carniol was my teacher and mentor. for a social action approach to
social work practice.

21. Campbell. Manuel. Cardinal. and Adams. voiced their concerns. about
socio-economic conditions of Nehiyâw'akPeoples in the Seventies.

22. see Battiste and Barman. and Battiste. for current discussions of Nehiyâw'ak
education strategies.

23. Laughter is Nehiyâw'ak. Traditional. Law. "When you are alive, you give
homage to the Great Spirit, and you will do favours for others, and then you
will enjoy yourself. If one does not do those things, he will explode within
himself. These three things are the highest in law. Realize this. These are
truths, so be it" (Ben Black Bear, Plains Elder, in Beck and Walters 1977: 40).

24. Italics indicate quotes. taken from my Speech to Honour Grads. May. 1988.

25. already an active resistor of hierarchy. western. patriarchal. domination.
groomed by Feminists with AWARE (Alberta Women Against Rape and
Exploitation), and MACSW (Manitoba Action Committee on the Status of
Women. Gifted me much learning. practical applications of consciousness-
raising. activism. collective process.

26. Starhawk discusses Power. PowerOver. greatly influenced my thinking
AtThatTime. "Power-over motivates through fear. Its systems instill fear,
and then offer hope of relief in return for compliance and obedience. We fear
the force and violence of the system should we disobey, and we fear the loss
of value, sustenance, comforts and tokens of esteem" (1987: 14).

27. see Leonard for a critique of Fatalism. and SocialWork practice.

28. a Nehiyâw'ak word for Helper.

29. If. you want to know more. about dangers of immunization. you can read
what first influenced me. Chaitow 1987. or more recently. McTaggart 1991.
also. Alternative Health magazines.

BACKING OUT DOORWAYS. BE AWARE
WATCH YOUR TAIL. THEY BITE BACK.

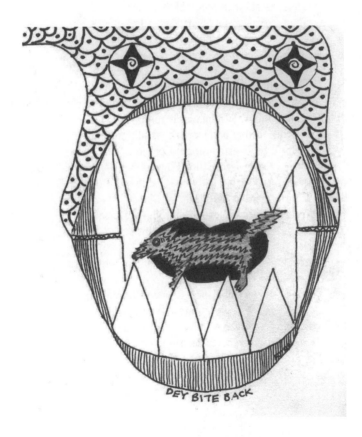

dey Bite back.
it Hurts. when yer scrawny carcass. gets stuck between their Teeth.

I Watch. Listen. Wait.
    then act on what I learn. Activism.
    challenge institutional Hegemony.
            Argue. Teach against. multiple forms of Hierarchies
               that affect my Life. Sexism. Homophobia.
                        Racism. Eurocentric imperialism.
I swim against mainStream.
I Organize. Persuade. Orchestrate. Construct.
I actively participate. in socio-political cultural Life.
        help to articulate critical Currents. already Flowing within it.
dian marino and I have figured it out.
Peoples' consent to Hegemony. RulingOrder.
        is Never one hundred percent.
Consent is a process. established.re-established daily.
        "There are always a few ledges, a few cracks,
        in the seemingly 'monolithic' wall of consent."
I Story to make Consent.Resistance. responses. Visible in Narrative.
    work to break open. Cracks in Consent. is Dangerous.
        might bring Wall tumbling Down. On us.
when we are Violated. react to Defend ourselves. attempt to change Systems.
    Authorities. Institutions. Systematically respond.
        with further and more devastating forms.
        to Re-establish our Consent.
        to re-secure their Power.
I call upon Power of Wisakecahk.
    Trickster. Transformer. to Assist me.
    to represent Powers of learning through Reversal.
                InsideOut Lessons.
Wisakecahk Tales.
    show us Multiple. Competing. Reflections of our Selves.
    Not as a Mirror. a Circus Mirror.
        Images shown Unbalance. Reorient. Reveal.
        reflect Ordinary events in New ways.
Wisakecahk rolemodels necessary Courage.
    examine Uninvited. Uncomfortable. Threatening. Confusing Moments.
    as they Erupt in My Life. in Our shared spaces.
        Strong reactions are Inevitable when creating Change.

"I DREAM THIS JOB"

I'll tell you. One BitingStory. [14]
    One I'm still learning to tell.
        because of how Hard. how Strong a Feeling. I have for it.
a Wisakecahk tale. a Dream tale.
    of Nehiyâw'akControlledSchool.
    done OurWay. based on Nehiyâw'ak Traditions.
        Administratively. Pedagogically.
set in BeautifulSacredValley. nestled in PreciousMounds of Our Mother.
I Dream this Job.
    although I can't see my Face. and Vision gives me a chill.
      ChillWinds blow through me.
I Think. Decide. want it to be.
    just fierce NorthWind blowing off Ocean.
I accept a surface picture. BeautifulSacredValley. a Dream fulfilled.
          I take a Risk.
SoCalled Nehiyâw'akControlledSchool is Not.
      is bureacratically Mooniyâs.
    this is biggest Heartache. biggest Disappointment of Dream.
as I Uncover. Unmask. oppressive relations.
    to myself.with others.
my classroom becomes a Site of this Struggle.
    of this learning.teaching. Paradox.

Anyways. here I am. Chalk in Hand. teaching Theory of Oppression. around Medicine Wheel. it takes all Morning. ThatFatefulDay. We have a double class. I begin Afternoon. I say: "Now. does anyBody have an example we can work with?" a few are mentioned. OneWoman speaks at length. She knows about Oppression. She Has a Story to Tell. a Story she Has to Tell. She Had to Tell It.

here she is. SingleParent. FullTimeStudent. works PartTime at TheSchool. just that Day. at Noon. She went in for her cheque. She is told she is laid off. "I am Laid Off!" OneWoman gasps when she tells it. "but. Why?" she asks.

"Now. you are Student Council President. it's a Conflict of Interest." They tell her. "Conflict of Whose Interests?" She asks. "You can not Possibly have Time. to fulfill Duties of Both. Studies and Politics. and juggle Paid work. especially being a Mother and all." She is told. She Was Told!

Later. She protests to us in Class. "I Need TheJob. why should They decide. what is Best for me? Why Should They Decide? why should they?

should they?"

It. is a classic example. a Teachable moment. I listen Respectfully to Whole Story. when she is Done. I go to TheBoard. We begin to Work. "We'll take this model. Wheel of Oppression. We developed this Morning." I say. "and apply This problem. what do we Get?" We work all Afternoon. EveryOne is Energized about It.

It. is all drawn out. right here on TheBoard. Sociopolitical. Gender. Race. Class. and Historical context. of OneWoman's "personal" problem. We strategize then: "given this analysis." I ask. "how can this picture change? how can she get what she needs? who will she have to talk to and how?" by close of Afternoon. She has KnowHow. If. she Chooses. she can Act on her own behalf. has Support of her peers to do so.

She does lobby Administration. and she does get her Job back. She Got Her Job Back. It. is a beautiful Lesson. I am proud. Proud of my work. of her Courage. It. is a Clear and compelling example. right in their Daily Lived Experience. Analysis. Action. and a happy ending. a Happy Ending. only in FairyTales you say. Well. You are Right. almost a happy ending.

Until Later. I hear. I Heard. there is someone Lurking. outside an Open Window. as Lessons progress. a Spy from Mooniyâs Administration. who reports what little She saw and heard. What Little she Saw and Heard. out of context. Out of Context. of course. I know Then. What I teach. in what Form. in my classroom. is Contested Terrain.

It. seems to me a Paradox. Wisakecahk at Play. They hire a Nehiyâw'ak Teacher. but. They really don't want one. don't want one with a RedHeart. They want a Token. I am supposed to deliver same old message. in same old way. TheWay it has Always been done. in Mooniyâs Systems.

some are building their Lives. Careers. GreatWhiteLeaders of IndianEducationMovement. old too-familiar colonial pattern. which I recognize and resist. Recognize. and Resist. Recognize in my Head. Resist in my Heart.

I Learn. Structural issues. quickly become personality problems. Personal Problems. I become TheProblem. All of a Sudden. They. Administration. begin to mention to me. in cozy little Chats. behind ClosedDoors. "maybe. you are Unhappy here." "I'm Unhappy?" I parrot back. QuestionMark attached. "maybe. you are Not Comfortable Here. Not "Fitting In." I am told.

I partially agree. "I am Dis-Enchanted. my workload is a bit Too heavy. Too Heavy. and Things. Well. Things are Not as they first Appeared. No. but. I am Surviving. Thank you for your Concern. I have

Good Days. Good Moments in my teaching. I'm making nice Connections. Good Friends in Community. I'm learning and teaching lots. Lots
and Lots. Inside Classrooms and Out. both Inside and Out." I clarify.

Short Time Later. their Message shifts. from you are Unhappy. to you
are Leaving. I Am Leaving??? I Have Resigned??? Maybe Fired??? What???
"She is Leaving because of Conflict." They say to Some. "because of
complaints. Complaints from Students." What? I am Confused. "what
Students? when?" I ask anyone I can.

I am Dizzy. I am Sick. Sick at Heart. it's all happening Too Fast. Who?
Who? Who said What? to Who? When? Why? Where? What? Who?
Who? I Sound like Owl. even to myself. this is Too Much for me. What
to do? What to do? "GrandMothers help me." I pray. What to do?" I pray
whenever I can remember to.

here I am. in Nehiyâw'ak territory. where OurWays. Circles. Stories.
Ceremony. Experience. Voice. Should. be used as Pedagogy. where our
Histories. Experiences. Oppressions. Should. be Content. to understand
Mooniyâs institutions we are Encountering. I Felt Safe. Open with my
Politics. Beliefs. Practices. Open. Teaching from my Heart. Mistakable.

I want to Know. why do I find myself frequently Counselled.
Disciplined. by those in positions of institutional Power. "it will be Less
Trouble. If. you just learn to Get Along." I know. Now. I read between
Fine Lines. They mean to say. "You are forbidden to teach Skills. Tools.
Attitudes. required to Heal Nehiyâw'ak Peoples. to recover from Abuses
of colonialism."

Then. I am Naïve. I am Unprepared for BackLash. Fears of White
Authorities. how Words. Actions. of mySelf and my Students are Twisted.
Twisted and Used against Me. Twisted and Used against Students.
Twisted and Used against our Traditions.

I Can Not Rest. I Could Not Rest. Students are turning against
Students. Gossip fuels divisions. between Administration. Students. and
Me. mostly. I withdraw. I Withdraw and listen. Listen and wait. Wait and
burn Sweetgrass every Day. EveryDay. I am hurt. Hurt and Sad. Sad and
Mad.

OneDay. I do go out to see Elija Harper.[15] when he comes to
TheTown to speak. a moment of Light. Inspiration in a Dark time of
Despair. after. I see ElderMay downtown. a beautiful SacredWoman. who
Works at School. who is my neighbour on TheRez. when we first arrive.
"how are you? How Are You?" She asks. touches my Arm. a soft CareFull
caress. "what to do? what to do?" I ask. "What To Do?" "If. you call a
Circle. I'll come." She tells me.

So. I do. I put Word out. to Community members. Students. Colleagues. Administration. Family Community Relations. Elders. I especially invite some MedicineKeepers. to help with Circle. I feel too Shaken. too Empty. I know. I will Not be able to Properly attend to Process. to give full Energy to Circle. I will Need. to be attended to. I will Need Support. for myself.

Finally. a GoodDay for Circle arrives. EveryOne. is all in a Circle. about Fifty in all. a Big Circle. filling all Space in Room. most of my Students. many Community Supporters. some members of Administration.

MedicineKeeper. Husband of a Student. Friend. burns a special Sage Smudge. a Traditional Way to Open Circle. PipeCarrier. my Student and Friend. loads his MedicinePipe. offers Blessings to Four Directions. Passes SacredPipe. giving us each Opportunity. to acknowledge Personal Responsibility. within Greater Circle Today.

TalkingFeather is passed to ElderMay. She speaks First. Right of Elders. She speaks from her Heart. leads us by her example. She tells of her Concern for me. for her GrandChildren. my Students. for her Community. for TheSchool. for BeautifulSacredValley. their Home.

ThatDay. She shows Interconnectedness of all of us. "in Circle." She says. "People Speak Openly of Our Hearts. Voice our Part in Story. We must all see Web. Connection. what holds us Together. during Times of Struggle." She teaches Tradition.

TalkingFeather moves to East. in clockwise manner. Traditionalist who burns Smudge. Speaks next. about rules of Circle. "EveryOne speaks in turn." He says. "Circle goes round. an' starts round again. till everyone Speaks. all that Needs to be Spoken. when I come to Circle. I speak from my Heart. this is what we talk about. Here. We talk about our own Selves. what we know. each of us." and he does. He does and we all do. We All Did.

Circle progresses. seems to be bogging down. Bogging Down. two People have Spoken and Left Circle. Spoken and Left Circle without listening. Without Listening to Others Speak. This. is considered Very Rude behaviour. by Some who Know Better. Some Know Better.

Then. MedicineWoman comes. with her EagleFeatherFan. She Sweeps Air Clear. She swirls and twirls. Swirls and Twirls. and she Flies. Flies around Circle. Moving Air. Moving Air. Changing it and Charging it. Re-Charging it and Us. Pain lessens. Sssssshhhhh. Air lightens. Aaahhhh.

I can breathe easier. Haaaaaah. We all feel better. All Felt Better. She works as we work. She Works as We Work. We Worked as She Worked. to create new PositiveEnergy. out of this Horrible. Horrible Time. out of this Struggle.

I pray. "let me Learn Lessons. what I need to know. let each one Learn our Lessons. so that we can walk on a GoodPath. Walk a GoodPath with clear knowingness. of our past actions. how to make It Right. GrandMothers. what do I need to know?" I pray silently.

We all Circle. for as long as we are able. As Long As We Were Able. Our Energy is ebbing. YAWN. Time goes on. I am getting Tired. We all are. OneStudent. Ella. Friend. Wife of PipeCarrier. Mother of Others. has TalkingFeather. She speaks CollectiveConsciousness. Voice of Circle. "I'm Tired. I need a Hug. I want to Close Circle. does AnyOne here. still Need to Speak?" She holds out Feather. No one Needs. to speak. All has been Said. All Had Been Said. for Now.

closing begins. She turns to her Daughter and Hugs. moves on to her Husband. all around Circle. Circle members follow her. her Daughter. then. her Husband. then. All of us in turn. All Circling. All Circling and Hugging. Hugging and Talking. Talking and Crying. Crying and Laughing. and MedicineWoman is Flying.

I Face. each Person. Connect. Hug. Handshake. Speak. any or all. I say or do whatever I need to say or do. and move on. then. as Circle circles back. each Person. Faces me. once to Talk. once to Listen. a Balance is Created.

Beautiful Energy. I feel Community in that Circle. Community I carry in my Heart Today. Ceremony integrates. I shed my Isolation. am restored to Harmony. with mySelf. my Students. my Purpose. that Day. Circle is for Me. For me and With me. With me and Intimately About me. Me and my Relations with Others. my Sense of my Self as a Person. as a Traditionalist. as a Teacher. are all called into Question.

I stand Strong on Tradition. call on Support from that base. in my Greatest Need. I feel Power in Circle. Collective Knowing. Power of generating a Circle. with that much Help. Smudge. SacredPipe. Elders. MedicineKeepers. Feathers. GrandMothers. Strength of All Community Members who know Powers of Circle. who know through Experience how to Intensify Circle. through Power of Voice. Speak from Heart. through Power of Silence. Listen Respectfully. pay Mindful Attention. really Hear what each Person has to say. What Each Person Has To Say.

ToDay. I carry SacredBundle myself. to use in Healing and Teaching. Smudge. TalkingFeather. EagleFeatherFan. Sacred Pipe. I love Circle. I Love Circle. apply it as Pedagogy. use it in political Collective Building.

in Healing Ceremonies. and Conflict Resolution for others.
Circle is a SafePlace. where All Voices can Speak. If. they Wish to.
UnInterrupted. UnAnalyzed. UnArgued. UnChallenged. We each speak
our Own Truth. and be Heard. and Be Heard. Being Heard is a
requirement for HealingWoundedHearts. being Heard is essential when
breaking Silence. when giving Voice to Pains of our Woundedness.
when I give Voice to this MedicineStory. my PainFull Woundedness
still Healing. some want to know. "so what happens? do you get your Job
back? is it a HappyEnding after all?" I ask them. "what's a HappyEnding?
I don't get my Job back. I wouldn't be here telling it if I did."
but. I am Happy. Happy about it. Now. I learn lots. influence many
People. Strongly. more than I yet know. recently. I am Gifted. by
WomanStudent AtThatTime. Now. RespectedElder. She is so affected.
by my BraveHearted WarriorWomanSelf. She presents me a MedicinePipe.
Acknowledgment and Honour. for my Sacrifice. for Strength and Vision
I inspire. Happiness is. surrendering expectations of outcome. Being
Open. to learn from experiences. especially PainFull ones.

Imagine my Surprise

Imagine my Surprise.
     when my Ears are asked to Hear.
          that I. Métis Traditionalist.
"Should." or pardon me. Could ask. "Permission."
     that is. "see if anyone minds." before I Burn Smudge.
               in Heart of Métis Territories.
                    only a short Journey.
                         as Magpie flies.
                              from Batoche.
                              from TheForks.
my Heart beats a PainFull Thud.
          bangs inside Cage of my Ribs.
               Metaphor of my Confinement.
Wisakecahk howls.
     did AnyOne Ever ask Nehiyâw'ak our Permission?
          before engaging in European cultural practices?
          for Generations. Schools. Churches. Hospitals. Governments.
               All Services. have been Forced upon us. Literally.
Now. why is Eurocentric mono-cultural reality. TheExpectedNorm.
                              on OurAncestralLands?
                              in All of our Classrooms?

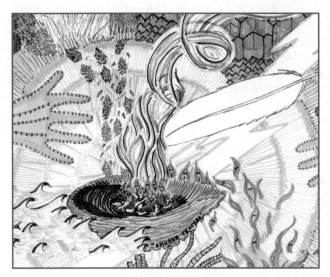

Smudge Teaches.
All Elements offer
themselves.
Together.
help Humans.
prepare ourSelves.
ourSpaces. for
Healing.Teaching.

why do I find myself frequently counselled.
        by those in positions of institutional Power?
        "it will be less trouble. if you don't burn Smudge."
what about Equity in UniVersity?
        where is DiVersity? another False Promise?
        how about a MultiVersity?
Freedom needs to mean more. than an empty Word.
        how can we reclaim Freedoms. after generations of Repression?
Smudge is Ancient. deeply significant HealingTeaching tool.
        who will understand my Right.
        to enact a simple Smudge.
        to prepare my Self. my teaching Space?
"Speak to Elders."
    I am formally advised.
    I am well taught.
        whenever ThatMessage comes.
        regardless of Messenger. Listen. so I do.
ToDay. Wisakecahk helps reveal. Powers of Smudge.
    how one five-minute experience.
        can surface Prejudice. unmask Racism.
        can challenge Personal.Systemic. Eurocentrism.
        can Teach us holistic lessons.

MENTAL LESSONS
what do we need to Know. about Smudge?
    it is for Mental Cleansing.
        to prepare Minds. to be Receptive. to be Aware.

We clear our Minds.
shift from hustle. Bustle. of EveryDay fast-paced Lives.
manifest in overCrowded. Scattered. Confused Minds.
Smudge allows us to Focus.
direct our Thoughts. to opportunities available in This Moment.
at This Time.
Imagine my Surprise.
some People express very firmly.
They desire to be taught in TheExpectedMode.
I am to teach Exactly what Calendar says.
"this wasn't listed as a Native class." One complains.
"tell me Again." I say. "what do you Mean. If. I Smudge.
when it is Not a Native Studies class. it Confuses Students?"
I hear Wisakecahk's howl. She speaks to me.
"Smudge. is to clear Not cause Confusion."
"I need Smudge. Right Now!" MySpirit says.
"If. Confusion is a Problem." KindAcademicElder advises.
"put it on your CourseOutline. Underlined.
right here on page one. 'Smudge will be conducted to open each class.'"
He says. with a deep chuckle.
"after all." He says. smiling broadly. His ObsidianEyes twinkle brightly.
"They are Always telling us.
'spell out your Expectations. in your CourseOutline.'"
We know. Smudge brings Illumination.
lights up closed-mindedness.
shows face of Dominators.
OneWiseElder. shares her Story of Smudge.
"All People need to Know.
how to Honour our Traditions." She says Strongly.
"They come to our Homes.
If. They show no Respect. won't Smudge with us.
I throw them out! I go complain to their Supervisors. I Fire them!"
She nods briskly. affirming Truth in her Words.
"what good are they to us? to me and my Family?" She asks.
assuming we Both know answer. She continues.
"I tell them. 'You are Not paid to be Christians. but to help us.'
how can they help us Heal. if they are Afraid of our Traditions?"
She wisely asks.
Resistance to Spirit. takes many modern forms.
"but. I already took Indian Studies 101." Another tells me.
is he trying to believe. taking One course.
means he knows. all he needs to learn?
my GreenEyes open wide.
how many classes. do Nehiyâw'ak Students take.

in Mooniyâs Studies?
Wisakecahk wants to ask.
SPIRITUAL LESSONS
Smudge prepares us. for Ancient Spiritual Ceremonies.
for Encounters with Others.
for Challenges in daily Life.
as SweetSmoke encircles all. Our Spirits sing in Oneness.
OurAncestors gather with us. pass on SacredTeachings.
a Time for Opening. Love. Light. Peace.
many are Honoured. to be Gifted. an opportunity to Share.
a Sacred moment Together.
Imagine my Surprise.
when she says. "I saw Spirits come in. and I was afraid."
how Sad I muse.
She cannot recognize her Gift. to see Spirits.
Christians have taught. Many to Fear.
Many Fears.
Fear Dark. Fire. Devils. Spirits. Pagans.
Fear all but one God.
Fear God. Creator. Supreme Spirit Being.
She is Afraid. Because. this is Not TheTradition.
She has been Indoctrinated to follow.
I can Respect her feelings.
I can help her name their Source.
I will Reject her wishes.
Her Discomfort. will Not control my actions.
will Not disallow me my Freedom.
to burn Smudge on these Lands.
Lands of my Ancestors.
to burn Smudge in my classroom.
even in a Eurocentric context.
"after all." He states. all too smugly.
Arms crossed tightly. on his Chest.
"If. We are Not Allowed. to start the Day in Our classrooms
with TheLord'sPrayer. than why should You be Allowed. to burn Smudge?"
Imagine my Surprise.
Wisakecahk whispers. "I can't believe it. can you?"
No! I can Not Believe. after all these hundreds of years.
Religious Conversion. Indoctrination by BrainWashing. Strapping. Rape.
many RationalScholars. UniversityAdministrators.
HumanRightsActivists. UnionStewards.
SchoolBoardTrustees. ConcernedParents.
equate Smudge. with their Right to Preach. do Prayer in Schools.
"after all." one UnionSteward says.

as he leans towards me. to emphasize his point.
"even if a Christian fundamentalist. thought starting class with Prayer.
was a good learning tool. it would not mean. it was his Right to do so."
"perhaps." He lays his Finger. along side his hairy Chin. stroking it ever so
deeply.
    "If. he did it Once. and explained the Significance.
    He would get away with it.
    but. Not as a way to begin EveryClass."
He sits back in his chair. exudes Confidence. in his analysis.
I scratch my Head. what am I to Understand?
    what is Spiritual messages in these Words?
"sounds like Compromise." Spirit translates.
    "maybe. it's Okay. burn Smudge for OpeningClass."
but. do not push it. I learn. I am expected. to Stop Ceremony.
    Stop. before those with unexamined issues. get Uptight.
"be sensitive to Context." TraditionalistAcademic cautions me.
    "even in a Nehiyâw'ak program. We talk a lot about Spirituality.
before we let them experience Anything." He says gently.
Nehiyâw'ak too. have been Indocrinated to Fear.
    to feel Discomfort. if asked to participate in Ceremony.
"because of missionization. some are especially sensitive
    If. they feel they are Expected. to do AnyThing. Spiritual."
    offers Nehiyâw'akColleague.
I wonder. is Margaret Swan's advice to Manitoba Chiefs meant for me?
"It's counterproductive to poke a stick in someone's eye
while you're attempting to get them to listen to you."[16]
    is burning Smudge too ForceFull?
    even if I do Not offer it to Students?
through Smudge. we call Ancestors to Witness. be Present. give Guidance.
        on matters beyond Human comprehension.
in Eurocentric contexts. Traditional Teachers.Healers. Need. All help we can get.
Spirit is Necessary. for Holistic paradigms.
    how many Teachers.Healers. talk Holistic talk?
    how many do Spiritual walk?
why is Smudge seen. as "too much trouble"?
    even for Nehiyâw'ak Educators?
    even when Nehiyâw'ak Students predominate?
    even when All Students need to learn Skills. Tools. Attitudes.
        required to TeachHeal Nehiyâw'ak Peoples.
        struggle to recover from Abuses of colonialism?
    even when Accreditation demands
        "the curriculum shall ensure that students have an
understanding of oppressions and healing of aboriginal peoples."

EMOTIONAL LESSONS
Smudge brings Healing Powers.
   Emotional Cleansing. Calmness. Gentleness.
Smudge brings us Together. a feeling of Caring. Community. Connectedness.
   We share a Physical. Metaphysical experience.
Smudge brings Health. Healing to all who Open themselves.
Ceremonies appeal to Emotions. Imaginations.
       brings Intensity of feelings to individuals.
               to group as a whole.
Elders teach.
   All Ceremonies must be entered into. with GoodHeart.
Imagine my Surprise.
   I am Dismayed.
       how can such a small Act. produce such a large re-Action?
   "GoodHeart." laughs Wisakecahk.
       as I recoil. feeling metal points. Daggers. Wound my Heart.
           cold anonymous statements. express unveiled hatred.
   I am Evaluated. Accused. by Some.
       of Pushing my beliefs and Traditions.
       "She should not force her personal beliefs on her classes. and subject
       them to an activity they do not wish to perform."
           "Her spirituality should not intrude onto others."
               "Instructor needs to be free of personal issues and cultural
               biases to effectively deal with sensitive issues."
   Authorities tell me. Teaching based on my value system.
                       is "not fair to the group."
   Education is not fair to me. or my group. I want to say.
       in my twenty-three years as a student.
           I was only ever taught. one course by a Nehiyâw'ak Teacher.
   other Teachers. bring their value systems. to Classrooms.
       most frequently happens to coincide. with dominant World.Views.
           their Bias remains Invisible. Unnamed. Hegemonic.
                       Whiteness. Mooniyâs.
All education is Political. I am Political.
   I challenge All to acculturate. to my Traditional norms.
   I will Not. sit in Rows. I Circle. in Rooms. Round or Square.
   I will Not. churn out identical cogs. oil wheels of Industrialism.
   I will Not. leave my SpiritGuides. or Wisakecahk. at Door.
   I will Not. reproduce Linear. Cognitive UnReality.
   I will Not. reinforce Cognition. as Separated from Spirit.
                       Colonial Mentality.
Anxiety. Insecurity. Disorientation. can result.
   Stress. Strain. Incongruence. is produced.
       when we have to Adjust. to Unfamiliar cultural demands.

to Competing World.Views.
some experience Disorientation. Daily. for Lifetimes. over Generations.
some experience it for first time. with Smudge.
as Ela says. People are *"being put on the spot with all their guilt and their*
defensiveness, and were blaming themselves and projecting that onto
other People."
I see thin veneer. of polished Politeness.
Political Correctness. goes up in Smoke
when they realize. MétisWoman is Teacher.
I am ExpertAuthority.
I say what knowledge counts.
what processes are pedagogy.
in this Classroom.
some do Not like NewRules.
want SameOldGame.
where they were Cowboys. GoodGuys. Comfortable. Privileged.
I see. how Smudge becomes focal point.
Weapon in hands of unHealed beings.
who seek to Humble me. Humiliate me.
to put me in MyPlace.
"She should not be Allowed to Burn Smudge. hold Circle.
teach the way she does." They cry.
read between lines. I have pushed too far.
Smudge becomes Contested. when colonial attitudes are Challenged.
SomeHow. Students know.
Mooniyâs Administrators. will Not support Nehiyâw'ak Teachers.
for practising OurTraditions in Their Classrooms.
even in cross-cultural studies.
bad enough to be a MétisWoman. in an Authority position.
but. to openly contest Eurocentrism.
unveil White privilege.
and revitalize Ancestral practice.
is this simply too much to take. in Western educational contexts?
I am Discouraged.
perhaps. I will abandon Battle of Eurocentric consciousness.
as too dangerous on Their turf.
"I Am tired of Struggle." I hear myself say. Others hear.
ConcernedElder responds to comfort me.
"that's where Systems are failing." He says.
"We may be developing our own programs. for Indian People.
but. what about cultural awareness for Mooniyâs?
They are as Racist as ever." He states in a matter of fact tone.
Sadly shakes his Head.
I agree with Him.

"I know from growing up in a WarZone." I respond.
"close proximity of Nehiyâw'ak and Mooniyâs.
does Not necessarily bring about Understanding.
sometimes it produces more Antagonism.
less Respect for difference. Helen Betty teaches us that."
We nod our bowed Heads in agreement.
        WoundedHearts beat in shared Pain.

PHYSICAL LESSONS
as we bring Flame to light Herbs. nestled in AbaloneShell.
      Fan with EagleFeather. Smoke encircles us.
           Cleansing Body. Mind. Spirit. Heart.
a Time to relax. Breathe deeply. Ground ourselves.
    remember our Connections. to Self. Others. Earth Mother. All of Creation.
    Empty ourselves. Release negativities. Receive learnings.
Imagine my Surprise.
    I wonder. why are some Repelled?
        lurch back as I approach.
           "Cough. Cough. cough. I don't know what it is
           about the .... what did you call it ?"
           "Smudge ...
           "but. It. closes in on my Throat.
           I can't seem to Breathe ... gives me a Headache."
           "are you allergic to other smoke ?" I ask.
           "a bit. I guess." She says.
           "do you go to Bars? Shop in Malls? Sit in Traffic?"
                        I want to know.
           "Yes. All the Time." She laughs. "of course I do!"
                She exclaims.
           "They are all Necessary parts of Life." She laughs again.
Wisakecahk laughs too. Smudge is Life Giving.
    Bars. Malls. Traffic. are Spiritually numb.
                Toxic to Earth Mother.
"No Smoking. No Perfume.
this is now a Scent-Free Environment." I am told.
Imagine my Surprise.
    I don't think to consider Smudge Burning.
        to be Smoking. or Perfume.
           Smudge is Healing Herbs.
                burned in a Sacred manner.
Then. Notices are posted.
        on all fours walls of my teaching space.
        placed in my mailbox.
        announced at staff meetings.

"No burning of Any substances." I am explicitly told.
I am Devastated. Puzzled. Raging. Then. Resistant.
I question. If. we are All. so Health. Environmental. Conscious. Now.
why? are those who wear Toxic HairSpray. Perfumes. Colognes.
Not banned from class?
are some allowed to duck out front door to Smoke Cigarettes.
leaving Non-Biodegradable butts to litter Earth Mother.
for generations to come?
why? do some run in. for "a few minutes."
leaving CarExhaust to seep in my open window?
why? are rooms and bathrooms. "Cleaned.""Deodorized."
with ToxicChemical products?
why? are buildings and office Furniture.
built with FormaldehydeLoaded pressed board.
which takes at least two years to de-toxify?
then. where does it go?
why? do most eat ChemicallyProcessed. Irradiated. HormoneInjected.
BacterialInfested. GeneticallyModified. "Foods."
wrapped in "Disposable" PlasticWaste.
why? are some willingly shot with radiation everyDay.
through CopyMachines. Computers. Scanners.
Televisions. Microwaves.
Yet. Authorities Choose to enforce Regulations. against Smudge Burning.
because of Health Concerns.
Smoking byLaws. potential illegal drug use.[17]
SecurityGuards bust into Rooms to enforce rules.
throw SmudgeBowls into back alleys.[18]
as Authorities BackLash against Smudge.
Smudge becomes. a form of Spiritual Activism. Again.
Ancestors are present. know Battle is ongoing.
I hear Their quiet chuckles.
They light up Friends. dark cloud Foes. Swirl and Twirl.
They teach Wisakecahk Tales.
Try my Patience. Mock my Perseverance.
Love my Beauty. Honour my Strength.
Good GrandMothers. Good GrandFathers. I Pray.
What to do? why does this Violence ensue. everywhere I go?
"You are a Teacher.Healer. Warrior."
OneWiseGrandMother counsels.
"You actively Choose Classrooms. to fight your Battle.
You are bringing Healing. Cleansing. to these Systems.
You are Uncovering immense Pain.
Recovering Systems long Numb. from Toxic Dis-Ease.
do you think. it will be Painless. Easy. work?"
She rhetorically asks.

MAHÊ'KUN BITES HER TAIL

OneNight. Not too long ago. Not too far away. Mahê'kun is hunched in her Den. with a puzzled look on her Face. She just came back from TeachingLodgeCouncil. She is Hooted at by Owl. because some Apprentices are complaining about her.

"Twoowoo Beings left Circle. are still holding on to Hurt feelings. Sad. Confused. Not able to express openly." He shakes his Beak at Mahê'kun. and turns his Head right around. before piercing her deeply with his YellowEyes. "it's Not right. Beings are sharing their concerns. Outside Circle. Restlessness. Anxiety. Conflict. brings Dishonour to our Lodge. what will you do-woo about it?" Owl Hoots at her Loudly.

"Who? Who? Who-woo said what to who-woo? I want to say." laughs Mahê'kun later. really trying not to cry. "my Head is Buzzin'. like a bunch of horny Fireflies. zippin' around dark Night air. ideas are flittin'. Here and There. I can see Sparks. but. They never really land. or shed enough Light to see anything." Mahê'kun whines down. starting to lose her false.brave. Mask.

"I try to keep my Ears open. like you teach me." She says to OldOne. "but. Owl's Words fly right by me. I am Startled. Worried. Confused. Hurt. All at one Time." She howls mournfully. and puts her Paws over her Head.

"der. der." Consoles OldOne. patting her Shoulder. "tings always seem darkes' before Dawn. searchin' for Truth is like chasin' Moles in da Night. sometime' you'll trip on a Hill. an' hurt yer Nose." OldOne howls. something seems to tickle her FunnyBone. "stick wit whatcha Know. Our OldWays. Beside'." says OldOne as she turns to retreat to back of her Den. gently letting Mahê'kun know to go Home. "I'm sure it will make a great Story SomeDay."

on her way Home. Mahê'kun worries. "Oooowr. how am I ever going to make sense of this situation?" She whimpers to herself. as her Paws surefootedly carry her along familiar trail to her Den.

"no wonder. I'm Confused." She thinks. "so many mixed messages. 'Welcome. Teach what you Know.' They say all nice like. then. as soon as I turn around and get started. They say. 'Not like Thaaaat!' can I ever please anybeing? never mind everybeing." She whines to herself. as she curls up with WolfCub. trying to sleep. "fall on my Nose. Hhrrump. this whole thing is a big pain in TheNose." She thinks as she lay. listening to WolfCub's heavy breathing.

Mahê'kun Dreams. Long and Hard. She awakes to see Spider. weaving a gossamer Web. thick beads of Dew shine in Dawn's Light. "Spider." Mahê'kun hears a High Voice. "She spins and Lives in a Fragile. but. Strong. potentially Deadly. ever Wonderous Web. Web of AllThatIs." "She Does?" Mahê'kun wonders quizzically. "what kinda Message is That?"

then. in a Flash. She knows. what she must Do. She will be Wolf-Hearted. take OldOne's advice. Face them in Circle. She will Weave her Words. and theirs. Together they will learn about Healing conflict. through her strong Leadership. "weave their Words and mine." She hums to herself. as she strolls to Circle.

it's a GoodDay for Circle. Cloudy Fall Skies hang down. Grey and Blustery. threatening any moment to open up. a few rumbles of ThunderBeings ring in Air. Everybeing gathers in Grove. a good Circling place. on such a Day. Tall Birch and Fir. spread their Arms overHead. ready to catch any drops of Rain.

Mahê'kun greets each Circle member. as they arrive. takes special care to be extra friendly to All. Who knows Who is Not Happy with her Teachings. Her friend BlackBear always says. "You can catch more Ants with Honey."

Anyways. Mahê'kun burns a very small Smudge to begin Circle. She knows. Onebeing has complaints about Smudge. She asks Cardinal to open with a Song. He tosses his bright red feathery Crest back. certain he is most beautiful Bird in Grove. and Sings a perfectly Sacred Song to open Circle.

when he is done. Mahê'kun opens her Mouth to speak. "Ahem. Awrllll." Mahê'kun clears her Throat. tries to stop her Voice from shaking. in a Flash. She knows. "I am feeling Terrified of these Ones."

"Oh why? Oh Why? do I do this to myself. Moon after Moon?" Mahê'kun thinks to herself. "always trying to bring Teachings into Others' places. to Ones who have Forgotten. or never learned OldWays." She shakes her furry Head. Back and Forth. a few Times. and takes a deep Breath.

"ToDay. We are going to have a Circle. about Conflict and Leadership." She says. She can immediately see Eyebrows raise. Eyes widen. Ears. Hoofs. Paws. Wings. All start moving around nervously. Mahê'kun plunges ahead. "I heard from Owl yesterday. some of you are concerned about Circle. and my Teachings. Ripples of discontent. are moving under surface Calm." She says. a Ripple of murmurs and rustles. sweeps around Circle.

Mahê'kun opens Circle. "what Feelings does each Being have? what are Spirits moving us to understand? where we go from here? I welcome you to Share. I will listen and learn." Mahê'kun says. StoryStone begins to Travel.

BaldEagle speaks first. with a shriek. "I'm glad Mahê'kun brings Conflict. to Circle. I hear a few Words on Winds myself. I agree. We need to learn. how do we catch Fish? swimming underneath surface of CalmPond?" She stretches her Talons out. just at thoughts of it.

Stone travels to Marten next. "I feel a little Sssccccared. I'm not sure. I'm Not rrrreally rrrready to be here. I know. I am rrreal good at climbing. and can out jump most squirrels in this Grove. Bbbut. I'm not sure I'm serious enough to be a Healer. Yyyet." tucks up his short Legs. under his furry Body. long bushy Tail. twitches rapidly. as He speaks.

Stone moves to Rabbit. who is shaking like a leaf in Windstorm. long Ears wiggling as fast as her Nose. "I dread Circle." She manages to say. Her anxiety is obvious to all Beings.

Mahê'kun's Ears tingle. so does her long Nose. She puts on her most friendly face. keeps her Mouth closed with a little smile. Ears tilted back ever so slightly. GreenEyes real round. She nods her Head sympathetically at Rabbit. "of course. Rabbit Will be Afraid." thinks Mahê'kun. "little wonder she came here again. after Last Circle."

Mahê'kun flashes back for a moment. how Rabbit ran out of Circle. "I just reached out to take Rabbit's Paw. to bring everybeing in closer together. to give Thanks to Creator for our Lives. She is gone in a Flash. and. you know. how fast Rabbits can run when they're Scared. it's all a big Misunderstanding." Mahê'kun laughs. when she tells her Sister GreyWolf.

Now. she wonders. "was it Rabbit that complained to Owl? Na. too unlikely. She's more scared of Owl than me." She decides in an instant.

Mole sits next to Rabbit. blinking her tiny Eyes. spade-like Paws out front. holding Stone. Her little Nose sniffs repeatedly. smelling more than most can See. "I have to say. I'm a bit Uncomfortable. sitting in Circle with You. Mahê'kun. not just Mahê'kun. but. a lot of Predators around here. just gives me Shivers. and all this Light. a lot to Cope with. like I said. Not just you Mahê'kun."

Mahê'kun is beginning to feel Sorry. for herself. Again. then. Beaver speaks. "I find Mahê'kun's approach Strange. but. truly Wonderful." She slaps her paddle-like Tail a few times. to emphasize her point.

Otter agrees. "I am very Excited. I Enjoy coming here. there is Magic and Mystery. I wouldn't change a thing. Not One Thing." She opens and closes her BigBrownEyes. rapidly. then she continues. "I like Smudge. We can Stop. Slow down. Be. here and now. I say. Be. open. Go with Flow. like River. Oh. I so Love. a Good Swim." She gushes on as Otters do.

Buffalo shakes his shaggy Mane. Up and Down. "I enjoy Smudge too. a way of gettin' rid of Bugs. ones I am carryin' wit me. when I get here. a good Smudge helps prepare me. before goin' on a Journey. like Sheddin' an ol' Coat. Standin' in a strong Wind. or Rollin' on a grassy Plain. You gotta take Time. to Clean Up."

Red-HeadedWoodPecker. sticks out her very long Tongue. with its spiky Tip. In and Out. of her sharp black Beak. Anybeing can see. except maybe Mole. that she is preparing to speak some Truth.

"We're all Different. I don't have much in common with Mahê'kun. but as Healers. we really need to learn to embrace. with open Wings. All beings who cross our Paths. Be it Sky. Water. Forest. or Underground." She moves her RedHead rapidly. and asks one of her pointy Questions. "is being Comfortable? more important than taking a Risk? or changing what needs to be changed? I don't think so?" shrieks WoodPecker in her preachy Voice.

Stone continues to Journey. "I feel fortunate. I am being given a chance. to Scratch and Peck at surface of Mahê'kun's Culture. and Teachings of OldOnes. So. if Mahê'kun is adapting OldTeachings. I accept her ways. I don't know. what was said. or how Things were done long ago." OnceWildTurkey gobbles. Wobbles his red Comb. "many of our WildTeachings are Lost. a lot of us are just Too Tame. I'm Happy to be here to learn."

Mahê'kun is just beginning to Feel. pretty darn Proud. of herself. as a Teacher. She has caught a Glimpse. how bringing OldOnes cultural practices can create Community. Here. Now. ToDay.

Then. PolarBear gets Stone. Her turn to speak. "I travel all this way. come here to learn how to Heal. Not to burn SweetGrass. We don't burn SweetGrass in my Lands. doesn't even grow. There." She flexes her powerful Arms. picks her Teeth with her sharp black Claws. stares with her BlackEyes. right at Mahê'kun.

"some of Us. We don't think it's Fair. Not to All of us. to all Beings. that Mahê'kun uses Smudge and Circle. to teach Healing. based on

Teachings of her Pack. and OldOnes I've never met. I may Not be Mahê'kun. but. I Live with Wolves. UpNorth. I Adopted two WolfCubs. So. I already know a Lot. about Wolves." She growls in a gruff know–it-all tone.

it's all Mahê'kun can do. to Not roll her Eyes. She knows. what That means. lots of Others think they know Wolves. better than Wolves know themselves. Her Clan has been given a very bad Name. because of past Misunderstandings. Mistranslation of OldOnes[19] Stories.

PolarBear is not done. yet. "but. what about Others' Ways? Mahê'kun isn't being Neutral. that's not Fair. I say." PolarBear growls. thumps ground with her Paw. as she speaks. Glares around at Others. Mahê'kun works hard. to Not drop her GreenEyes. as PolarBear returns to stare at her. She does not want to seem Scared. or back down from PolarBear's Anger.

"PolarBear. like you. are Visitors to dese Territories." Counsels a WiseOldOne. Later. "differences in Traditional understandin's. you know. you can Expect it." She says softly.

"I am surprised to hear about her Cubs." She tells BlackBear. Later. "I wonder where they came from? They may be Ones lost in DarkMoons. when many WolfCubs were taken." Bear growls. "Bears an' Wolves. we're not much alike. 'ow will she raise dem to be deir TrueWolf selves?"

StoryStone continues to move. BobCat speaks next. twitching his short stumpy Tail. spotted Fur stands up on his back. He asks. "don' we all bring what we know to Circle? 'ow can anybeing Not be who dey are? ya know. what dey say about my Cousin's Spots. beside'." He growls real low. "what ezackly is Neutral?" BobCat asks. Claws involuntarily pop out of his Paws. "Neutral is jis how each Being expec' it to be?" Later. He confides to Skunk. "I work Mahê'kun's Lodge wit her. She works 'ard. an' I don' want to 'ear somebeing outside our community. treatin' her wit disrespect."

of course. Coyote Laughs. loudly. when it is her turn. Mahê'kun winces. never knows what to expect from her Cousin. "I'm surprise at how cranky y'all are. Meself. I could care less. what Mahê'kun does. or doesn't do. up to 'er. If. Mahê'kun want to share 'er Teachin's. I'll take 'em as a Gift. 'er Giveaway."

Coyote Laughs. again. "Hooorrrrlllllll. I say. It's On You. Mahê'kun can force nuttin' on me. Take it or Leave it. I say. jis lighten up. don' take yerself so serious." Coyote laughs again. flicking his Tail.

Mahê'kun's Jaw drops open in Surprise. "for one time. in his Life. Coyote made good sense." Mahê'kun says to an OldOne. Later. "I'm not

Surprise'." OldOne responds. "Circle takes on a Life of his own. Truth sometime'. jis pops outta Mouths. Unexpected like. even to dem. even to Coyote. I reckin'."

Crow caws loudly. like she always does. when she thinks she has something important to say. "Everybeing has a right to be heard. why should anybeing be put down?" She puts her shiny black Head to one side. and caws thoughtfully. "even troublesome ones. They should Not be pressed. or have to argue their Reasons. If. you don't want to follow Mahê'kun's ways. Don't. Pressure is unnecessary. and unkind." She glances around Circle. especially at BobCat and Coyote. "We all need to accept different views. Not very Wise. to expect all beings to agree." She caws.

"All'n'all. It seem' to me. like it musta bin a powerful lesson." says OldOne. Later. "Ya say all dis happen. cause ya burn Smudge." She says sort of puzzled. "sometime it happens thatta way in Circle. nice at start. den break out Scrapin'. like a Storm[20] hits. like when WholeClan gather."

OldOne howls in glee. at her thoughts of last Gathering. "of course. Bein's are goin' to fight when dey get togeder. dat's Natural. it's whatya learn from it." She says still chuckling to herself.

RedFox speaks next. shows everybeing her keen abilities. to weigh out issues. "You gotta wonder though. look at all sides. not just obvious. SomeTimes. when I complain. about how things are goin'. I can really be sneakily circlin' around. tryin' to attack Leader. cause I'm Not getting' what I need."

Later. Mahê'kun wonders with OldOne. "Fox is probably right. She'd know about being Sneaky. I wonder if it was her?" "na. She wouldn't Tell. on 'erself."

Then. Fox asks. fluffing her red Tail with her Claws. as she speaks. "should some Surrender to what otherbeings expect. or work in OldWays? Nobeing wants to be Bullied. by over–Bearin' ones." Coyote laughs at that. "ArArArArAr." Mahê'kun gives him a sharp glance. intending to quiet him down.

Stone moves to Skunk. Her bushy striped Tail. is lifted up quite high. "She must be feeling Threatened." Mahê'kun thinks to herself. Immediately. always one to pay keen attention to other animals' behaviours. Skunk sniffs loudly. "Somebeings say they have no Voice. yet. They express very strong. about how to teach. want ways They are used to. what They expect. some Teachers talk on and on. On and On. They don't Do what they teach! or Preach!"

She squeals. and lifts her Tail a little higher. Everybeing starts getting real nervous. Then. She continues. "We all travel here to learn. Didn't we? You can't teach. what you don't know. OldOnes can tell me. 'If. yer bein' chase' by Mahê'kun. lift yer Tail an' spray'." Her Tail twitches at her thought. "but. until I have to do it. I don't really know if I can."

Mahê'kun doesn't really like that kind of comment. being made about her or her Clan. but. She knows. She has to continue to listen Respectfully to Skunk. "I'm here to be a Healer. to Heal my being. to talk about my own Self." Skunk sniffles again loudly.

Mahê'kun nods. She is pleased. Skunk has clearly learned. at least that lesson. Mahê'kun finds herself thinking. about an OldOne. who always used to say. "even if ya tink yer talkin' about some other beings. Yer really jis talkin' about yerself."

"of course. Skunk would get it." howls her SisterTimber. Later. "Everybeing is always talkin' about Skunk. after all. She has such a Reputation to live up to." They both howl over that one.

Skunk is still holding Stone. "once we question our Leader. We're lookin' at Her. We should all look at our own selves. I tink da whole thing Stinks!" concludes Skunk.

"what do I want from a GoodLeader?" Moose asks. when Stone arrives. She waves her big Antlers though Air. "Somebein' who can bring out my Best? can help me change Bad behaviour?" Mahê'kun isn't sure what to think of Moose's questions. "I wondered if she thinks I'm a GoodLeader? or Not?" She confides her Insecurities. to BlackBear. Later.

Moose continues. "a GoodLeader shares Power. Power means. I can do what I Choose. Da more Power I have. Da more Choices I have." Moose snorts. clears her Nose. as if to say more.

next. Stone moves to Porcupine. She bristles her Quills. "when we raise questions of Power. We threaten Freedom. for those who have it. Wise are always ready. to defend themselves." She says quietly. Mahê'kun can't help herself. lets out a small whine. at Porcupine's comment.

Much Later. Mahê'kun howls in Pack. "there I am. Teacher. do I have Power? to do as I Choose? I feel like Owl. WhoWho? Who has Power? Who is Attacking? Who is Defending? Why?" after Pack. She walks Home with OldOne. "maybe I am too ForceFull with Teachings." "don' be to 'ard on yerself." OldOne responds.

Anyways. Porcupine has more to share. "EveryThing can be a Power Struggle. to some. Conflict can take over. every Relationship. If. we let it. in our Dens. Circles. Groves. and outside. let's not let it be that way. Here. We can be GoodLeaders. Ourselves."

Stone travels. PrairieDog takes a turn. Nods at everybeing. She says in her best socializing Voice. "let's all just Try to get along." Weasel stands on her Haunches. surveys Circle with her BeadyEyes. and squeaks. "I'll go. with. what Others want." and sits down.

Spirit of Conciliation is getting stronger. holding Stone in her Wings. Pelican nods her Head. Pouch waggles. Up and Down. "what ever Circle decides. is Good with me." She says.

Finally. Mahê'kun speaks to conclude Circle. Her Head hangs down. "Surrender." She growls. "is not easily done by my Pack. or by me. OldOnes lost their Lands. Lives. Teachings. and their Hides. but. I offer my Word. It. is Done." She opens her Throat. and howls Honour Song. to call AncientOnes to hear her pleas for Healing. for allbeings in Circle that Day.

"is It. consensus?" Mahê'kun asks AnOldOne. Later. "well." AnOldOne replies. "did everybeing support CommonGood? did anybeing Compromise? give up something Important. dey need. or believe in?"

Mahê'kun doesn't have to think. very long. or very hard. "it is a Compromise. for me." She howls sadly. "I knew. Somebeing has to be willing to give in. I gave up Smudge." She guiltily admits. "I've been fooled. gave up OldWays. because of a Bully." Mahê'kun howls. covers her Head in Shame.

Crow caws. Later. to anybeing who wants to know. and some who don't care. "can you believe it? Mahê'kun Compromised. Surrendered Smudge. Can you believe it?" She caws real loud. "gave up Smudge. for sake of Harmony." Coyote Laughs. loudest. always able to appreciate Backwards. InsideOut moments.

ThatNight. BlackBear stops by Mahê'kun's Den. on her way UpNorth to hibernate. "there's always sometin' to lose in Compromise. lookin' at you. I don't need to ask. Who lost. Who lost a few strips of hide? Who smells like Skunk? and Who smells like Rose." Bear growls in a grouchy tone. yawns wide. ready to sleep. "sounds like ya bit yerself. Bit yer own Tail. Agin."

"BlackBear might be wise. but sometimes she's a little too Honest." GreyWolf consoles her Sister later. "sometime' ya 'ave to ear Trut' about yerself. even if ya 'urts." OldOne howls. "Trut' 'urts".

Then. She takes a good long look at Mahê'kun. "come 'ere my Cub." She says. Pawing ground right beside her. Mahê'kun moves over close to OldWolf. Ears cocked ready to hear. She doesn't know what. "Ya've learn' well from OldOnes. only teach whatcha know. a 'Ealer mus' 'ave 'Eart. Ya show yer WolfEartedness ToDay. be Proud."

Small whine of Gratitude. escapes Mahê'kun's Mouth. Her Tail wags slightly. "Ya show Courage. Ya face yer Enemies wit 'Umility. Ya listen wit yer 'Eart. an' change wat ya can. It's yer call to make. Yer Bundle to carry. when to pick a Medicine up. when to put it down."

"Sacrifice is made." OldOne continues. "Pain is to expect. on MedicineWalk. tru Circle dere Words an' yers are woven. All is as it should be." growls OldOne in a loving tone. Mahê'kun lays down on Ground. bares her Neck and Belly. to OldWolf.

"Seasons change. from Spring to Summer. Fall to Winter. tings change. We 'ave to Accept. tings 'appen for reasons. We don' always understand. good yer 'ere." OldOne says. gently licking Mahê'kun's Wounds.

Mahê'kun learns. Time. Patience. and Relationships. are all required to Heal. to Teach in Traditional ways. "dere is no quick recipe for zappin' OldWays into anybeing. Ya can't change da essence of who anybeing is. Ya can only change yerself. even dat is Hard." OldWolf croons softly. as her Tongue rasps over Mahê'kun's Fur.

Notes

1. Versions of this piece have been published as "Lived Experiences of an Aboriginal Feminist Transforming the Curriculum" in *Canadian Woman's Studies,* Spring 1994 (Volume 14, Number 2: 52–55) and *Experiencing Difference,* Carl James (ed.) 2000. Fernwood: Halifax.
2. Elija Harper is an infamous Nehiyâw'ak politician, from Northern Manitoba. who is credited with speaking. "No!" on behalf of Canadians. to stop the Meech Lake Accord.
3. Margaret Swan. once Grand Chief of Manitoba Assembly. was quoted in Windspeaker.
4. in one location. reasoning is. If. Smudge is burned. Then. others would insist on right to smoke marijuana.
5. happened at Friendship Centre in Winnipeg. as reported by O'Hallarn in *The Winnipeg Sun.*
6. like BigBadWolf. in ThreeLittlePigs. or LittleRedRidingHood.
7. Gladding. would be proud. We were Storming. "Anxiety, Resistance, Defensiveness, Conflict, Confrontation, Transference" (1995: 104) were all there.

HONESTY IS A DOORWAY
SLIPPING INTO SILENCE.ING.

EagleWoman Heals GrandMother Moon with her Fyre Breath.
Healing Breath. manifest in Prayer.Song.Voice. is required to stop. all forms of Exploitation.
of our GrandMothers. Mothers. Daughters. GrandDaughters. EarthMother.

I Story to Know. Tell. Ask.
Whose Voice gets Heard?
in Life. Homes. Parliament. Pulpits. Media. Society. Classrooms.
an ongoing Political Struggle.
my Voice is often Unheard.
throughout years of Life. University.
I continue to Grow. to Speak my Truth. Stories.
as I age. I get Stronger in my Words. Stronger in my Conviction.
I will not remain Silenced any more. No More.
Now. as a Métis Traditionalist.
Feminist. Mother. Healer. Scholar. Activist. Artist.
I Story. to bring Together. my Life and Work. Life.Work.
Within and Against. Eurocentric. Patriarchal contexts.
have you Noticed?
my Story is highly Contradictory.
Very personal. Ultimately political.
it is in these Contradictions that I Exist.
on an Hourly. Daily. Monthly. Yearly basis.
these Contradictions inform my Voice. FirstVoice.
Voice of experience. I share with you Today.
Nehiyâw'ak Elders Teach.
We all have a Story to tell.
We All Have a Story to Tell.
I learn. in Eurocentric classroom settings
Not All Voices. Not All Stories.
have Healing Medicine.
Not All Speakers are Rooted.
differences in Consciousness. History.
different Experiences of Voicefulness.
Tonguelessness. Exist.
some Voices need Expression.
some Voices need Silencing.
it is Personal. Political. a Privilege thing.
Yikes! did I say. some Voices Need Silencing?
what you say? what?
isn't that against Emancipatory Voice?
against rules of Collectivism?
opposing values of Respect for All?
Internal. Critical. Cultural.
Voices Debate. Dialogue.
sometimes giving Voice. Giving Voice to my IdentityPolitics.
Paradoxically. can be a lesson in Silencing. mySelf. and Others.
Being. in Nehiyâw'ak Consciousness.
when I am also in Mooniyâs Classrooms.

OOOpppps.
        can be Dangerous ground. Slippery Slope.
          sliding into quicksand. quagmire.
           competing. contrary. realities.

NAME THE.R.WORD.

for those willing to Risk. Speak up!

in many Places. Times. Spaces. I witness slurs spoken. often Silenced. I discover Anger. towards myself. about my Silence. After. Now. I teach people. Speak up! I'll Tell one Story. when I try to teach others. Name The.R.Word.

in my Journal I write. *I am beginning today, after third class to journal write about my experience as an Aboriginal educator with a predominately white middle-class group of … students. I am beginning to experience confusion and fear, and feel a need to seek clarity in some form. I find if I externalize painfull experiences as I live them, it can sometimes help me gain* insight.[1]

I begin class in my Traditional manner. Talking Circle. Students have opportunity to Share. raise Questions. tell Stories. illustrate Concepts from earlier classes. Race. Culture. and Privilege. we complete a full round. NoOne mentions any overt acts of Racism.

I sit in silent Surprise. I know at least six witnesses. in this class. Nehiyâw'ak members of our Support Circle told. processed TheIncident. a couple of Days before. I am confident. SomeStudent will bring It up. in Circle. I think. Then. we can discuss It. use It as a critical example. It. is Not raised. I am stunned.

I hesitate. Do I raise It? What does their silence mean? Do they not recognize what happened as racism? Did It not impact on them? Are they afraid to talk about a Prof? Might get back to him? Or is it more complicated? Like, are they silenced by some commonsense recognition of an informal taboo about speaking about another faculty member or School policies to an "insider" like myself as prof? What is happening? my Mind is racing. multiple criss-crossed directions. simultaneously.

I have good reason to be cautious … losing a job in the recent past for using students experiences as classroom material for analysis of oppression … shattered my illusions about "safety" or "freedom" in classrooms.

but what choice do I have? As an educator, do I pass up the "teachable moment"? Particularly as several of these students said they had not experienced any racism that week!!! How could they ignore such a blatant act? We just discussed that very term last week.

How can I be an anti-racist and ignore an overt act committed within my workplace? Do I want to be or be seen as an upholder of institutional norms of silence, of neutrality around issues of race and racism?

I know. being anti-racist requires transformative action. Taking a stand. Working to remove conditions that oppress people. Neutrality. reinforces institutional Racism.

I wonder. Collegiality. What does it really mean? Do I owe allegiance to maintaining the surface of community amongst colleagues? Or do I align with my RaciallyDefined Brothers and Sisters?

I know it is even more complicated than all that!!! What a double bind! AtThatTime. I throw caution to Winds. dive in. open second round. "an act of Racism. was committed this week. in front of several class members. I am surprised. NoOne mentioned it." I try to drop clues. jog their memories. Hope SomeStudent will relate TheIncident. All look Puzzled. Bewildered even. glance around at each other. Eyebrows raise. uncomfortable Silence grows. People begin shuffling around in their seats.

It is obvious. too late to turn back. So. I just forge ahead. summarize. give a much shortened version. of TheStory told. at Support Circle. by Nehiyâw'ak Students. Those who also witness TheIncident.

Mariah brought TheStory to Circle. She was in Class. when It happened. "A professor at University used TheN.Word. in Class yester-day. in a real nasty. insulting tone. maybe trying to be funny. I don't know. He's talking about Black protestors. The thing in the news lately. " she says. "Maxine. OnlyBlackStudent. in Class. a Woman. speaks up. she says. 'That is a racist remark.' I don't really know her personally. but. I was real proud of her. I think. I'll make more of an effort to talk to her. Now. She's got guts. More than I have." She pauses. takes a deep Breath.

"Holy Smokes. I can't believe my Ears. Well. I guess. I can. the guy's an A-Hole. Excuse my language." she looks around. Apologetically. especially at OurElder. a couple of members nod in agreement. "Can you believe it?" she continues "TheProf's response is real bad. I am still shaking my Head. Trying to get it out of there." She shakes her Head. back and forth. "'Racism, smacism'. TheProf says. "There are a lot of stupid people in this world ... stupid Blacks, stupid French people....' He names a bunch of ethnic and minority populations." she says.

I end TheStory there. when I tell it in class. that Day. but. Unfortu-nately. it goes on. Nehiyâw'ak Students' sorry Tale. TheWholeStory. is always much longer. we are well socialized to tell all. to explore full details.

Eagle takes a long view. Mouse sees up close. Never know. what lessons
are we learning? or teaching? So. tell all.

Anyways. Mariah continues. "I am Shocked. just shocked into
Silence. in that moment. I think. most of us are. Maxine is so upset. She
jumps up. and leaves the room. She never comes back.. I feel real bad for
her. I want to jump up too. and go after her. but. I don't. Nobody does.
I feel bad about That. We leave her all out there. on her own." She hangs
her Head. as she passes Stone on.

Nootka tells next. how he replies to TheProf. "So. I say. 'You missed
da bigges' stereotype. da stupid Indians'. I tol' 'im. Seein' as dat is one of
da mos common ones. ya know." he tells it. We all nod in unison. Every
one of us have been deeply affected. throughout our Lives. and still today.
by that One.

"Can you believe da guy?" Nootka shakes his long black mane. "'E
agreed wit me. 'E Agreed wit me. 'E rubs 'is chin like 'e was thinkin' about
it. Den. 'E says. 'yes. dere is a lot of stupid Indians. in fact. I meet a lot of
dem right 'ere at da School.' Can you believe it? Can you believe dis guy?
Teachin' people to work as helpers. E's Scarey!"

EveryOne at Support Circle is already Shocked. Offended. but.
TheStory goes on. Nookta continues his version. "I wanna jump right up.
an' wipe dat grin. right offa 'is face. but. I work so 'ard on my Recovery.
Don' want to go back to Childhood violence. I wouldn' let myself stoop
dat low. Not for da likes of 'im. I am Livid. I jis 'ad to Laugh. at 'ow Stupid
da guy is."

"That really got to me." says Rebecca. "Seeing you laugh like that.
Then. I think to myself. 'no. he's not actually finding it funny. just coping.'
So. I let it go. but. what really got me goin'. I mean. Really got me goin'
was when he goes on to tell us. his view. 'Workers don't have to worry.
about what they do to Clients. Because. they already have had it so Bad.
So Bad you can't really Hurt Them.' You Can't Really Hurt Them. He
says that. He Actually Said It!!" Rebecca is literally almost jumping off her
chair. as she speaks. Her cheeks flame red.

"Well. I've been one of Them." she continues. "and I've been really.
Really Hurt. Hurt by what Workers have said. and done. Said and Done.
to me and my family. What Nehiyâw'ak person hasn't been victimized.
by ignorant racist Workers. Welfare. Child Welfare. Workers. Hmmphhh.
All of Them. do more damage than good. and we all know it!"

Rebecca glances around Circle. makes Eye contact with EveryOne.
before she continues. EveryOne in Circle nods. We all know. Experience.
Witness. many. many. sad Stories of abuse. Abuse of Nehiyâw'ak people.

by so-called Service Providers.

"Well. I just can't take it anymore. I have to say something. before I can stop myself. It just jumps out of my Mouth. 'Bull Shit! Workers can further oppress Clients!' I say. I am kinda proud of myself. for speakin' up. Usually. I don't say anything. but. I guess. I'll thank Maxine for that. and you Fyre." she looks over at me. I smile back. "You're always encouragin' us to speak against injustice. and showin' us how. You walk your talk." she says. I feel Honoured. Responsible. and Uncomfortable. All at the same time.

"but. Really. Truth of it is." Becca adds. "I just can't take anymore of his Crap. my Heart is pounding so hard. I think it is going to burst. Fly out of my Chest. but. you know. it doesn't do any good. afterall. He just takes up the word oppression. and goes off again. 'What is oppression? but a weight on the back of a Person. They can throw it off.' he says. sort of over his Shoulder. as he goes to continue on. with what he is writin' on Board. 'Basically.' he says. 'it is up to the individual. whether you are oppressed by your Life. or not.' It is wasted." concludes Rebecca.

Art. who is also studying at ThisUniversity. speaks next. He nods his Head. rubs his Fingers. through his long Braids. "If it's up to an Individual. whether or not you are oppressed. in your Life. or not. Why would We? Why would AnyOne? It sounds like those NewAgers to me. OneTime. I was mistakably Sharing. with YoungWoman. I met her once. like at a Gathering. Sharing about being sexually abused. as a Child. Then. she says. 'you choose your Parents. you know. You must have wanted that experience. in this LifeTime.' I am flabbergasted. I never even said it was my Parents. She seems kinda cute. and nice. before that. but. that is too Flaky. even for me." He laughs. and so do others. as he admits that to himself. and to us. Art always is one for Women.

"Anyways. it reeks of victim blaming. to me. Pure and Simple. Let's not dress it up here. The Guy. is out to get himself. and all his privileged buddies. off the hook." Art concludes. We dialogue. long and hard. about TheProf's ignorant words. in our Circle. that Day. as I sit and listen. to Nehiyâw'ak community members process. I fume inside.

Having other faculty preaching these types of ideas. makes me feel really Marginalized. very definitely an Outsider. in This Program. It is very obvious to me right now that my hiring is an act of Tokenism … I am TheOnlyOne. TheLonelyOne.

Misel. OurElder. speaks last. "Everyone 'as somethin to teach us. like Coyote. We learn from tings. Even ones we don't want to see. from SomeOne who makes Mistakes. in front of us. We can see 'ow foolish dey look. 'ow much pain and problems. dey bring on to demselves. to da community. We learn 'ow we don' want to be. what we don' want to do. Some of you. you witness dis wit' your own Eyes. You will tell TheStory. to teach others. 'ow Not to behave." Misel tells us.

"dere is always some Truth. in every message." he continues. "it is up to each of us. to look for it. like me. I went to ResidentialSchool. I can remember. whenever I want. 'ow much it 'urt me. to have my 'air cut off. or 'ow much Shame I feel. when dat OldPriest. put 'is 'ands down my pants. I can get really mad at Mooniyâs. for what dey 'ave done. don't misunderstand me. I 'ave already spent many good years. bein' mad. wantin' revenge." Misel is careful to clarify.

"Now. I'm Old. I can See. I can choose to see dem Priests. as pitiful 'umans. makin' mistakes. I can forgive. and move on. Because. if I keep lookin' at my Pain. over and over. I just sink deeper. and deeper. into a pool of Alcohol. Yeah. you all know. I've been there. Too." He looks around Circle. at each of us.

"or. I can look at what is Beautiful. what I Love. what I am Grateful for. keep tryin' to better my Life. dat's where my Choice comes in. I'm 'appy to be alive today. on This Beautiful Day. I'm 'onoured to be 'ere. Sittin' in dis Circle. wit' of all you Smart People. You'll be able to figure it out. I wish everybody a Real Good Day." He says. as he closes Circle.

Our dialogue in Support Circle. fuels my need to raise TheIncident. with TheClass. even if I end up getting Hurt again.

as Circle talk continues. in TheClass. about The Racist Incident. I express praise for OnlyBlackStudent. who had made her Voice known. "She overcame several layers of structural oppression. Race. Gender. ProfessionalPower."I say. I chastise.question. WhiteStudents for not speaking up. "Is Racism only a Black issue?" I ask Them. a WhiteMale made TheRemark. were they stopped by Gender? by student–instructor Power? by their own Ignorance? 'Did you not recognize The.N.Word. as an act of Racism?' I ask Them. I remind Them. how we discussed that very term. among others. only one week before.

I see myself. very consciously teaching. about StructuralPower. how that informs our use of Language. in ClassRooms. and elsewhere. I think of what Rita says. in SupportCircle. "what I'm thinking about. Right Now." she says. "is how much Students believe anything. AnyThing TheProf says. Because. He is Professor. He must be Right. Must Be Right! Because. He says The.N.Word. or other Slurs. He makes it Acceptable. makes it Okay for others to use."

"I'm thinking about my Daughter." she continues. "She comes

Home. from School. with some awful ideas about Nehiyâw'ak people. from her grade four Teacher. They are studying us. Right Now. Even when I explain to her. how We see things. she has to believe what TheTeacher tells her. to get it Right. I don't think that changes much. especially with Racism. because it's reinforced. at every level. Education. Movies. Books. Everything."

We have all heard The.N.Word. We all know what The.Word. means. We just Wish We Didn't. Wish We Didn't Know It. We especially wish we didn't hear Teachers. people in Authority positions. use It. so casually. using their Power. Position. Privilege. Voice. to teach Racism. to reinforce Racist ideas.

That Day. I am thinking about my Daughter too. I use my Voice. to raise critical questions. Why those who witnessed TheIncident. did Not bring it up to Circle? *Bejay* confides in Journal later. *I always thought that if someone was making racist remarks or telling racist jokes, and I remained silent, I was letting it be known that I did not approve. I now know that silence equals compliance, and that it is important to speak out and educate people as to how harmful these things are.*

I conclude Circle. by teaching about AntiRacistActivism. "Speak up. take action. record Racist remarks verbatim. and report to Instructors. TheDirector. or TheCommittee on AntiRacism. let Authorities know." I leave it with Them.

After Class. Don. says to me "I didn't think TheProf was trying to be Racist. he was just trying to make a point. about how Others saw Blacks." I raise my Eyebrows. "Trying to be Racist." I wonder. "Some people don't have to Try." I think to myself. I cautiously respond to him. "there are other ways to make a point."

Don continues. Trying to clarify his position. "I didn't see It. as Racist." "He really doesn't get it." I think to myself. carefully assessing his non–verbal cues. I say quietly. "you are a WhiteMale. you view TheIncident from that perspective. what about the OnlyBlackFemale? who spoke up in class. and said She saw it as Racist? Why do you want to excuse another WhiteMale? Minimize his actions? Because of his assumed lack of intention?" I pause. Don is just looking at me. with a confused look.

"How do you know. that he is Not a Racist?" I continue. "when he is using Racist terms? How can you know his Intentions? the Fact remains. he did use The.N.Word. It was taken as Offensive. when he was directly Confronted. he did not Retract. or Apologize. he used further insulting comments to Rationalize his own position."

Don is perfectly still. I could go on and on. keep Trying to explain.

Instead I wait. Wait through his murky Silence. Finally. he starts to nod. and says. "I am Beginning to See. what You mean."

Several other Students. Those who are still lingering around after Class. Observe our exchange. Some are nodding their Heads. agreement. I almost let myself feel a glimmer of Hope. Hope that it is worth the Risk I take. "Maybe something positive has been learned." I think for a moment.

Then Sandy. a WhiteFemale. new to class that Day. burst my bubble. with her helpful comment. "Maybe we should have him in to explain his point of view?" she says over her shoulder. as she turns her back. and leaves room. at least. she relieves me. No need to respond. to her Liberal FairMinded suggestion. Silently. I fume.

"Just what I do Not need. to use Class time. in TheOnlyCourse in the curriculum on Race Relations. to give Voice to one more WhiteMale. rationalizing his role as Oppressor!" I say to Lannie, a White Feminist Ally. Later. "I feel very much put in my place. right in the minority position now!!" I tell her. She sympathizes. of course.

That Night. I Nightmare. Nightmare. Tossing and Turning. Talking. I wake Up. I Wake Up in a Cold Sweat. Terror. I am dreaming. Dreaming. Dreaming other dreams. other realities of calling Racist. giving Voice to this Word. Racist. The.R.Word. to describe Authority. particularly WhiteMaleAuthority. and Being Hurt. Being Hurt. and Being Fired. Being Fired. and Being Trashed. Oh. No. Oh. No. I don't want to. I Don't Want To! I don't want to be. in middle of ThisBattle. of ThisParticularBattle. right AtThisTime. Right at this Time! on shifting new grounds of employability.

"What to do? What to do GrandMothers?" I pray. as I Smudge. I try to prepare myself. to calmly greet a new Day. Phone rings. its shrill buzz. makes me jump. I grab it. Zabet. my BestLifetimeFriend. "How Are You? I am Dreaming about you? Is everyOne. everyThing okay?" She asks in a concerned Voice. "Oh my Goodness. Zabet." I say. all in a rush. "Am I glad to hear your Voice. I'm in deep Trouble. and I don't know what to do about it." "Slow down." she says. "take a few Breaths. and tell all." So. I tell her. TheStory sofar. All details. She listens. puts in a few sympathetic mmmms. once in a while. to let me know she is Listening. Caring.

"I am Nightmaring about it. Last Night. TheIncident. how I Voiced in Class. pointing out his Racism. Privilege. Now. I feel totally Vulnerable. before This. you know. I was feeling Confident. Optimistic even. I imagined to myself that I am InCharge. have a grip on unfolding

ClassRoom processes. Now." I say. finally slowing down a bit. "I question TheWholeThing!"

"I regret TheWholeThing. It's not worth it. I just can't. no matter how hard I try. even if I say I'm just going to keep my Mouth shut. Especially if I say That. next thing I know. out something pops. Especially in Circle." Zabet laughs appreciatively. "You are a speaker of Truth." she affirms. "ThunderTouchedSpirit speaks Truth. It's one of your great qualities. as far as I'm concerned anyways. You are a rare species. in our phoney world. but. Yeah. it is Dangerous. why do you think other endangered species are protected?" she laughs.

"yeah. right. I already put myself in a Cage. this is a Zoo. Really!! Why do I continuously do this to myself? build my own Cage? to separate myself from Others?" I ask. I do not really expect an answer. I don't wait for one either. "I see and say Racism. as it happens. I'm confident in my analysis. AtTheTime. After. I am Regretful. Fearful of Retaliation. my Voice is Dangerous all right. OnceUponATime. I thought I could take Them on. act to change Them. from within. but. Right Now. I don't know anymore." my Voice trails off. disappears like my self confidence. Poof. Gone. up in Smoke.

"I hear ya." says Zabet. very sympathetically. "of course. you are Afraid. You have every right to be. I'm thrilled you are back here. but. it wasn't that long ago. when you went off to Nehiyâw'akCollege. and got dumped on. and chased out. for speaking Truth. I remember. You were really Devastated by that."

"Yeah." I sniff. Tears finally release. "I am hurt badly. when People miss-frame my honourable intentions. Right Now. I Am Fearful. I feel all Alone. I need Support. Community. I know. I am Not going to bring down Mr.TenureTrack.White.Patriarchy. on my own. neither are Students."

"Yeah." says Zabet. "Students are often not able to do it either. They have too much to lose. too little power. They just want to get their Degree. and get out. I can remember being like that myself. AtOneTime." Zabet confesses "You??" I raze her. "You're always so good at putting People in their Place. You're my role model." "Hah!" she responds. "the feeling is mutual." We both laugh. "You know for yourself." she continues. "I wasn't always this good. It's a learned skill. but. you gotta pick your Battles. Anyways. I'd love to talk more. Later. but. I gotta get to School. Phone me. Love ya."

I hang up. My mind is reeling. a critical Question is: *Can I strike a balance between using the material for "teachable moments" without creating a political mess—where I end up being pinned as the agitator?*

I Know. News about "What TheProf Said." travels fast. I Know. Who will ask Who. to Clarify my Nehiyâw'ak meanings. in StudentLounge. I contact members of Nehiyâw'akSupportCircle. and Tell Them. I Tell Them about Circle in Class. CircleInClass. and what I Said. in CircleVoice. how I called TheR.Word. and how I Dream. how I Dreamed. and how I am Afraid. How I was Afraid. and how I Pray. What to do? What to do GrandMothers? We think. We talk. We strategize. We Know. what has to Happen.

Because. I Fear. have to Fear. Because. of my Past. Experience. History. I.We. decide to encourage Silence. Encouraged Silence. Emphasize to Students. What is said in Circle. is mean to be kept in Circle. What is Said in Circle. is Meant to be Kept in Circle. Kept in Circle. I.We. invoke an ethic of Confidentiality. Confidentiality?

I encourage Silence. Don't Talk. about what I Talk about. Don't Talk About What I Talked About. Silence to cover Fear. an Old. Deadly. combination. well known to many. many Generations of Victims. I invoke Silence. to paper over my Fear of Voice. when what is needed. What was Needed. to intensify. provoke Change. is Lots of Talk. Lots of Talk to Silence His Voice.

but. AtThatTime. I am Glad. I Was Glad. It turned out as well as it did. Student chitchat settles down. Problems remain. but. I imagine that I escape. not caught in middle. I think. I will Not be Martyr. for a change. at least for that moment. I am temporarily relieved of burden of MartyrDoom.

Authorities. I Assume. never hear of TheIncident.

Much Later. as twists and turns of Fate will have it. OneDay. as I am leaving MyOffice. I stop to chat with ConcernedStudent on steps. We speak for a few minutes. casually. Then. we part. a few weeks pass. I find out. she was on her way to Meeting. called by Students. to complain about Racist remarks made by TheProf. SomeOne saw us chatting. and assumed. Assumed I am giving her Last Minute Briefing. Assumed I am Involved. Organizing. Orchestrating Student dissent. against this Racist Colleague.

AtThatTime. I am so wrapped up in my own Work. I have no idea Confrontation is going on. Of course. I could safely assume. TheProblem. is ongoing. that Casual Chat. fueled an already escalating WildFire. eventually led to my BurnOut. Out of ThatSystem.

Temporary Insanity I plea. I know. Now. it is Impossible. NoOne can be seen by Administrators. Colleagues. Students. as Impartial. or Collegial.

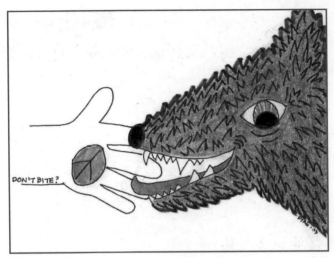

don't bite
GrandMothers
Wisdom. "don't
Bite da Hand dat
Feeds ya."
Mahe'kun prefers
to feed herSelf.
will Bite.
to escape
confinement.

when teaching RaceRelations. in Racist environments. as Sherene Razack tells it. "Stories of racism and genocide are profoundly shocking … because they deeply upset the dominant group's notion of self."

as hard as I try to be Collegial. that is. to avoid direct Confrontation of colleagues. No point. a NoWin situation. as Patricia Monture-Angus tells it. "And when I speak and the brutality of my experience hurts you, you hide behind the hurt. You point the finger at me and you claim that I hurt you." And when I am forced to leave. Leave now Poisoned Work Environments. Mooniyâs can Comfort each other. they Know. their Hurt. Discomfort. justifies their actions. against me. against me and my kind. I.We. are TheProblem.

I learn Then. and know Now. Over and Over. over and over again. I learn. Resistance produces Backlash. Activism. big or small. has Risks. Denial and Defensiveness. Appear Disappear. Re-appear. in each and every. Each and Every encounter. in challenged Systems. If you ever Question. their Actions. or their Good Intentions. re-Action happens. Challenged Authorities re-act. I learn. over and over again. Don't Bite Hands that feed you. They will Bite back. and their Teeth are Bigger. and Sharper.

R.E.S.P.E.C.T.[2]

OneDay. I Slip. Slide. inadvertently. into Silencing many Students.
Silenced Many. of my Students.
after Class. I went Home.
feeling Upset. Angry. Hurt. Sad. Confused.
I. Needed to Recuperate.
Students had been highly Disrespectful.
Highly Disrespectful!
Not paying attention.
Not Paying Attention to process.
made Little Effort to Understand.
to Even Understand.
Expectations of Circle.
So. I tell Stories in Circle. about Circle.
try to give Traditional instruction forms.
Subtle. Indirect. Methods taught to me by Elders.
Ineffective in ThisClass.
I began to Share. my experiences of ThisClass.
with other Colleagues.
"Some talk too much.
especially when others are talking. or I am.
They are busy talking. or talking off topic. or chatting.
They are Not listening.
I find Them Disrespectful." I say.
I do. I find Them. Disrespectful.
my Ears are surprised to Hear.
"Some are just Like That. it's not just YourClass."
I know. Respect is a much needed lesson in ThisClass.
I decide. rather than Swallow It.
Swallow It. and keep trying to affect change in Subtle ways.
I will. SpeakOut. about my feelings. in Circle.
Speak Honestly in Circle.
an expectation in Nehiyâw'ak Communities.
I journal a SpeakOut.[3] about Respecting self and others.
to increase Awareness. Sensitivity towards others' Feelings.
Teach lessons about. recognizing.
Multiple Interpretations of TheSameReality.
during CircleTime. I Speak from my Heart.
I Speak From My Heart. about my Feelings.
I am feeling those same familiar Emotions, and Body signs,
that tell me I am experiencing Oppression.
I Tell how I have been Dreaming. about ThisClass.
Envisioning. Experiencing ThisClass.

I am attempting to engage you in a process. Which reflects my culture's values of cooperation and shared learning through Voice and Experience. I am experiencing this as a destructive process for myself and an act of disrespect for Circle.
I Share how. They are Showing Disrespect.
    to my Ancestral Traditions.
It is my observation that you are Not paying attention to difference, to different expectations in this class, which I find disrespectful. Are you resisting the process? Or are you so used to always having the same teaching style that you just do not realize that my expectations are different?
I give general and specific examples.
    ask Each Person to take Responsibility.
I am internalizing/interpreting "your"—I say the collective. but mean to have each Student internalize what of their own actions/attitudes were disrespectful as racist, sexist or oppressive. I do not want to carry the weight of your collective unknowing.
I begin to Feel. HeavyHeartBurden lift.
I do Not want to be Appropriating Tradition.
    or Not Honouring Ancestral practices.
I warn if Attitudes. Behaviours.
    do Not change in Specific Ways.
    ThisClass process Will Change.
I will continue to cover content, but we will Not be using Circle or other Sacred Ways in this Class.
I recognize Source of their Actions. Mooniyâs Consciousness.
    I see and name. Saw and Named
    Ignorance as an Act of Privilege.
You are acting out your White privilege and need a lesson in how others have been silenced and continue to be silenced by your need to be verbal continuously. While Whites have lots of training to verbal aggression, we (Aboriginal, Black, Acadian) have had training to silence—to take it.
I express my Teaching Vision.
I want to help White Students become more conscious of what a gift their "freedom of speech" is, and what the cost is to others. Please be quiet. Listen.
my SpeakOut is very profound.
  Very Profound Experience. for everyone.
    EveryOne. including me. Especially Me.
next Class. I pass Feather.
  Pass Feather. to give opportunity for Voice.
    few speak. Black and Nehiyâw'ak Students.

one MooniyâsMale. No others.
No Others Speak. They are Silenced.
Silenced. I am Surprised.
my Eyebrows shoot up. I do Not respond.
can Not Respond except to say.
"I do not mean to Silence you."
over next few Days. I reflect.
at First. I think. maybe. what I said. is Profound.
was so Profound. it provoked Silence.
maybe. It. Was?
what proves Really Profound. for Me. is realizing.
what Silences Students. is Not necessarily my Nehiyâw'ak "Voice."
teaching Respect for Tradition.
it is Power. invested in Professorial Voice.
that's what is Important. to Students.
that I. TheProfessor. said. It.
that's what makes It. SchoolTalk.
SchoolTalk.
They talk. and they talk.
They talk to Other Students.
to Nehiyâw'ak Students.
"what does she mean? what Did She Mean?"
"maybe She's Just Angry. taking it out.
Taking it Out on Us!" some say.
"She's right. I do it myself." others confess.
some Students Learn. Silence is necessary.
to practise Proper Conduct in Circle.
some continue to be SameRudeSelves.
some record strong Reactions. mixed Emotions. in Journals.[4]

Surprise. Shock. Anger. Fear.
I feel scared now to say anything for fear of it being offensive.

Guilt. Responsibility.
I also feel so responsible and guilty for whatever I have done that contributed to her pain ... I feel like an oppressor tonight—in a major way. Not a nice feeling.

Admiration.
It must have taken a huge amount of courage to do that and I certainly admire her for It.

Attacked.
I commend anyone who has the guts to describe specifically when, where, and how they are oppressed. However I found Jean's style to be so open and honest

that it left me feeling I was personally attacked.

Tia's journal is most lengthy. a detailed description of her Feelings.
    an example. of someone Actively engaging. in Learning.Healing.
        extracting Lessons. from a potentially "Negative" experience.
            breaking through Denial. at least for ThatMoment.

The first Word to describe how I felt was Denial. My immediate reaction was denial and that I could never be a part of a group or collective of People who could oppress another person. WRONG! When I look back at the size of the class itself and the fact that a majority of the People in the class are white and maintain a white culture, this is a form of oppression in and of itself. As a group we want to share and voice our experiences yet not being silent and learn/listen to other first person experiences. This act alone silences those who have so much to offer.

Another feeling I was experiencing was anger. I felt angry because I was being grouped with a bunch of People who were oppressing someone and we didn't even know it. This angers me the most, that I am so privileged that I couldn't even see/feel what was happening. I also felt angry because you thought enough of us as People to tell us how you were feeling, but all I could feel at the time was that I was at fault and being blamed for something I could not see or feel.

This is when I began to feel scared and afraid. Oppression is so deep and so interwoven that it has become a way of Life. I am afraid because if you were feeling this way, others may also be feeling oppressed in a classroom with a majority of white Students. I am also afraid that the Words I voice may silence others and contribute to this damned oppressive society. I want to be part of change, not silencing People.

Finally, the Word that stands out in mind is strength. It is not right that you have to explain you're being oppressed. Yet you shared this with a room full of strangers to assist in our awareness. You shouldn't have to explain anything. We should be able to see, feel what is happening in this classroom. I have a long way to go but, I would like to thank you Jean for your honesty and strength in wanting a group of (Students) to know, see and feel what you were experiencing—AWARENESS.

Being. Silenced. often in my Life.
    as Victim. Student. Colleague.
        very much Affects me. my Teaching style.
            my Reaction to Students' Reactions.
                especially My Reaction to Students' Reactions.
                    I am Shocked. Shocked at Myself.
                        Shocked to be Thinking well about Silence.
                        Silencing as Positive.
                        Silencing as a good Lesson.
OneStudent. wrote me a Poem.[5]

So
you've decided
to tell us
like it is

Someone said
Courage
is acting in the face of fear ...
I'm sure fear
wasn't the only
thing you felt—
the only barrier to action
... but perhaps one of many

Well, you know
it's hard to hear
And I'm sad, defensive, guilty ...
will it sound patronizing
If I say
I'm glad you did it
Thankful you have the courage, conviction, strength
to say what white people—me included—need to hear
Thankful you are willing to do this work with us ...
as oppressive and angering as it can be ...
as we can be ...
because
it needs to be done
And
I'm strengthened and humbled
by your feelings, your words, your actions

We talk of white privilege
And yes I do have it, use it, live it
but it's a privilege to be here in this room
To be part of this
To be challenged
changed
enriched
and challenged again

I guess this is what I have to say
right now
when I tell it to you
like it is
for me.

positive Feedback. provides Confirmation.
          nourishes my Soul.
Later. as all good Academics do.
  I Rationalized. Contextualized. my experience.
  I know. it is Rooted in Nehiyâw'ak pedagogy.
      Not Acts of Silencing. Honouring Powers of Silence.
      Respectfully Listening. Power of quietly Observing.
      Quietly Observing. Not Questioning. Not Asking Why...Why?
      just sitting Quietly. usually out in Nature.
      Being. In. Silence. In Silence. learning by Observing.
      as Larry Bird tells it "you don't ask questions when
      you grow up. You watch and listen and wait, and the
      answer will come to you. It's yours then, not like
      learning in school."[6]

in Defens'ive Truth. don't Deny me.

*Winds of Change.
Healing. Truth. can
be like a Tornado.
swirling Rainbow
Winds. sweeping
through. Bending.
Twisting.
Uprooting that
which once seemed
Strong.
Unbendable. comes
with Cleansing.
Rain.*

I Story. ToDay. to reclaim my Voice. to get to Truth.
    to Crack open Great Black Chasm called Denial.
    to Slip through Tightly Tangled Bars of Defensiveness.
        to get to Heart of what really matters.
        a Dangerous mission indeed.
I am learning. through Decades of Experience
    Activist. Healer. Artist. Academic.
        Denial is fused with Defensiveness.
            conveniently covers cracks in crumbling Kings' castles.
            NoOne. wants to know. Emperor has no clothes.
                Some. will do anything to Hide. this Reality.
Denial.Defensiveness. are Highly Complex.
        Physiological. Psychological. Sociological.
        Manifest as Mental Traps. Social Cages.
they Appear. Disappear. Re-appear.
    in Each and Every. Each and Every Encounter.
        with Individuals In Charge. in Challenged Systems.
        Patriarchal. Eurocentric. Heterosexist.
        Capitalistic. Bureaucratic. Hierarchical.
    Systems which Currently Control All of Our Lives.
        on this Planet. Our Earth Mother.
    Systems that Discriminate Against Some. Oppressed.
        Deny Voice. Services. Support.
        Rights and Freedoms.
    Systems that Provide Access to Some. Privileged.
        Encourage Voice. Services. Support.
        Rights and Freedoms.
Open your Eyes. Minds. Hearts.
    recognize Denial.Defensiveness. in these Quotable Quotes:
        "I'm Sure she didn't Mean It."
        "What do you Mean you're Hurt? Angry? Sad? etc...."
        "You're Just Over Sensitive."
        "Over Reacting."
        "Over Critical."
        "Are you Sure you're not pre-menstral? on a sugar low?"
        "We've Never had These problems before You came."
        "Can't you Just look on the bright side. for Once?"
        "I've Never had that happen to Me."
        "I Don't Believe it."
        "It Can't be True."
        "I Never thought of It before."
        "It's Just policy."
        "It's TheWay we've Always done things around Here."
        "Don't take it Personally."

"Racism is *Just a theory.*"
"Just because he used Slur.
Doesn't mean he's Racist."
"*We've done Everything we can*
to make *You People* Comfortable here."
"*I support Affirmative Action.* but ...
I don't think hiring Someone
Just based on Race. or Gender. is Fair.
Do You?"
"What is Fair about Historic Discrimination We Face?"
I am often left to wonder. Aloud. to myself.
Who here has Not heard. TheNowClassicTale?
"NowaDays WhiteMen. are *Just* as Oppressed as AnyOne.
in Fact. EvenMore Oppressed.
Why just TheOtherDay. I Heard about JoeNo. WhiteMale.
who was Refused Entry into RCMP
(or any Government Services position)
because of Equity *Quotas* in place."
and TheStory goes On and On. *ReverseDiscrimination*[7] They cry.
Open Your Ears. Hear Key Code Words.
Sure. Just. Never. Always. but. You People. Quotas. Reverse Discrimination.
Fortress of Privileged. is Defended by Denial.
Denial is a Brick Wall. We Slam into Head First.
We Crack Our Skulls.
Blood Oozes Out.
from around Graciously Given
Tiny BandAids.
We are Expected to Gratefully Receive.
Quietly. Happily.
Staunch BloodFlow.
We Weep. as our Tears Stream.
Our Self-Confidence. Courage. Erodes.
Health and Vitality Seeps. out of Our Eyes. Skin. Blood. Hearts.
Our Visions Dim. Lives. Livelihoods. are Lost.
Defensiveness means to Defend Whatever is Said or Done.
rather than Examine your position.
Some Defend WECCP Systems. through Denial. Minimizing.
Patronizing. Antagonizing. Blaming.
Denial.Defensiveness.
High Costs to Some. Maintains Benefits for Others.
What do I do. when my Voice is Unheard. Mute.
Echos in an Empty Room?
when Basic Services are Denied me?
when Family. Colleagues. Administrators. Unions.

Refuse to Support me?
when HumanRights. Justice Systems. Evade me?
when Freedoms.
do Not include me?
Break Through!
Break Through!
Break Through Defensiveness.Denial!
What Do You Find?
What Do You Find on TheOtherSide?
Do YouKnow?
have I Gotten Apologies? NO!
Commitments to Change? NO!
Compensation for Injuries & Losses? NO!
Detoxification for Poisoned Work Places? NO!
Break through Defensiveness. Denial.
and what do You find on TheOtherSide?
Do YouKnow? Do you Care?
If. you Believe in Voice. Services. Support. Rights. Freedoms.
If. you have Them. help renew my Hope.
Be Open. Be an Ally.
Can you Learn from my Stories. Experiences. Pains. Triumphs?
Can you Learn what Needs to be Done?
to make Inclusion. Equity. Equality.
more than Words
Mouthed to fulfil hollow Federal promises.[8]
Can you Teach me. how to Believe?
Can you Teach me. why I would want to Trust?
I don't Know what Truth. lies Beyond Defensiveness. Denial.
it has Not been my Reality. Yet.
I do Know. Experience. Learn.
when I Push on Authorities. to See Truth.
Truth of Discriminatory Systems.
Truth of Inequities.
Callously reproduced in name of Affirmative Action.
when I Tear thin veil of Denial.Defensiveness. from their Eyes.
what do I get? BackLash.
BackLash is my Reality. Inevitable. Continuous.
Action will be Taken by Challenged ones. especially those in Authority.
in-relation to Any form of Transformation
Attempted or Enacted. in Any context.
can you See. how I Story.
to Understand. Heal. Teach.
how First Voice. Traditionalism. Activism.
produces ongoing BackLash.

BackLash wears many Masks.
 like Personal Slurs.
  OneTime. I am Yelled at by AngryMaleStudent.
   name.called. across Classroom. Slurred.
   I attempt to complain about Him. to Administrator.
   I find out. He has complained about Me.
   I am advised. "You should examine your teaching style."
Threatening phone calls.
  including harassment by *Frank* magazine.[9]
Anonymous hate-filled notes.
 on office door. in campus mail. home mail. email.
Withholding Necessary information.
 by Colleagues. and Administrators.
 about changes in Deadlines. meeting Dates. Times. Places.
Five-page memos. outlining my Wrongs.
 using Anonymous written course evaluations.
  conversations Solicited from Students in Hallways.
  about classroom process.content.
  and Their personal Satisfaction.Dissatisfaction. with Me.
InformalChats with Administrators.
 about my "inappropriate" family relations.
 my "non-collegial" behaviour. for mentioning blatant harassment.
 "Narrowness" of my research.
 Indigenous World.Views. Healing methods. Research paradigms.
  Race relations. Equity. Education.
  "Native Studies.""Cultural studies."
  "Women's studies." Family violence. Feminism.
 "Misguided" focus of my CommunityWork.
  actually in Nehiyâw'ak or Women's Communities.
     instead of UniversityCommunity.
Ongoing "review" of my course outlines. even once approved.
Interrogation for Being.
 too Critical. AboriginiCentric. Feminist.
 one Time. for being too Lesbian.
  I included a case example. a LesbianCouple wanting to adopt.
  a thirty-minute exercise in a three-credit course.
    Thirty minutes too much.
Overturning of failed grades.
 assigned for Incomplete. Unsatisfactory. Students' work.
Failing completed Students.
 based on NewRules. like "selfPlagarism."
Issues Escalate on their Own.
 even when I Ignore them. try to BeNice.
InformalChats quickly.

become OfficialReprimands.
Disciplinary meetings. Withholding increments.
Non-renewal of contracts. Bad references.
results in TenureWars.
refusal to Reappoint.
denial of Research. Travel funds
Cyclical. Ongoing. BackLash has Substantial Impacts.
on my Personal Life. Professional Life. Life for my Family.
BackLash. Unhidden. despite Multiple Guises.
like when I am Told.
I "have an Attitude Problem."
am "Too Angry All the Time."
I "put a Negative spin on Everything."
"TroubleMaker." Paranoid. Christian,Bashing.
I have been Chastised for "Intimidating" others.
told to be less "Accusatory." warned to be More Collegial.
like Seema Kalia.[10] I am left Wondering. "is it Me? or is it Them?"
I agree with Chandra Mohanty.
for Systems to conduct BusinessAsUsual.
while facing overwhelming Challenges we are Posing.
Conflicts must be Personalized. Psychologized.
Problems of Race and Difference.
are reformulated into Narrow. InterPersonal Relations.
Historical. Contextual Conflicts.
are rewritten as manageable Psychological Problems.
I often experience BackLash as Personal.
BackLash is decisively Political.
must be Acknowledged. as a Critical issue.
for Workplace Health and Safety.
Unions. HumanRightsCommissions.
those working to achieve AcademicFreedom for All.
Wisakecahk teaches.
Discomfort is a Critical Political issue ToDay. threatens AcademicFreedom.
Institutions are increasingly Driven. by market Demands.
commodified learning. Satisfy Customer.
my so-called AcademicFreedom is Conditional.
Satisfaction. of Every Student. in Every Class. I Teach. is Required.
when some are Uncomfortable. Dissatisfied.
because. They. are Challenged to critically See.
what They. have been Conditioned to Ignore.
my Livelihood is Challenged.
those Projecting. Fear. and Anger.
are consistently part of Every work environment.
whenever Administration decides.

PersonalAssassination is Required. to Deflect political Heat.
Dissatisfied Students. are Recruited.
given Voice. given Power. PowerOver My Life.
Wisakecahk teaches.
deep Personal Commitment to Change.
leaves me Open. a Target for BackLash.
PersonalAssassination plays a large role.
de-activates political activism.
I Story to help myself. and others.
to learn.teach. be more Self-Preserving. in our Activist efforts.
to learn.teach. don't internalize
PersonalAssassination is a political Weapon.
it's Hard. what does it Take. to Keep Going?
how do I Stay Motivated.   to want to Continue.
Continue to make a Change?
how do We Sustain. struggling Force.
in midst of All Pressures?
what happens to Us. in our Lives. to Exhaust Us?
to keep Us Down?
to keep our Minds off.
our Activist work?
I Story to Learn.Teach. Survival Tactics.
Remember History.
Negative labelling is always produced. escalates with Resistance.
Need to Dehumanize Us. historically arose.
to Justify actions taken by Colonial Powers.
to maintain Control. in face of Nehiyâw'ak Resistance.
No longer Wards of QueenMother.
Political Nehiyâw'ak are treated as RebelChildren
Spanked for Acting Out.
Keep Focused. on Politics behind Personal Attacks.
Remember. BackLash is very Real.
expect it as part of Activism. one strategy for Survival.
Remember. creating change Helps some. poses Threats to others.
Always brings a CounterAction to Our Selves.
BackLash. can cause us to Spiral into Hopelessness. Helplessness.
Fatalism. serves Dominators. preserves Hierarchical Order.
Personal. Collective. Survival. Strategies are Lived with Others.
Shared in Story. offered as Condolences.
given Reciprocally. among community members.
remain Real. Visible. part of Community.
Support others for change to Occur.
Support helps us remain Strong in our Desires.
Support is required to Challenge. Change. Oppressive People. Systems.

Change occurs on a Daily. Weekly. Monthly. Yearly basis.
Not All change reflects an Inclusive agenda.
   forces of Hegemony continuously exert.
     PowerFull Erosion of Any. All. Movements.
        towards Personal. Cultural. Social. Political. Change.
Learn our Wisakecahk. Mahê'kun. tales well. Be Open.
  Learn.Teach.Heal. from lessons embedded in our Daily Encounters.
  with Systems. with People. those who Hold.
            Enact Power. PowerOver Us.

MAHÊ'KUN GETS BIT

OneDay. Not too long ago. and not too far away. Mahê'kun is trying Hard. as usual. to teach Respect to disbelieving Predators. even those who are used to Tormenting. or Eating those unlike themselves. are required to learn about Respecting others. to enter Healing.Teaching Lodges. "I always seem to be TheOne asked to teach about these issues." Mahê'kun is heard to complain in her Pack. Later.

Anyways. ThatDay. She is just concluding a tiresome conflict ridden Circle. when something awful happens. Hyena interrupts Mahê'kun. shouts at her. "can you believe it?" Mahê'kun tells Story to WhiteWolf. "He Interrupts and Shouts in Circle? Interrupts me. and Shouts at me. in Circle?"

AtThatTime. Hyena accuses Mahê'kun. "You're taking sides. supporting LittleOnes and not Others. who are you? Judging Predators! You eat Rabbits. and Mice. You lie like Snake. that's Not right. You are Wrong. Wrong. Wrong! This Time. You are Wrong!"

Snake is offended. Hisses out her complaint. "why doesss sssomeone hafta mention SSSSnakeee." She says softly to Robin next to her. ThatDay. Everybeing notices that Hyena is particularly Rude. even for himself.

He Clawpoints at Mahê'kun. shrieks loudly. shows his Teeth. and clenches and shakes his Paws at her. while yelling his tirade. He even uses Mahê'kun 's name in a Very Nasty tone. like a Slur. many are Shocked. and Afraid.

He is obviously one VeryAngryHyena. and not afraid to use his

Weapons. Not afraid to threaten Teacher. Later. GreyWolf consoles Mahê'kun. "Hyena is definitely havin' BadDay. He's known for his hot-headed temper. He's always so full of himself. eh? very unWolfable of Him." She says. when she hears Story.

luckily. ThatDay. BlackBear came to visit. from OverTheHills. She got there just as Circle began. She had been out picking Blueberries. digging for Ants. She growls to Mahê'kun after Circle. "I don' know 'ow you can take it. Time after Time. dos Ones wit Paws an' Legs cross. grimaces on dere Faces. talkin' to each other across Circle. jumpin' up an' leavin' Circle. whenever dey feel like it. laughin' out loud. when OtherBeings express dere feelin's. it's Terrible. très Terrible. where are dose Beasts from?" She growls a real low.

Then. Bear continues. "even I find it frightenin'. do you want me to stay for a while? I'd invite a couple of WolfGuards to DarkShadows. If. I was you. some of dose Predators were starin' Hate at you. whole Circle."

Mahê'kun is very Happy. takes BlackBear up on her offer. "not only do Beasts disrespect Circle. They patrol my Den. every Moon. I find big Branches down at my Doorway. but. that's not the worst of it." Mahê'kun's Voice becomes a very low growl. in back of her Throat.

BlackBear moves closer to hear. "OneDawn. I nearly step in a large coil of stinking Merde. at front of Den. Merde! can you believe. It! what kind of Beast would do such a thing?"

Mahê'kun growls under her Breath. "I wonder if some LargeDog from HumanWorld. came in Night to leave it. do you think any Beast from DarkShadows. can be that disrespectful to a Teacher?"

Mahê'kun can see. BlackBear is visibly Shocked. She's sorry she's been so hasty to tell her. but. She never had a chance to tell anybeing. since It! happened. and is just bursting to get It! out.

BlackBear growls real low. "don' let dem get to you. don' feel afraid. We'll go to Ceremony. I 'ave ProtectionMedicine. I can Share." Mahê'kun gains Courage. She trusts ProtectionMedicine. Ceremonies.

later. one FullMoonCeremony. when WolfPack gathers UpInHills. OldOnes tell Story of WolfCub and RattleSnake.

"OneColdMornin'." WhiteWolf begins. "a young kind-'earted WolfCub. is walkin' down a Trail. when 'e ears a small Voice. callin' out to 'im. "'Elp. 'Elp me". Now. You all know. WolfCub is curious by nature. goes over to See.

it's RattleSnake. lyin' in a 'eap on Ground. "I am freezzzin' Cold." hisses RattleSnake. "Pleasssse help. pick me up. wrap me in your Fur. and Warm me. Pleasssse."

OfCourse. WolfCub is immediately afraid. as 'e should be." WhiteWolf looks around at all Cubs. to make sure they are Listening. convinced they are. he continues.

"No!" WolfCub says. "If. I pick you up. You'll bite me. an' I will die." Now. Snake is shiverin' with Cold. "Noooo." says Snake. "I will be sssssso very very grateful. If. you ssssaved my Life. Pleasssse. help your Brother SSSSnake."

"now. as I said." WhiteWolf goes on. "WolfCub is a kind-'earted Cub. 'E 'as bin raised in WolfPack. So. OfCourse. 'E recognizes Snake. an' All Creation. as 'is Brothers an' Sisters. So. OfCourse. 'E can Not resist 'is plea for 'elp. So. 'e lays down. and curls up round RattleSnake. Warm 'im in 'is Fur."

"wasn' dat good of WolfCub." a YoungOne breaks in to Story. while his Mother nips his Ear hard. WhiteWolf growls. "well. mebbe. Listen up. leastwise. till I'm done."

WhiteWolf continues. "jis as WolfCub is gettin' drowsy. cuddled up in Mornin' Sun wit Snake. 'E ears a small sound. "Rattle. Rattle. Rattle. Rattle!" an' WHAAA! Snake bites 'im."

"can you believe Snake bit 'im?" YoungOne asks her Mother. "WolfCub couldn' believe it either." says WhiteWolf. "den. WolfCub jumps up. on 'is little Legs. Tears in 'is little GreenEyes. 'but. but. you said. You Said. you would Not bite me. If. If. I saved you." 'E whines at Snake. Snake hisses. "SSSSSSooooo. YouKnow. I am RattleSsssnake. when you ssssnuggle me."

Mahê'kun is inspired. "Yes! this is It!" She thinks. "Perfect Story for Circle." Later. on her way back to Den. She wonders. "am I like WolfCub? or am I like RattleSnake?" even Later. as she makes her Rounds before Bed. She is still wondering. "who will be Snake? and who will be WolfCub? in Predators' eyes?"

NextCircle. Mahê'kun puffs up her Chest. and tells Story. uses her best Voices. "I did a great job." She confides in GreyWolf. Later. but. what a reaction!! Mahê'kun is stunned. "Some seem to think I am calling Them. Snakes. Think I am insulting Them. how come They don't see me as a Snake? If. They think I am so Bad?" She asks BlackBear later. "I guess. mebbe dey like you deep down inside. an' don' like demselves dat much." offers Bear.

Mahê'kun nods quickly. not really expecting BlackBear's response. She goes on. "I can't believe it. One even thought I called him Satan. can you believe it?" She howls. "surely Bible is Furthest thing from WolfMind. I hardly only think about it. maybe once in a great while. when

GreatGrandWolves howl about Humans. like on Remembrance Moons."
"musta bin somebein' recently Caged. by 'umans." growls BlackBear.
"Story is a powerful Teacher." WiseOldOne growls wisely. when she
ears. "You need caution. who's listenin'? what meanin' will dey take from
it? You 'ave to pay attention. to everybein's Ears."

Soon after. Mahê'kun hears. AngryOnes want to get her banished.
from DarkShadows. "After all. She is using her Voice. in Circle. to Judge.
Degrade. and Insult us." Some tell CouncilHead. Elk. "Mahê'kun has a
chip on her shoulder. She's just causing Trouble. there was No Problem
before." They accuse.

Mahê'kun retreats. avoids Elk. by this Time. He is getting anxious.
wants to discuss with her. "why would you be NameCalling Apprentices?
especially Satan?"

meanwhile. Hyena. misses Circle. ever since he attacked Mahê'kun.
OneDawn. He appears at her Den doorway. He tells Mahê'kun. "I don'
want to be in Circle wit you. but. I still want to be Initiated in Teachin'
Lodge." "You'll have to meet with CouncilHead for that." Mahê'kun
replies as politely as possible. not wanting Confrontation. EarlyMorningSun
is barely up.

Hyena does not waste words on pleasantries. cracks Jaws repeatedly.
quickly informs Mahê'kun. He already spoke to Elk. and several Others.
including International Council for All Beings. "Dey keep sendin' me
back to you." He bares his Teeth in a lopsided grin. "Dey say I'm supposed
to come back to Circle. but. I want to be Sure." He growls low in his
Throat. "Sure dat. YouKnow. dat I am Not Sorry. for what happens."

Mahê'kun's GreenEyes snap open wide in Surprise. Hyena continues.
talking quickly out of side of his Mouth. "I am Not apologizin' to you.
I mean to Attack you." He says. "I feel Attacked. some things You say.
I 'ave a right to Defend myself." He growls loudly. Paws and Legs crossed.
Teeth bared. His Anger stands out as clear as Spots. on his shaggy yellow
Coat.

Mahê'kun listens to him very carefully. reading every cue. when he
is done. she growls. "I can see you are Angry. You do Not have to Attack
me. You are Bullying me. and Others. this is Not acceptable." Mahê'kun
responds. She is Not going to back down from Hyena's force. even if she
Lives to regret it. Later.

"You can come back to Circle. when You are ready. ready to agree
to behave Respectfully. towards me and others." Mahê'kun insists with
a quiet growl. Hyena laughs real loud. and says. "I will Never agree."
Mahê'kun knows. right then and there. in her Heart of Hearts. Hyena will

Not own up to his bad behaviour. or Change.

Time passes. Hyena returns to Mahê'kun's Den. "I understand. You think I'm an arrogant tete de peuch.[11] Well. I am. No apologies for that." He says. LongTongue pokes out his Cheek. "I will Apologize. I twist your Name into an Insult. ThatDay." He whispers in a serious tone. glances around himself as he speaks. hoping no one else hears him. "but. I still don' wanna come back to Circle." He insists. showing his true Hyena nature. "can't change a Hyena's Spots." Mahê'kun thinks to herself.

Mahê'kun knows. he is just trying to suck up. and she doesn't want to listen anymore. "why does he always have to arrive. before Breakfast?" She wonders to herself. "YouKnow. CouncilHead is who you want to talk to then." growls Mahê'kun. crossing her Paws. and showing her Teeth. She just seen BlackBear. looking around in BerryBushes beside Birch. so she feels somewhat safer. and she already heard more than enough from Hyena. enough to last her a LifeTime.

Finally. Hyena. Tail partly between his Legs. returns to Circle. "too little. too late. as Ma would say." Mahê'kun confides in her SisterTimber. Later.

"I am Not recommending him as a Teacher. He Never apologizes for his Hurtful comments. or expresses any Good Feelings for Others. He does Not show me that he Lives any Circle Teachings. He only focuses on his own Self. and how badly he is treated by me. and by all of us." Mahê'kun contributes when Council meets to review her decision. "He is not ready to be initiated into Teaching Lodge." She shakes her Head. Strongly.

"Imagine my Surprise. when I see Hyena parade by. all slicked up. looking good. big grin on his Face. right along with Others from Circle. at Initiation Ceremonies. He is going to be a Teacher. after All that happened. I can't believe my Eyes. I blink a few Times. just to be sure." Mahê'kun howls to her Pack. Late That Night.

GreyWolf says. "I hear Elk is afraid of Interference. from International Council of All Beings. so he calls a Circle. and they decide to Initiate him. It. is all hurried. hush-hush." Mahê'kun whines. "I feel so disrespected as a Teacher." to AnyBeing. who will listen.

"I was never so glad to leave any place. at least my WolfCub won't have him as a Teacher." Mahê'kun howls to her Pack later. Breathing heavy from her long run. "He's prob'ly goin' to go back to wherever Hyena's come from. Mebbe dey jis want him to finish. So dey could get rid of him. real quick like." WiseOldOne offers.

Mahê'kun learns. It's not that great to be either WolfCub or

RattleSnake. She now teaches. "I learn. there are a lot more Snakes than
gentle-hearted WolfCubs. in Circles. DarkShadows. and ElseWorlds."

WHAT PART OF NO DON'T YOU UNDERSTAND?[12]

to Crazy Horse, Lakota Medicine Warrior.
so skilled was he in Arts of transformation. of his physical "reality."
he could not be killed by bullets. they could not pierce his Body.

What part of NO don't you understand?
I wonder many. Many Times.
    as I am berated over and over.
      Sign.
      Sign.
      Sign.
      Sign on TheDottedLine.

"AcademicFreedom includes everyone. YouKnow.
   You already have it."
   I am patronistically assured by TheKing.
as MétisWoman
   I do not feel Included or Free.
   more than twenty years a full-Time academic.
   with different institutions. across disciplines.
     Pressuring me to Acculturate.
     Disciplining me for Resisting.
     has taught me OtherWise.

They offer "accommodation" as a possibility.
They will "*permit* use of those cultural customs which are *well established*
as being an *appropriate* part of the pedagogy of a particular discipline."[13]
   when in Eurocolonial history on ThisContinent.
   in ThisWorld. AtThisTime.
     has Eurocentric. Hegemonic. Canon.
      permitted Nehiyâw'ak philosophy. Nehiyâw'ak pedagogy.
      to be seen as *appropriate?*
      to be *well established?*
how can I collude in this ruse?
   to tighten noose around our Necks?
   to confine our already limited Freedoms. further?

They argue.
   Collegiality. cannot unilaterally be removed. from tenure criteria.

We can't challenge Collegiality. without Due Process. without an Uproar.
"I'll personally bring it to the bargaining table."
TheKing solemnly promises. convincing nobody but himself.
"YouKnow many things get dropped in bargaining."
Mousie speaks quietly.
I know. Collegiality is Sacred. Popular Academic Discourse.
Privileges only some.
often used to Marginalize. Minimize. Control.
Mouthy. TroubleMaking. Minorities.
many will acknowledge.
I find non-collegial Stick. too convenient a Weapon.
used to Bludgeon me into Submission.
if I challenge Mooniyâs Hegemony.

Pompous TheKing roars.
"an External Complaints Mechanism.
University won't hear of it. They'll walk away"
"let Them." I say.
I have been already victimized by infamous ProLow.
InternalComplaintsInquiry.
like Elephant. I am slow to Forget.
how my pain was Minimized. Denied. Objectified.
how ProLow's version of MyStory. OurStory.
was misUsed to Deny. my Rights.
"You cannot apply for reappointment."
was misUsed to cover up Discrimination.
Racial harassment.
Homophobic abuse.

"BadFaith clauses are standard.
OfCourse. it does not mean that They *will* retaliate.
if They don't believe Your complaints.
of Racism are justified."
TheKing unconvincingly argues.
I know better. I am ill. ToDay.
because TUNA retaliated against me.
ten years later. They *still* think. I am acting in BadFaith.

Believe it. or Not. it can get Worse.
when we refuse to agree. to BadFaith language.
as Reasonable. in ComplaintsMechanisms.
BadFaith is inserted. in proposed RetaliationClause.
They want Rights to Retaliate. If. we *allege*. They are Retaliating.
Now. If. I Surrender. there will be No RetaliationClause at all.

"it's TheBest we can do."
Sign.
Sign.
Sign.
Sign on TheDottedLine.
    I still wonder. is this how it feels to sign Treaties?

Finally. after Six years of Delays.
        One year of grueling *internal* processes.
        Four NUTS Lawyer changes.
            each of whom had to rehear MyStory.
                all over again. from Beginning to End.
        Two Arbitrators.
            One who resigned barely a week before opening arguments.
        Four months of PressureFilled.
                NonProgressive. NonSettlement. NonNegotiations.
                    held in my Absence. but. requiring my Consent.

TheDay Dawns.
I arrive in Anticipation.
        Fear tingling my Spine.
        Blood boiling. Close to surface of my red. Too Red Skin.
            Stroke level HighBloodPressure.
                remnant of Victimization. I come here to Remedy.

Restless. Sleepless. I arise. to meet Him. Hero.
        long anticipated. through years worth of Delays. Denial.
        He is Gray. Small. Lean.
            Smiles a wee Smile. Gives a warm Handshake.
            BlueEyes twinkle. "Finally! We meet." Hero says.
        Arbitrator may be Human. I gratefully muse.

No!We will not go ahead. Today. They Decide.
        We need more. More UnSettling. UnSettlement. talks.
I am Misled. to believe something New. Interesting. is being offered by TUNA.
        "Pressure has built." They say. "TheManagement will reOffer."
I am Fooled. Tricked. Hope once again. for TheImpossible.
        Soon I hear same Old. Same OldLies.
                another SOUP ploy to Conform. to get us to Settle for StatusQuo.
Sign.
Sign.
Sign.
Sign on TheDottedLine.
Long. Longer. Longest.

Tortuous Day transpires.
TheKing desperate to Settle.
     BOG will agree to Education of upper Administrators.
              Uncleverly disguise it. as Systemic Remedies.
They go on and on. On and On. They Go.

Finally. Badgerous˙ confronts.
   "You want to crash TheArbitration."
      Backs rise. Hackles up.
         Defensively They Deny. take Personal Offence.
            "We are Not Liars. OfCourse. We will go ahead!
            We just want. what is Best. for TheGrievor."
               They sing in chorus.
I think. I am Not fooled.
   Yet. against all Sanity. I retain a glimmer of Hope.
I speak NO!
No.
No.
No means No.
   I will Not sign.
      I do Not want. a Gag order.
      I do Not want. to satisfy a Desperate Desire for my Silence.
   Fear of my Voice. gave rise to TheGrievance.
      I will Not be. Battered. Frightened. Coerced. into Submission.
      I will Not be. Silenced.
I do Not want. to sign off All rights. to other forms of Action.
I do Not want. to be CoOpted.
I do Not support. your NonSystemic. Racist. Discriminatory. UnRemedies.
I will Never agree. to Less than a BandAid.
      on a Gaping. Oozing. PusRidden. Festering Wound.
I will not be AParty. to SOUP's Complicity.
      Covering for TheInstitution. renowned for its Revolving Door.
         Chews us up. Spits us out.
No.
No.
No.
No means No.
   I will Not sign.
   I know. What needs to happen for change to occur.
   I know. What has been Done to me. is being Done to many others.

We have proposed Reasonable remedies.
   through months' long NonNegotiations.
      where I am consistently Banned from TheTable.

No means No.
tiny FyreJean stands
Strong. asserts Voice.
No means No. in face of
Racist. Sexist.
Homophobic.
Institutional Violence.

where only StraightWhites are welcome.
to discuss Mere Allegations.
of Racist Homophobic Discrimination.
where all Real Remedies are given away.
by TheKing and NUTS.
only Empty Shells. remains.
TheKing goes on and on.
in his monotone ministerial drone.
continuing to convince only himself.
about my "BestInterests."

I begin to silently Slip. into a deep murky Mire.
of SelfLoathing. and Disgust.
am I Fated. to SellOut?
will I Sign? this NonSettlement.
to Escape. Flee. Ongoing Humiliation. Terror.
Intense. TensionFilled. DoubleBind.
Cage of Oppression. is being constructed around me.
How am I to Decide?
How can I Choose. from a select set of Bad Choices.

and remain True to self?
I bow my Shamed. Silenced Head.
a Sob erupts my strangled Throat.
TheKing drones on and on. On and On.
Irreverent. Irrespective. Disrespecting.
Ignoring my Needs. and Feelings. I am NoOne.
TheKing only stops. when LaLa calls him off.
"Enough. let her have Time to Think."
Until Tomorrow. I am told. take Night to Think. about it.

I Dream.
Flail Legs and Arms. Twist Blankets into a tight Ball.
I Scream. Jaws. Fists. Clenched.
"What part of No don't you understand?"
my now TongueLess self. Mouths.
to many Abusers. bending over me.
I am Trapped. Caged. Motionless.
They are poking me with Sharp Sticks.
trying to put things under my Skin.
in my Head.
in my Mouth.
I don't want it.
I Don't Want It!

I Awake. Sit up. GreenEyes wide open.
I wonder. Am I Weakening?
is my Spirit strong enough to withStand?
I remember Auntie Eva. Helen Betty. Papere. Ma.
Forty hours of labour for MyDaughter.
Four years of FourDayFasts.
I remind mySelf. I have withStood.
Strapping by MissionSchoolNuns.
Raping by WhiteMillBoys and Truckers.
Brainwashing. twenty-six years as Student.
SpinDoctoring. twenty years as Academic.
in Eurocentric. Patriarchal. Homophobic. systems.

Dreams. Ceremonies. Elders. Guides.
Give me Strength. Give me Answers.
AtThatTime. I am reading Paula Gunn Allen.
when my GreenEyes pop out.
"She has to be willing to forego pleasures when necessary and put
herself in whatever danger and inconvenience her spirit guides
require of her. She must be disciplined and committed enough to

follow the requirements of her path, regardless of the pain it causes her."[14]
I Smudge. lift SacredPipe. consult Ancestors.
> Guides teach: Never choose Greed.
>> Seek TheHighestGood for TheMost.
>> Truth must Speak your Voice.

Truth is. I can Never be. ultimately Clear. Who my Enemies are.
> When They hire me. They want me. want to be my Friends.
> When I speak Truth to Power. They want my Silence.

Truth is. I have Not changed who I am. They have changed their Minds.
> I am Dangerous. when I Challenge their agenda.
>> I Destabilize their status quo.

Truth is. University Administrators. Management. can Abuse us. Slur us.
> Strip our AcademicFreedom. Breach Human Rights.
> Let us Die in Poisoned Work Environments. Fire us.

Truth is. The.SoCalled.Union is Majoritarian. will Not defend our Rights.
> Grievances are a charade. Bureaucratic Maze. Get Lost!
>> Intended to Lull us. into a false sense of InSecurity.
>>> Delay us. into Inconsequentiality.
Now. I know. Truth Hurts. Nobody wants to Hear.[15]
I know. Be Aware of TheWeber[16] precedent.
Now. All UniversityWorkers. require their Union to seek Justice.
> to be Protected from Management's reign of Terror.
Commonsense ideology.
Unions are supposed to act. on behalf of All their Members.
Hegemonic public Discourse. I learn to Reject.
We have been Lied to. Again.
> Trickster opens my GreenEyes wide to Deception.

Finally. Morning Sun rises. PeachFlame above Horizon.
> I Think. I am ready. to hear and speak Truth.
> I Sit. hear Mannequin. open and close.
>> Open and Close. her MinorityMouth.
>>> She speaks shameless Word Webs.
>>> SpinDoctor. TheKing. creates.
> "WE do Not Think. it is in TheGrievor's BestInterests.
>> or in TheUnion's BestInterests. to go to Arbitration.
>> We want to Settle. We want You. to agree to This."
>>> I am told. I Am Told.
Sign.

Sign.
Sign.
Sign on TheDottedLine.
    I am told repeatedly.
        Over and Over again.
"do what We want. Or Else."
      is now no longer a Covert Threat.
        it is Overt. Painful. Visible.
            on TheTable for All to see.
No longer a *Conspiracy of Silence*.
I am being Blatantly Coerced. by TheKing. WhiteChristianPatriarch.
        in front of six female witnesses.
        including Mannequin.
            Oppressed. Co-opted.
            most Junior. Inexperienced.
            RacialMinority. Female. Lawyer.
            assigned by NUTS. Only two weeks ago.
        Now. She gives Voice to His.
            The.SoCalled.Union's. position.
I Remember. Only one year ago.
        TurnCoat. "Defender of AcademicFreedom for All."
            calmly re-assures me. Face to Face. at NUTS AGM.
            "We want ThisCase to go ahead.
            It. is Important. Precedent Setting Case.
            for All Aboriginal. Racial Minority.
            Academics. in Canada."

my Jaws clench. Pain ricochets through my Skull.
      TMJ. another Lifelong Legacy of abuse. suffered in TUNA's employ.
    We all sit MotionLess. exude our PowerLessNess.
        in face of TheKing's overwhelming Arrogance.
            till Badgerous jumps up. leaves Room.
            She does Not want to be AParty. to Treason.
            She does Not condone. Collusion.
Wolvereene shrieks out.
Fur stands up. all over her Back.
            "Cowards. All of You".
She questions TheKing's morality.
            "How Much is Your Cut?"
Her inquiry lands like a Thud.
        His face Blanches. Contorts.
We all Know. He is Desperate. to achieve his own Ends.
        He is visibly Shaken. but does Not back down.
        His Needs.Desires.are Greater than Mine.

are Greater than Natural Justice.
Due Process.
Fairness.
His institutional Power. is obviously Greater than Mine.

I am enraged to Tears. Again. left to Think. Again.
Finally. TongueLessNess subsides.
We Think. and Talk.
Badgerous suggests quietly.
"ask Him. What part of No Don't you understand?"
I stare at her through Fog. Mind flips back to Night's Dream.
I give Head a quick Shake.
I want. No Need to Know.
"how can I get rid of Him?"
Patronizing. Missionizing. Sermonizing.
Demonizing. Dreadful. Pompous. Disrespectful.
Deceitful. so called "Ally of mine."
We seek advice of Tigress. Queen of strategy. True Ally.
who Shares my circumstances.
who Cares about our SocialChange agenda.
"don't try to get rid of TheKing. Yet." She counsels.
"You do have 'reasonable apprehension of bias'.
ask for your own Representation. You have a Right.
They have a Duty. 'A Duty of Fair Representation'."
We craft MyLetter.
I ask for what I am Entitled.Denied.Deceived of.
"Fair Representation."
my Hopes are rekindled. Once More.
maybe I can have more than Mannequin.
fed her lines by a disHonest Traitor.

Hopelessness ebbs. only for short while.
OnceMore. Morning Dawns.
TheLetter arrives. delivered by Mannequin.
looking yellow under brown. BrownEyes Hollow.
Mouth expressing Sorrow. "I'm Sorry. how Things turned out."
I try to talk about Testimony.
I am still preparing. EveryMinute. EveryNight.
pondering over large Boxes.
stuffed with Bad. Bad memories.
I have Exhibits to add. to ThickBlackMultiTabbedEvidenceBinder.
"We are Not Arbitrating."
She shakes her Head. as she retreats.
"It. is in TheLetter."

I am Stunned. Hopes dashed. OnceMore.
    I have No Rights.
    I learn. in that moment. Sad.Sad. Truth.
        SoCalled.Unionized. labour has No Rights.
        beyond what Leadership decrees.
Thanks for Nothing. Weber.
All avenues are closed off.
    TUNA can Abuse me. Racially harass me.
      Confine my Family with their Homophobic edicts.
      Humiliate me. Dismiss me.
        Foolishly leave a Trail. Clear Evidence on Paper.
      Not just my Word against theirs.
        TUNA provided all Proof we could possibly need.
          in their own Documents.
Sad. Sad Truth is.
    I am truly TheGrievor.
    I Grieve. I can Not achieve any Justice. through SOUP or NUTS.
    I Grieve my Losses.
      TUNA took my Home. my Partner. my Livelihood.
        my Security. my Health. my Love of my profession.
    SOUP. NUTS. took my Hope for Justice.
      my Faith in Due Process.
my Cupboard is Bare.
    I can Cry and Rage. Write.
      but. I have No Political. Social. Economic. Legal. Recourse.
when Majoritarian. Eurocentric. Patriarchal. Homophobic.
    SoCalled.Union. leadership.
      denies me Standing. I have None.
"She is Not a Party" to TheGrievance.
    They. argue to Arbitrator. Hero. GrayHairedOne.
      Now. No twinkle in his steely BlueGreyEyes.
      Head tilts to one side. weighing arguments made carefully.
        repeating their assertions. as if he can't Believe his Ears.
You are de-"functus." They declare.
    "You have No Jurisdiction. TheArbitration is complete.
    Settlement has been achieved. by TheParties."
He. We are Told. over and over. Over and Over. again.
No.
No.
No.
No. I have Not signed.
No. I have Not agreed.
I am being Coerced.
    YesterDay. I wrote MyLetter. to TheParties. and Arbitrator.

"TheSettlement is Unconscionable. I require Representation."
I am advised to write. Legalese.

Too Bad. So Sad. Sad Truth. Grievors have No Rights.
ToDay. We are all done. I can Not argue for Party Status.
I can Not speak my experience of Coercion.
I can Not get Legal Representation.
They. TheParties. Collude to conclude. Settle. Without my say so.
No Signature required from me any more.
at least. this is a small relief. I momentarily wish. to myself.
Arbitrator says. "I must think about This. I will answer in a Week."

Finally. Long Agonizing Day is done. All prepare to leave.
I am Amazed. Dazed to hear. TheKing's voice drone on.
"If. you Need to Talk to Me. about Anything.
YouKnow. where to Find me."
Nightmare continues. I can Not wake up.
I cringe. Slump in Chair.
Head Down. as low as it can go.
Tears Rising. to fill my GreenEyes. Chest Hard with Pain.
Blood Pounding. from Temples to Toes. Stomach rock Hard.
reminiscent of years of Digestive Disorder.
Unnoticed. Unremedied.
throughout Abuses suffered at TUNA.
that brought me to ThisDay.
my SoCalled DayInCourt.
TheKing drones on to himself.
On and On. He drones. saving Face.
as if. As If. I care to hear his pitiful condolences.
As If. I would turn to him for support.
Wolvereene cuts him off. slices into his monologue.
lays clear Boundaries. Curses him.
"Go Suck Up Somewhere Else." She Snarls full Teeth bared.
in Shock. Silenced. TheKing retreats. at last.

I shut Down.
I can Not cope with him. or his Voice.
I feel Ashamed.
Ashamed. by Wolvereene's brawling tactics to Protect me.
I feel Ashamed. of myself for my Shame.
Ashamed. of my PowerLessNess. TongueLessNess.
I am sucked Dry.
I can Not believe. TheArbitration is Over.
No testimony. No cross-examination.

It. is Done. I am Numb. Struck Dumb.
Justice is de-functus!
I am Spinning into dark Void. Despair.
They will stop at Nothing. to vindicate their Authority.
Close doors to Unions. Nail coffins shut for Grievors.

from far.far. away. I faintly hear. High Pitched Voices.
mouthing Words. Shock. Surprise. Strategy.
Allies trying to decipher. "what to do? what to do next?"
I sit in Silence. Tears creep down my Finger covered Face.
Women run. get tissues. squeeze my Shoulders.
a Wail. rises up my Body. lodges in my Throat.
it is Not Safe to release Here. in land of StiffUpperLips.
even surrounded by Sympathizing. Mothering. WarriorWomen.
my Throat closes. Teeth clench. Neck aches.
I Disassociate. I am Lost in a Fog. I move In and Out.
WarriorWomen's Voices. Rise and Fall.
Criticize. Strategize. Sympathize. call others to Inform.
I try to Retreat. into small Space. Back. Black. of my Mind.
I try to make sense of Guide's advice.
"Seek TheHighestGood for TheMost."
in this moment I have Failed.
Fires of my Hopes. Desires for Justice.
have been Extinguished.
All Smoke and Ashes. Now.
I have lost TheBattle. how can this be TheHighestGood?
I want to Breathe Fire. like Pele. Melt All. in my Path.
I want to Rise Up. to Rant and Rave. Berate my Guides.
I can Not.
"As often as not, medicine women find themselves taking jobs for which
they feel unequipped or have little affinity—or even that they actively
dislike—because their medicine guides have instructed them to do so."
my Body will allow. only all consuming Grief.
I am truly TheGrievor.
Solitary. alone with magnitude of my Losses.
Loss of Hope. Loss of Trust.
Loss of Opportunity. to make a Decade of Pain.
Oppression. TongueLessNess
count for SomeThing.
Loss of Opportunity. to set clear Precedent.
to vindicate my Reality.
to change Inequities.
remediate Unjust systems.
to support Aboriginal

African-Canadian
Asian
Allies
Lesbian and Gay
Colleagues across Canada.
World.

Very Soon. Chatter begins to Irritate me.
I struggle to Unclench my Jaws.
        open my Aching Mouth.
        find my Lost Tongue. to Speak.
I feel. like I did. at my Papere's Funeral.
      while I Suffer. Deep Loss. my Life Changed.
      EveryoneElse. carrys on.
      almost as if. Nothing happened.
           Just one more Move. in an ongoing chess Game.
I find It. Intolerable.
      Finally. I manage to Croak.
      "Go elsewhere to Talk."
I want to Flee. this macabre Scene.
      there is Nothing left for me. Here.
      I feel too Vulnerable.
         afraid of continuing Abuse.
         afraid they still want me to Sign.
                     Sign.
                     Sign.
                     Sign on TheDottedLine.
I Must get away.
I am Grateful. I have Family to take me in.
         Friends to Console. Comfort. Commiserate.
I did Not lose my Soul. my Spirit is Intact.
I did Not sell out.
I preserve my Integrity. force them to Face their lack.
I sprang Trap of their Deceit.
I will Live on.
      See How I am Wounded.
        I am Limping. but. I am still Walking.

Battle continues.
      Frenzied submissions. of Legal positions. by all Parties.
        Seven copies of TheSettlement.
          I receive. by fax. mail. email. courier.
            with phone calls to confirm my receipt.
               Sign.
               Sign.

Sign.
Sign on TheDottedLine.
Pressure continues.
We await Word.
of our now Regression Setting. Arbitral decision.
can TheParties. make obvious to Arbitrator. to all present. their flagrant
Collusion?
can TheParties. fore-close. TheGrievor's rights?
can TheParties. fire Arbitrator. rather than respond.
to TheGrievor's plea. for Fair Representation?
can TheParties. overtly force upon TheGrievor.
an UnconscionableSettlement?
Twisting. Turning. ShapeShifting.
once PrecedentSettingGrievance turned Upside Down.
Arbitrator agrees. Hero is rendered "functus officio."
will Hero will lead us down. many Roads less Traveled?
Private Pro-Bono Litigation?
Human Rights Tribunals?
Supreme Court of Canada?
United Nations?
If. SoCalled.Unions. are Not required. do Not have a Duty.
do Not provide Fair Representation.
do Not take Instruction from TheGrievor.
WhatGood are They to Us?
If. soup and nuts. can de-"functus" Arbitrator.
eviscerate Grievance processes.
rather then Defend our Academic Rights.
WhatGood are They to Us?
How. can They be made to Represent? Us.
Represent needs of Dispossessed Members?
If. They can Not Represent Us.
WhatGood are They to Us?
How can They help Us?
when Fear. Loathing.
Oozes from Their Pores.
can be Smelt in every Breath.
Sad Truth is. Tough to Stomach.
Majoritarian. Eurocentric. Capitalistic. Patriarchal.
Hierarchical. Bureaucratic. SoCalled.Union. structures.
serve Themselves. Not me. Not me or MyKind.
deep-rooted Denial. Defensiveness. evidenced in recent Decisions.
are Visible. to All who Dare to Look.
Sad Truth is. soup and nuts. are No Friends.
No Allies to me.

They have shown their True Nature.
No Colour. Texture. Flavour. or Substance.
We. Me and my Allies. are WarriorWomen.
We seek Change. in these institutions. of so called Higher Learning.
We have been Abused. Demeaned. Desecrated.
by SoCalled.Unions. Management. Colleagues. Students.
No Thanks. to Hero. Arbitrator.
Now. SoCalled.Unions are Free. to Continue to Act On. Us.
Not For. or With. Us.
Now. I Grieve. False Promises of Allegiance.
False Promises of Support. to take ThisCase forward.
in the name of AcademicFreedom. for All members.
maybe winning OneRaceCase this year. [17]
is Good Enough for some.
but. I know. NUTS Abandonment.
leaves me Distressed. Devastated. Disillusioned.
how do I reconcile my Losses? reach deep into Spiritual realities.
"Each increment of power one gains along the path of power requires
sacrifice and exacts its toll of suffering and pain. In the universe of
power everything has its price."
OldOnes remind me. "Ya knew dey were Rattlesnake. when ya pick dem up."

Sacrifice
BuffaloNation.
made ultimate Sacrifice.
near Extinction.
once Free. now in Captivity.
they continue to Give. Forgive.
toDay.
like Neheyaw'ak people.
like me.

Forgiveness. Owwwr. easier Said. than Done.

being Raped. Silenced. Devalued. Objectified. Repressed. Oppressed.
　　Guilt. Anger. Grief. from deep Losses.
　　　　　can cloud what I Feel. See. Hear. Speak. Represent.
　　　　　Alienate. Isolate me. is a HeavyHeartBurden.
　　　　　　　　takes a toll on every aspect of my Being.
　　it takes more than Time. to work through Trauma.
　　　　　　　whether my Pain is caused by Cruelty. Neglect.
　　　　　　　lack of Respect.
　　　　　　　Ignorance. Arrogance.
　　　　　　　or even Fate.
　　to Heal. I must say my Truth.
　　　　not only my Regret and Pain.
　　　　　　what Harm is caused. what Anger. Disgust. I feel.
　what desire for Self-Punishment or Vengeance. is evoked in me.
　　　　　　Elders Teach. what Destroys. can only Destroy itself.
　　　　　　what Nurtures. will continue to Create.
　　　　　　Natural Law. Balance. will always Prevail.
　　　　　　　　over Time. Time and Time again.
Healing requires Release. and Forgiveness.
　　　"Owwwwrrrr. Not Forgiveness?" I say. "Anything but That!"
　　　Elders. Guides. Events. regularly Remind me.
　　　　　to remain Balanced. Responsive. Aware. is Required.
Imbalance can spell Disaster.
Not only to myself. to members of my Family. and Community.
Forgiveness of others. a slim possibility.
　　　　　only if we Love. Forgive our Self.
　If. Forgiveness has many Layers. many Seasons. many Choices.
　　　I can Choose. to continuously Forego.
　　　　　take a Vacation. Stop thinking about it. for Now.
　　　　　give Healing Balms. to my WoundedHeart. Self Care.
　I can Choose. to willfully Forbear.
　　　　　Stop talking Negatively. Stop acting out Hostility.
　　　　　Refrain from unnecessary Punishing. of Self. Others.
　　　　　strengthens Integrity of my Soul.
　I can Choose. to consciously Forget.
　　　　　Don't keep straining my Neck. looking Back.
　　　　　Look ahead. Look now.
　　　　　Create new Life. new experiences to think about.
　　　　　　　instead of old PainFull ones.
　I can Accept. LifeLessons.
　　　　　give up my resolve to Retaliate.

see Forgiveness as a GiveAway.
release Self. Others. from Imprisonment.
from Guilt. Anguish. Hurt. and Anger.
OnlyThen. I will not be Waiting. for AnyOne.
I will not be Wanting. AnyThing.
there will be no Snare. around my Ankle.
stretching from WayBackThere. to Here.
I will be Free. to move on.
to experience Happiness.
giving Love. and being Loved.
Acceptance. Forgiveness. easier Said than Done.
Begins and Continues. Never Finishes. is my LifeWork.

Notes

1. AtThatTime. I am keeping Journal. of my Experiences. I am Beginning. to systematically evolve *Circle Works (1998)* healing.teaching. model. some Words. Passages from relevant entries. woven in this Story. appear in *italics*.
2. thanks to Aretha Franklin.
3. *italics*. represent excerpts. from my Journalled Speech. to Students.
4. *italics*. represent responses from StudentJournals. resubmitted for research project.
5. OneStudent. gave me permission to publish this poem with an article. Some Time. after TheIncident. happened.
6. Larry Bird is quoted in Tedlock 1975: xxi.
7. I'm sure there are other examples. If. you want to find them. but. I am familiar with Beckwith and Jones.
8. TheFederalContractorsAgreement. a piece of legislation. enacted in 1994. requires CanadianGovernmentalInstitutions. including Universities. to implement. document. progress for EquitySeeking Groups.
    see Employment and Immigration Canada. 1994.
9. *Frank Magazine*. a political satire newspaper. somewhat akin to *The Enquirer*. on EastCoast of Canada.
10. Kalia. Mohanty. Ng. James. share their Experiences. Race Relations. within CanadianUniversities.
11. Mitchif term for stubborn. hardheaded. One.
12. written November 1, 2000. on plane ride Home. from NonArbitration. empowering to write my Anger. Days after being Abused. Not having to wait. thirty-five years. like I did with Helen Betty's Story. or No More. Some wish to Condemn me. for Still acting out my Anger. I take my clear.compelling. Narrative. of institutional Abuse. as evidence. progress in my Healing Journey..
13. Quote taken from final settlement offer by BOG (management). Things always get BOG ged down here.

14. I was reading. *Grandmothers of the Light: A Medicine Woman's Sourcebook* 1991 for solace and inspiration. relevant quotes are *italicized.*
15. This Story. a classic example. submitted to several journals. Law. Feminist. Cultural. HumanRights. Aboriginal. Sent to hundreds of EquityMinded individuals. asking for assistance to Publish. No success. Now. Four years later. One version appears in *American Indian Quarterly.* (Graveline 2004).
16. see Weber v. Ontario Hydro (1995), 125 D.L.R. (4th) 583 (S.C.C.).
17. see "All Ends Well for Dr. Chun." FrontPage. *CAUT Bulletin.* October 2000.

★ • Acronyms.Pseudonyms. can help us remember. Humor is part of all Aboriginal teaching.healing. TheKing is President of SOUP (SomeOrganizedUniversityPeople). Mousie refers to Grievance Chair at TUNA (TheUniversityNowAnonymous). for legally binding reasons.
• ProLow. Professor of Law. is Internal Investigator assigned by President of TUNA. when I "alleged" Discrimination. TUNA (TheUniversityNowAnonymous). refers to a University in Canada. my employer AtThatTime. something very fishy about that place.
• NUTS refers to National University Teachers Society. SOUP is SomeOrganizedUniversityPeople.
• Hero is Brain Bruise. Arbitrator.
• Badgerous is Grievance Officer. and Ally to TheEnd. It. is over. Now.
• LaLa is Professional Officer. for SOUP.
• Mannequin is FourthLawyer assigned for NUTS.
• TurnCoat is ExecutiveDirector of NUTS.
• Wolvereene is Ally. from my Community. AtThatTime.
• Tigress is Ally. AfricanCanadian Lawyer.

SPIRITS OPEN DOORWAYS. SPRING TRAPS. KNOW NO CAGES.

RedEagle WarriorWoman.
WarriorWoman stands Strong. knowing she can take Flight.
Helen Betty's Spirit soars like RedEagle. many WarriorWomen are lost in Battle.

ToDay. Nehiyâw'ak Traditional Teaching.Healing.
requires Words thoughtfully Spoken. Written.
SacredTeachings of OurAncestors. Our Elders.
    Once. deeply Sung in to our Souls in Ceremony.
    Now. Spoken from our academic Lips.
       flow from our ever critical Minds.
       enter Anonymous eyes from pages of Books.
    Now. Words. Sounds. are reduced to written symbols.
          stripped of Mystery. Magic.
    to Write is still Suspect in Traditional Communities.
        great Orators are still Respected.
I Write these Words. in alternative forms.
    to be a Spark.
    to Fuel your desires for Change.
    to Transform us. and our Lives. Together.
I offer Images. my efforts to Heal.Wounded.Hearts.
    to integrate Nehiyâw'ak.Mooniyâs. Teaching.Healing. practices.
    to inspire renaissance of Sacredness.
    to manifest our will to Resist. Dominant forms. Now.
Sacredness and Resistance.
    both integral to my Life.Work. as Healer.Teacher.
        re-inventing Eurocentric Terrains.
Nehiyâw'ak Peoples. have always Resisted.
    "it is natural to resist extermination, to survive." says Russell Means.
    Honour is owed to Ancestors.
    keep Traditions Strong. despite many Persecutions.
We will continue to Resist Acculturation. Assimilation. Extinction.
        in whatever forms. including written ones.
have you noticed? my ongoing Life.Work.
    Transforming contemporary challenges. by Invoking Nehiyâw'ak.Traditions?
are you Aware?
    I have taken Risks to Teach.Story.Tell.
    ways that Spirit transforms my Realities?
am I challenging you to Examine.
that which you have been taught to Ignore. Discount. Despise. Demonize?
    that which you have been Indoctrinated to Fear. your Known Reality.
    I See. People's Fear of Smudge. Talking Circle.
        Ceremonies. Dreams.
        MedicineStories.
I Know. Live. Fear. Persecution for our Spiritual Practices continues. Today.
    I Courageously continue.
    to enforce my Right. to Practise Traditional Teachings.
        on these Lands. on OurLands.

ENCOUNTERING ACADEMENTIA

DefenceDay is nearing. I lay in Bed. Tossing. Turning. This way and That. Wondering. "what Questions might They ask?" so many issues seem to be getting complicated. like. who is MyChair? Now. right before Defence. both coSupervisors say. "I am!" Then. TaskMaster is added as CommitteMember. at last minute. I haven't even written for Her.

I am worried. I know. and Fear institutional Power. I suspect. many possible BackLash tactics. I am Internalizing. Analyzing. all administrative ScrewUps. as potential Plots. to target me. for my already infamous political work.

I wonder. in dark of Night. "can They fail me? at this late date?" my battered self-esteem is going Wild. "will my work be GoodEnough? AcademicEnough?" I know. it will be tough to Defend. in a Eurocentric.Patriarchal. institution. known to be continuously marginalizing Nehiyâw'ak.Women. easy to feel Less Than.

Finally. I doze. into chaotic DreamLand. in wee hours of Dawn. I Dream. a lucid Dream. FullColour. each moment Eternity. I am aware of brilliant majestic PurpleWalls. hard polished gleam of solid OakTable. Oval. too large to move.

I see myself. Small and Strong. engaging in Conversation. No. it seems more like Debate. each in turn. like Circle. but Not. I Debate. a collection of Animal and Bird kin. seated around OakTable. Fox. Turkey. Donkey. Parrot. and others.

They each Speak. in their own Language. Cackling. Braying. Gobbling. Barking. Some. are long winded. Others. quite brief. to each I give consideration. a thoughtful response. although in Dream. I feel a barrage of Emotions. from Anger. to Sadness. to Hysterical Laughter. I remain Calm. and Focus. Respectful and Honouring. of each Bird or Animal. as they Speak. I am considerate of their concerns. in my response. Dream lasts. it seems for Hours.

Suddenly. I am Awake. I realize. as I eat. that many Questions swirl through my Mind. placed there by Creatures in my Dream. I am well taught by Elders. always Respect. Power of DreamTeachings. I quickly jot down. all Questions that are present for me. in that moment.

I go about my Day. Questions continue to play in my Mind. for next few Days. as they make themselves known. I rehearse my responses to each of them. I am certain. I am being assisted. in my preparations.

DefenceDay comes. I dress in my finest RibbonShirt. one sewed especially for TheEvent. by my Sister. SongInTheWind. GreenFloral. for

enCountering Academenita.
I had a Dream.
helped me Survive. Thrive.
during my thesis Defense.
taught me Truth.
about Academic rituals.
actors.
dramas.

my Growth and Prosperity. Ribboned with four Colours of four Races. Yellow. Red. Black. and White. Honouring contributers. and contributions my work can bring. to Healing of Humanity.

when we. my Family and I. enter Room as assigned. I immediately Notice. OakTable. One present in Dream. I wonder. "what does It. Mean? what does It. Represent?" Later. I process with FriendAllen. "OakTable is a sign of Conquest." He states. "All that is Manufactured. Altered. Reshaped. Unnatural. Defined to suit needs of Colonizer?" We know. Table was once a mighty living Oak. Winds blowing through her outstretched Arms. Now. She is a Tool. for Human use. locked inside a Box. all Day. like Us.

AtThatTime. I glance immediately around. thinking to see PurpleWalls. No! just institutional off-White. stares back at me. like Hospitals' White. Education is like Birth. I notice. it has become Sterilized. it'll be a BrightNewDay for Universities. when they embrace Vibrant Colour. as an asset to boardroom décor. I muse for a moment.

We immediately engage in SacredSmudge. to Cleanse ourselves. and Room. We claim our seats. Together. at one end of OakTable. nearest Door. Later. I find out. I was supposed to sit there. Alone. Not flanked by Family. DefenceChair. is supposed to sit beside me.

We ready TobaccoTies. carefully made from material matching my RibbonShirt. Each tied with Prayers. LastNight. a Giveaway for each Person. to Honour their Presence. at this Transitional event in my Life. as People gather. I greet one and all. with a Handshake. Hug. TobaccoTie. "Welcome. glad you could join us." a festive occasion indeed. a Ceremony.

Soon. We are nearing readiness to begin. SecurityGuard arrives.

"what's ThatSmell?" He wants to know. "there's no smoking allowed. in this building." He states strongly. I take Him outside Room. I speak to Him softly. "I am about to Defend my PhD. I am an Aboriginal.Woman. You smell SacredSmudge. Not cigarette Smoke. We're all done now. Too late now. We're about to begin. my Presentation."

His frown Deepens. Arms cross. my Mind is Racing. "I really don't Need this. Now." I think to myself. "If. you want. We can talk later." I add. Smiling Sweetly. relying on OldTactics. once WellUsed. We Can Talk Later I Say. Simultaneously. trying to buy Time. Humour Him. and conclude our conversation. as quickly as possible. "Well. Okay." He says. lumbering off.

on that note. I turn. and walk back into Room. ExternalExaminer is arriving. She is Nehiyâw'ak. and wants a Smudge. so I oblige. reLight SmudgeBowl. what can I do? I am defending a Thesis. on Traditional Spirituality. in University context. I have to be Courageous enough. to burn Smudge. when requested. I put SecurityGuard. Out of Mind. He is. Now. Out of Sight.

I sit. look around OakTable. a little Smile. creeps onto my Face. as Animals and Birds of my Dream. come to Life. as Supervisors. Faculty. Administrators. and others. "Focus. Calm. Respectful. Honouring." my Spirit Sings to me. in her HighPitchedVoice. I am Ready.

GreatestChallenge is presented. by MyOldChair. at first. I am a bit Surprised. and Angry. that he is Choosing to Confront me. Publicly. on issues we have hotly debated. Privately.

Well. that's not exactly True. Not exactly Privately. OneTime. We argue in Stairwell. in front of MyDaughter. and her classmates. "Russell Means is Not a Reliable Expert. He is not Academic." MyOldChair says. I am Livid. and give him a piece of my Mind. as he attempts to retreat up Stairwell. "what did He do? He musta been real. Real. Bad. He made you all Red." MoonChild comforts me. with her little Arms around my Neck. Later.

Anyways. when MyOldChair shakes his RedComb. waggly one. under his Chin. and Stares at me. with his BeadyBlackEyes. I can Not stay Angry with Him. for long.

"If. You really believe That. that Colonization is as Bad as all that. for Aboriginal People. Stripped People of Language. Culture. Community. Identity. as You theorize. then how can You also argue. that Tradition can be revitalized. in TheModernDay? how can You be Certain. that Anything is left. that is Traditional. that is not already Tainted by Colonization?" He asks. like he really wants to know. Head cocked to one side.

We have been over. and Over. this one. and have only come to DeadEnds. He. MyOldChair. holds true. to his unwavering Eurocentric commitment. to Dualities. really Believes it is an Either.Or. situation. Either. colonization is beneficial in assisting Nehiyâw'ak People. to become Civilized. Or. It. is an annihilation. of all that was Nehiyâw'ak.

"Turkey." I think. I am ready for you. this Time. I speak my analysis of Eurocentric World.Views. as Essentializing. critique his tendency to Historicize. and Totalize. Colonization. as if a completed process. and conclude my response with Story. One that strongly impacts. on my own Faith in Tradition. and Our Ancestors.

"OneTime. when I Lived in Mountains." I say. "I met a MedicineWoman. and had opportunity to attend Ceremony with her. after SweatLodge. as we Feast. I express my awe to her. 'I can't believe we have been in this Valley for same length of time. only a few months. and you are already fluent in Languages of Peoples here.' She looks at me with Surprise. 'No. I am Not.' She says between mouthfuls. 'Food always tastes sooo Good. after Lodge.' She says."

"'You're Not?' I say dumbfounded. 'but I am sure. Language you were Praying in. was Same as Elders were Praying in.' 'It is.' she says. Laughing at my Confusion. 'It's Simple.' She explains. Later. 'Spirits of Lands speak to me. Speak through me. Wherever I am. I speak. in Lodge. Language of Lands. Teachings of Lands.'"

"ThatDay." I continue. "I finish my meal in contemplative silence. I am keenly aware. I have been Gifted a fundamental Truth. You can kill People. or Brainwash Us in Schools. or ConcentrationCamps. called Reserves. but. as long as we are on OurLands. You can Not kill Spirits of Ancestors. They are always available to Teach. Pass on Lessons we need to Survive. Flourish. and Thrive in Traditional ways." I continue my Story.

"That. is how We. as a People. Survive colonizing tactics. and can still talk. even ToDay. in an age of postmodern fragmentation. of Aboriginal Identity." I educate Examiners. and Guests. at my Defence. "through Ceremony. Song. Stories. our Culture remains with us. as a source of Strength. We are connected to Spirits. of these Lands. and will continue to Thrive. for Generations to come."

"DominantSociety Tries. to Strip our Culture. Rob our Souls. what they don't realize. is Souls cannot be Robbed. there is Innate. Genetic. material. that can't be Damaged. it's passed down. and remains deep within us. We hold BloodMemory.Instinct.Wisdom. embedded deeply in Blood.Bones.Cells. of OurPeople. That's Why We Have Survived."

my Voice quietly speaks this Truth. in a Confident way.

I can feel presence of Ancestors. come to Witness. I feel Proud. that I am in this Place and Time. that I am given this Challenge. and Teachings I need to succeed at it. "Thank you Creator." I Pray. as I turn to listen Respectfully to next examiner.

We conclude. several hours later. I realize. No Question is asked. that I am unprepared for. even one by PhysicsProfessor. who was only asked to come at last minute. to represent TheUniversity. He had not even read my Work. when he asks about Metaphysics of Circle. I know what to answer. MedicineMan I am working with. gave me all I needed to know. Weeks before. AtThatTime. I am only listening to humour him. until we get to TheTopic. TheTopic I thought I went to see him for.

Weeks Later. I see MedicineMan. I speak to him of my Dream. and Metaphysics Question. and thank him for his help. He laughs real hard. as he loves to do. whenever he's given slightest opportunity to do so. He tells me. "I know. You were Bored. but. I told you anyway. because I know. you need to know. Hee Hee Hee." He chuckles. as he slaps his Knee. I laugh along. I still feel WarmGlow. from having sailed through DefenceDay with Flying Colours.

Glory for me. in final few minutes. as Examiners rest. and open Comments.Questions. to others who are present. Four Women speak up. to Honour my Words.Work. Each brings their own perspective. to OakTable. as participants in my Classroom. Research. or as Witness to events of that Morning.

EachWoman who speaks. is a member of a different cultural Community. Nehiyâw'ak. Asian. AfricanCanadian. Mooniyâs. Red. Yellow. Black. White. metaphorically reAffirms for me. my Life.Work. is being realized. in that moment in Time. I have been able to affect. and will continue to impact. on All Races of People. Rainbow Teachings are a Gift. I Honour in my Lodge.Life. ToDay.

It. is a glowing. perfect. peachy. moment. as DefenceDay concludes. We file out to await decision in hallway. Congratulations are loud and long. Nehiyâw'akWoman. Filmmaker. tells me. "Now. that was AnEvent. I wish I would have known in advance. I would have brought my camera. how you handled ThosePeople. and their Questions. I found myself getting soooo Angry. I would have brought out Bear. and Bit them. If. I was you. but. You were. Soooo Calm. Sooo Good. Sooo Brilliant. Sooo Aboriginal. So Certain in your beliefs. You are a Beautiful Example. of how Aboriginal People can Thrive. even in these situations. Do it OurWay. You didn't give them an inch. Not An Inch!"

as she raves. on and on. I beam Proudly. I Smile inside. and Glow
outside. I am confident. I have done well. Afterwards. I lay some Tobacco.
Thankful for Spiritual Assistance. I know. Ancestors support my Success.

Recovery From Chronic Neutral.itis. Research.itis. Rational.itis.

can you Notice? as a Nehiyâw'akScholar. TraditionalTeacher.
  I Story First. my Ancestors. my Roots.
      my Self. my Cultural.Locatedness.
          this Was. Is. Conscious. a Political Choice.
are you ready to Recover from Chronic Neutral.itis?
      Recognize Neutrality. as a Myth.
          OurSelves are ever present.
              like our Skin. can Not be removed.
              whether we notice it. or Not.
                  Others will.
      I do not Pretend. that I do not care. Objectivity.
          I Research.Teach.Write. with Passion.
              I become deeply Involved.
                  Because. I am Related.¹
can you See. how mySelf is Shaped. by Traditional Teachings.
          Influenced. by interactions with Western colonial realities.
          constantly Confined. by concrete social conditions.
IndividualExperience. and CollectiveHistory.
              is central to Research.Classrooms.Relationships.
              leads me to my Stories.Knowledge.
      MyVoice. MyStory is a Materialization.
          exernalizes my internal Beingness.
              EveryBeing. in my Universe Speaks.
      MyPeoples. have historically been Denied Voice.
          have had Voice.Stories. Appropriated.
First Voice. Only those who Are Nehiyâw'ak.
          can speak about Being Nehiyâw'ak.
          can understand with any Depth.
              our meanings within Nehiyâw'ak perspectives.
          can Speak.Write. Research.Teach.
              about Nehiyâw'akCulture. Oppression. SocialMovements.
I Challenge widely held Eurocentric Patriarchal notions. Hegemony.
      WhiteMaleExperts can Not. Should Not study Others.
      Not ultimately speak For. on behalf of Us.
              We know Findings vary. depend on Values Chosen.
          Processes. and Results. Empower and Enfranchise Some.

Disempower and Disenfranchise Others.
Research.Teaching.Writing. are Not Neutral.
are Political Acts.
this is how. We become ThosePeople.
Uncivilized. Vanishing.
Disadvantaged. Dispossessed.
Why? don't more White Researchers.Writers. Teachers.
Unlearn Expertism. Unveil Privilege. Rethink Racism.
Reveal White racial identity development.
Remember European roles in Global colonization.
Recast "the Imperial gaze."[2]
Recover from Research-itis. Look at YourSelf.
I am. as Cornel West names. a "prophetic critic."
I am. Unveiling Power Structures. Discovering alternatives.
in Circle Works. I ReSearch. Observe. my own Lived experience as an Educator.
in concert with Students.Community Participants.
I want to know.
what teaching practices. Enacted through my Model-In-Use.
contribute to what kinds of transformational learning? for whom?
I attempt to Reclaim curriculum. as We Live.Lived. it.
Test my Conceptual description. against Our Evidence.
Students' journalled experiences. and Participants' Circle Talk.[3]
as Mac tells it: "I wrote from the heart and only put down what I truly felt ...
to reflect my inner struggle with these issues and to convey it
honestly."
I wonder. as I read. pages and pages of Journals.
why do we Select some events. and Exclude others?
why do we Acknowledge some feelings. and Repress others?
I know. Written accounts can Distort.
Distance us from. our Lived experience.
I begin to question. how can I possibly produce. One.Analysis?
how can I Reduce twenty-five. delightfully diverse. self reflective monologues.
into One document. metaNarrative?
I envision a fluid pattern.
Medicine Wheel as Paradigm.[4]
Circular. Flowing. Integrative.
Honouring Interconnectedness of All.
Balancing. Mental. Spiritual. Emotional. Physical. Dimensions.
TalkingCircle. Ceremony. Adapted. Enacted.
becomes Teaching. Research Methodology.
ElderSarah reminds me.
"This is not the practice, taking notes ... in a setting like this."
other Traditional participants want to know.
how are Laws of MoonTime. Abstinence from Drugs and Alcohol

addressed?
> it would be unusual in Academic.Research settings.
> and may be perceived as Abusive. of Individual rights to Privacy
> > > to Even Ask.
> what about ingrained potential for Appropriation.
> > by members of White Culture. asks *Charlotte?*
> > *"It's very tempting to borrow wholesale from North American Earth*
> > *Based Tradition because its much more recent. It's much more*
> > *intact ... but it's not right."* she recognizes.
> > *Elder Sarah* worries. *"I'd like the dominant society to learn from this. but*
> > *I don't want them to exploit it or to do damage to it, or make fun*
> > *of it. That's my biggest fear."*

Soon. I sit. with Ten TalkingCircles Transcribed.
> Contradictions immediately begin to arise.
how do I transform this Data?
> collected through Subjective. Circular. CommunityBased processes.
> into Individualistic. Rational. Linearity. required by Academic minds?
Dorothy Smith's messages echo in my Mind.
> I do Not wish to maintain status quo.
> I do Not wish to use dominant categories or processes.
> > to Name. Analyze. Assemble. what Actually happens.
Mooniyâs cultural Norms. are Revealed to me.
> > through what they name Editing.[5]
I learn. am Chastized. Acculturated. made to follow.
> > certain CommonSense. Hegemonic Rules.

RuleOne. ANONYMITY OR OBJECTIVITY.
Strip all Speakers. of their Personal Identities.
> No GivenName. FamilyName. Community.
> > > TribalAffiliation. Geographic Roots.
> Eliminate all Personal Narrative.
No identification of Speakers leads to Objectification.
> deContextualizes Voices. deCollectivizes Individuals.
Naming is highly Personal and Political.
> when Renaming is required. to reconstruct meaningful exchange.
> I solicit selfSelected pseudonyms. to Empower participants.
Naming Oneself. Unicorn. Redbird. Misel. Sarah. Hattie. Zabet.
Names are chosen for Cultural. Familial. Historical. Spiritual. reasons.

RuleTwo. CATEGORIZATION.
when I create Categories. Confine subjective data to linear form.
> I Dissect Lives into relevant themes. Partialize Stories. Clip and Code.
> I deContextualize People. from their Life Narratives.
> > Eliminate much of potential importance.

when I exclude Personal information.
    Interrelationships. between those in Circle.
        Stories. that do not directly relate to Topic.
            Supportive talk. by some participants to others in Circle.
                certain CommunityBuilding terms.
                    You know. Right. Like (so and so) said.
I render Invisible. Undescribed.
    acts of CommunityBuilding. Healing dynamics of Circle.
why ignore socially mediated nature of knowledge. in Discovery of Facts?
like Columbus ignored Nehiyâw'ak relationship to Lands. in his Findings,
constructed in Telling. Facts are like Stories.
    They are Shaped. by purposes. audiences. for which they are Told.
    These MedicineStories. have been Edited. Shaped. to be Told.

RuleThree. BREVITY.
I am Told. "this quote is too Long. has too much Text to it.
    Break it up. comment on the Content.
    Theorize: what do You think. They mean?"
Create Bridges. it is called.
    I am Stunned.
in Circle Talk. when Speaker has StoryStone.
    They talk. as long as They want. make their Own Connections.
        between. Self and Others in Circle. Self and topic. Self and Communities.
my task is to Shrink Stories. Cut Stories.
    Cut huge chunks. of so-called Extraneous material.
as I struggle to Insert my own comments.
    I intrude into Other's Stories. Stumble in. without an Apology.
    I tell Others. what They are saying.
I become increasingly. Consciously. Aware.
    Editing. is a polite CodeWord.
    for Actions viewed Disrespectful. Unacceptable. in Traditional Circles.

RuleFour. READABILITY.
when I edit out.
    phrases such as. Sort of. Like. I guess. Of course.
        I think. I'd say. So to me. It seems.
I make Speakers. express more Authority. on a topic. than they might Feel.
when communicating Emerging realities. Not made into Words before.
    it is natural to Hesitate. to search for Right words.
how do I help convey? Unspeakable. Unmentionable. Unasked for actualities?
    introducing Holistic paradigms. Critical Consciousness.
        Challenges participants to New Awakenings.
            We can Not Expect Coherence.
If. in name of Clean text. I edit Out.

BlankSpaces. UnfinishedSentences. Ramblings. Acting Out.
I leave. only Ideas given Reportable status.
those Sanctioned and Enforced by Authorities.
I eliminate how Relationships are Built. with Ideas. Words. People.
how we make up. or change our Minds. Hearts.
how we Signal articulation of alternative knowledge.
All are left Unaccounted for.
Now. I have Written. Published. Themes. Stories.
I return to reSearch Patterns.
Old thoughts made New.
Tradition reMade in modern contexts.
I wonder. what written methods can be created?
to make Visible. Unspoken. Silent. communication?
as Thought forms. Travel among and around. those Communing in Circle.
Collective Consciousness Grows.
as Cal notes. *"There is a union without the words having been*
expressed. We don't have to respond to everything,
There is a degree of understanding."
how can this Understanding. be Qualified or Quantified?
how can I Qualify.Quantify. Story.
Healing benefits Produced. and Received.
by All members engaged in Traditional Methods?
by All who recover their Own First Voice?
by All who learn to truly Listen to Others in Oneness?
with Open Heartedness?
by All who Deepen their Connection to All that Is?
I have Grown. Know. Story.
Aboriginal Tradition can be Adapted Respectfully.
enacted in multiple contexts Cautiously.
Traditional forms have Complexities. Simplicity Is an Illusion.
Physical forms may be easily Comprehended.
Spiritual and other dimensions are Not.
a sense of Humour. is Required.
Wisakecahk. is Always ready to teach unwary ones.
I Creatively cope. recover from Rational.itis.
by maintaining Medicine Wheel as organizing frame.
I learn. and I would Heartfully recommend.
Data collected. by TalkingCircle as Methodology.
MedicineStories told.
are best left unEdited.unAnalyzed.unLinearized
Preserve content Intact. Circular.Flowing.Interconnected.
If. They want to know. "what does it all Mean?"
tell Them: Read between Lines.
Notice Light between Bars. in your Mental Cages.

Create Cracks. to slip through.
maybe AllKingsMen. won't put Humpty together again.
Remember. when you were an Egg.

COYOTE LAUGHS. WHEN SHE SEES SUCH A SIGHT

to Coyote. always an irreverent Witness. StoryTeller

OneDay. Not too long ago. Not too far away. Mahê'kun tinks. as Usual. dat she 'as sometin' to teach somebeing. So. she calls a Circle. wit some Wolves she feels could 'elp 'er teach. an' some Others she tinks 'ave a lot to learn. like me. Dat's da way she is. always tryin' to teach others. about her Nation.

Anywuss. GoodDay arrives. it's a bit blustery an' windy. Fall leaves are swirlin' round on ground. Ya can see. Some. are tryin' to vie for spots. to sit by Beings dey like bes'. lookin' round Circle dat Day. Ya can see. Some. 'ave shiny eyes. expectin' great learnin's. Some. like meSelf. are a bit bored. Some. are jis plain uncomfortable. We're shufflin' our Paws. an' pickin' our nits. as we wait to see what will 'appen.

Mahê'kun gets up wit her Cub. to open Circle. She welcomes everybeing. flashin' 'er long white Teeth to show friendship. I 'ad to chuckle to see. a few Circle members flinch at such a sight. Mahê'kun sniff real loud. enjoyin' crisp air. as she lights Smudge. with Embers from Sacred Fire. She circle real solemn like. stoppin' for each one of us to Smudge. dere we all are. actin' Real Holy.

All of a sudden. sometin' unexpected like 'appens. my YellowEyes jis about pop right outta my yellow 'Ead. Every Sight. Sound. Smell becomes instantly bigger dan Life. in dat moment. in Dat Moment...

Mahê'kun's Tail bursts into Flames. into Flames. Imagine dat! I ear sizzle. sounds of Fire cacklin'. den I Smell. unmistakable smell of Fur burnin'. like 'ow it smells in ForestFire. when we're all runnin' faster dan Wind. to get outta dere.

Anywuss. Flames jump up 'er bushy Tail. onto 'er Back. She coulda bin a gonner.

Fox an' I laugh later. "it remind me of Tails of my Ancestors." He howl wit glee. "Remember 'ow OldOnes tell. 'ow Fox steals Fire for 'umans. sticks 'is Tail in Flames. I wisht I could 'ave been dere to see for meSelf." 'E cackles real long an' loud.

Anywuss. Mahê'kun yelp purdy loud 'erself. an' spins round in a Circle. look as Crazy as Dog chasin' 'er Tail. didn' help nuttin. brings Wind to Flames.

Later. Mahê'kun is whinin' her version ta me. "I spin 'round to Cub. is Fire on her? No! it is me! my Fur ... my beautiful. grey. black. long. Fur. Fear races. Then. my 'Eart Stops. my 'Eart Stopped. I could've howled. I could've wailed. I could've cried. my Knees bucked. as I swoon towards ground." She howls real pitiful like.

AtThatTime. I jis couldn' believe my Eyes. or Nose. So. I takes a quick glance round at Others. Dey smell it too. Dere Noses'n'Beaks are all pointy'n'stiff like. Fear was in dere wide open wit surprise Eyes. I am thinkin'. EveryBeing is jis goin' to stampede right outta dere.

lucky for Mahê'kun. She 'ad Friends. Family dere. Dey jump up and rush over. an' save'er 'Ide. literally. Save'er 'Ide. Imagine. four of dem. Tiny. Grey. Timber. and Spotted.

All wit Paws'n'Tails spread wide. Pattin'. Soothin'. Clawin' out. Smotherin' Flames as dey shoot up Mahê'kun's long Fur. up 'er Back. Torchin' a strip right down middle of 'er Back. Right Down Middle of 'Er Back. an' Skunk wasn't even dere to see it.

da whole sight was hard to believe. but. it was real good to see my Cousins. dem Wolves. Workin' Together. Givin' Support. Leapin' to save Mahê'kun. Dey put down dem Flames wit dere own Paws. Risk der own Bodies. All as One. Together. dey put Mahê'kun's Fur out. Save 'er Skin. Save 'er Life. Dey save 'er Life!!! Right in franna me YellowEyes.

even Mahê'kun knows. She was howlin'. Later. to 'er Pack. and any.all. who will listen. "an' dat whole feelin' of Community. Dey saved my Life! it's dat Strong!!"

SpottedWolf. EveryBeing. is all amaze. "I don' speak for anyone else." She 'owls to me later. "I'm 'owlin' only for meSelf. from my own 'Eart. what amaze me about dat Day. was dat when I 'elp to put Fire out. Not only me. dere is others. when I run over. an' touch actual Fire to smother it. We. I walk away witout a mark on me Paws or Ears. or Tail. or anyting. Nuttin. Not Even. Not one flicker of pain atall. it jis sorta amaze me. 'ow we could all walk away from dere. witout a mark on us."

I know it's 'ard to believe. Believe me. I'm dere. I want to Laugh so bad. I could Piss meSelf. I am crossin' me Legs. back an' forth. Wigglin' round. ready to run like a crazy one. but. I tink. I'll wait round a bit longer.

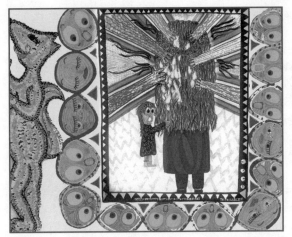

Coyote laughs.
Coyote is Trickster.
helps me Learn.Heal.
from challenging
experiences.
like this one.
LifeThreatening.
HairBurning. experience.

jis to see what will 'appen next.

I am glad I do. Cub. Mahê'kun's Cub. She gets a new Name. Now. StoneCub. stands. Ember carryin' stick still in her Paws. still as Stone. Silent. BlueGreenEyes wide wit Fear. Not even Breathin'. I hear she later whine. "I didn' know ... I didn'..." an' to GreyWolf she howl. "why didn' she growl at me? or bite me real 'ard. 'Er Fur is special to 'er".

even I. as 'eartless as I can be. 'ad to feel a little sad about dat. but. No time for Bleedin 'Earts round 'ere. I couldn' believe what my pointy Ears 'ear next. a Voice. Never did find out who's Voice it were. though some suspect Magpie. cause she can't keep nuttin to 'erself.

Anywuss. UnknownVoice says. like all full a awe. "I never seen anybody's Fur on Fire before." canya believe it? Dey says. "I never seen anybody's Fur on Fire before."

Ya could'a 'eard Acorn drop. a 'ush fell over everybeing in Circle. it was like 'ighCeremony. MaskDance. lots of Drama. "never a dull moment at Mahê'kun's Circles." We'll joke to each other. for a long long time to come.

Some. did wonder. Later. exackly what was she tryin' to teach us. dat Day. Imagine. Some. tought dat. tought it is part of Mahê'kun's plan. HaHa. Hooowrrlllhehhehheh.

Anywuss. dere I am. gettin' ready to rush out of dere. Agin. until I take one more look at Mahê'kun. She's pale an' shaky. look like she's goin' to lose her last meal. likely she wants to disappear down into a 'ole in ground. wishes she is like good ol' Mole. it's too good to miss. Mahê'kun is always dere. tryin' to teach me a ting or two. laughin' when tings don' go my way. which is often. of course. bein' who I am an'all.

den you could see TimberWolf take charge. She growl real gruff like. in Mahê'kun's Ears. guidin' her wit her Wisdom. "back to Smudge. back to Circle. We are 'ere wit you."

jis as quick as Mahê'kun goes to slump. Belly on Ground. 'Er SisterTimber grab 'er Back. wit her Paws an' Teeth. an' 'ols 'er up. Strong. Mahê'kun stares at 'er Sister in disbelief. jis for a moment. GreenEyes wide wit Fear. I can see White all round Green. I never seen no Wolf look dat Bad. before. den Mahê'kun shakes her 'ead back and fort. Quick. a few times. She must've shake it off. cause she straighten up. an' Timber let 'er go.

den. Mahê'kun motion StoneCub to front of 'er. sometin' she should've done before. If. she really value 'er Fur. I tink to meSelf. I already loss enough Fur to learn. Ya gotta keep an Eye. on dem RedHotCoals. They'll jump right off of dem Sticks. an' StoneCub was shakin' like a Leaf. 'oldin' 'ers out front. jis perch on da very end. of a tin bendin' down RedWillowStick.

but. I gotta give dem Wolves credit where credit is due. Dey carry on to complete Smudge an' Ceremony as plan. EveryBeing could see. dat Mahê'kun took teachins of OldOnes to 'eart. She show us. when ya start Ceremony. ya gotta carry on wit it. til it's done. No matter what. No Matter What. even if yer Ass is burnin' up. Harharharharhar.

OldWhiteWolf is dere too. She's always good for a good ol' Belly laugh. 'er wit is as sharp as 'er Teeth. but. what always gets me. is 'er advice. "Be yerself." She howls to us. "don't always be tryin' to change yerself. wanna be Taller. Shorter. Fatter. Tinner. Blacker. Whiter. Fluffier. Faster or Slower. Love yerself. Accept yerself for who ya are."

She tells us da ol Story of Wolverine cookin' BlackBear. cause 'e wants to be White. She is so 'ilarious. sittin' dere wit 'er Black as Black can be Coat. No sign'a 'er White Fur in sight. even Mahê'kun 'as to Smile. in spite of 'erself.

Me. I couldn't 'old it in for another minute. I start to Laugh. so 'ard. I 'ad to jump up. an' run into Woods. before I Piss meself. right den and dere. Too bad dough. I ear later. Dey 'ad a Roun' Dance. an' Feast. wit some real good Food. Duck Soup. after I leff.

TinyWolf stay right to end. tol' me all about tick Rabbit'n'Mouse stew later. "I couldn' believe it." she tol' me. "even after Cub torch Mahê'kun's Fur. Later. when Cub is tired from runnin' wit 'er friends in Woods. while Circle goes on'n'on. Mahê'kun cuddle 'er an' lick 'er Neck'n'Ears for whole Time. Stories. Drummin'. an' Roun' Dancin'."

"as Mahê'kun an' Cub sit dere togedder." TinyWolf tell me.

"EveryTime I look round Circle. an' see Dem cuddle up togedder. my Eyes fill right up to da brim. I don't tink I am such an old softy any more. jis goes to prove me wrong about meself." She howls softly almost to 'erself. I can see. She's still bein' all sentimental like.

Mahê'kun whines to 'erself. Later. I ear. when she gets Home. StoneCub tuck in Den. when she's all Alone. when she takes Twig to 'er Fur. Great Chunks of burnt to a cinder Fur. come wit Twiggin'. She drops to 'er Belly. an 'owls.

She 'owls to Us later. "I imagine meself Scruffy an' Bald. forever. why? what does It. Mean?" She whines to everybeing. Ya can tell she feels Real Sorry for 'erself. dat Night. Too Sorry to even go Out. an' 'owl at FullMoon. Now. dat's a Bad Case. iffin I ever 'ears one.

NextNight. TimberWolf an' some others are out howlin' till Dawn. howlin' da news to anyone who care to listen. "Mahê'kun is as Strong as GrandMotherStone. stands Strong wit 'er Pack. after Fire took 'er Fur. She stands Strong. carries On. We take care of our own."

Dey Howl on'n'on all dat night. Makin' us all tink about ourselves. Wonder. what 'appen to all'a'us sittin' in dat Circle. Ones who didn't jump to Mahê'kun's rescue? what 'appen dere? 'ow could we Watch. all google-eyed like? Not feel we 'ad to jump up an' do anytin'. We did nuttin. Nuttin'a'Tall.

I can understan' myself. Nobody ever done nuttin to 'elp me. I jis sit'n'stare. it's kinda amusin' after all. Well. Mebbe. I do feel a teeny bit bad. I musta. I find meself on me way to Mahê'kun's place. da very nex' Day. I surprise meself.

when I drop in. I'm kinda expectin' a crowd. Mahê'kun is by 'erself. lookin' pretty down an' out. "I fin' dis whole experience Confusin' and Alienatin'." Mahê'kun tol me. "Alienatin." I tink to meself. "Der she goes wit dem BigWords agin."

Anywuss. I am jis tryin to be Nice. but. ends up. I wanna get away as soon as I get dere. Jist den. Ol'WhiteWolf drop by. lucky for me. Mahê'kun jis carry on talkin'. "'ow could dey not notice my Fur on Fire? 'ow could dey? Mebbe. It. don' strike Beings strong enough. Dey don' bother Helpin' me. or even Talkin' to me about it?"

OlWhiteOne let 'er go on for a while. Den she says. "mebbe. dey were so shock at seein' you. Mahê'kun. Der Teacher. lookin' so drastic. Yer Fur all Flamin'. lookin' so Weak. an' Outta Control. dat dey don' know what to say?"

dat shut Mahê'kun up for a bit. jis as I was goin' to sneak out. get while da gettin' is good. BlackBear. who miss Circle. stop by to consol

Mahê'kun. "I'm sorry I wasn't at Circle. to help an' support you. I'm glad dat Others are dere for you. I curse ignorance of Some." She growl to me on da side. "I betcha it's Magpie." knowin' I love to Gossip.

"Yer Fur is lookin' pretty Shabby. I'm glad yer alive. I feel sorry for StoneCub. where is she? out playin'? Yer a good Mother. You know what to do. Yer Strong. You 'ave your Pack. I still Respect you. FyreMahê'kun. Teacher. I mean you as is." Bear gives Mahê'kun NewName. and a BigHug. as only Bears do.

GreyWolf arrive at Mahê'kun's Den next. wit an incredible six-foot long greenbrown intertwine overgrowed SeaWeed. She find it at LongLongBeach. I Love to scavenge. for dead'n'rottin' Fish an' Birds dere. MMMMMmmmm.

Anywuss. Grey give it to 'er Sister. Growlin'. "I'm not sure. why. dis Weed call to me on Beach. It. says. 'take me to Mahê'kun.' 'Ere. Yer new Fur. till it grows in."

FyreMahê'kun wipe stun look offa 'er Face. an' graciously accept' a green slimy One. I am glad dat I stuck round. cause Mahê'kun jump up. an offer us all some fresh Rabbit. dat she found at 'er denfront dat Dawn.

after eatin. I watch as Wolves work togedder. place SeaWeed. real careful over scorch Fur. It. cover Perfect. FyreMahê'kun growl at 'ow nice wet cool Weed. feel on her Back. "Ooorrrwwwlll. NiceMedicine." She appreciate It.

jis den. Crow flies in. after cawin' her compliments on da new Fur-do. She say. "I tink it's all very interestin'. fascinatin' even. an' for every Bein' dat was dere. dere's a differen' Story about what 'appen."

even dough Crow is tryin' to be nice'n'chatty to Mahê'kun. I tink I see Tears. springin' to Mahê'kun's GreenEyes. She brush dem away. as quick as dey come. She growls low in 'er Troat. "So. Everybein' Is talkin' about me. but Nobeing is talkin' To me. Not To Me."

Mahê'kun's Paws go up to cover her Eyes. "Oh no. 'Ere she goes agin. on 'er selfPity trip." I tink as I try to back my SkinnyLi'lCoyoteAss outta dere. as I sneak real quiet like outta Mahê'kun's Den. I can ear her go on'n'on. On'n'On. "it really makes me not want to teach 'ere any more. it make me scared to come outta my Den. I jis wanna cut meself off from everybein'. why am I puttin' meself out?"

"Mahê'kun's really goin' on and on." I tink. "Yeah. why is she puttin' 'erself out. Out to be so doll garn Important"? I can still ear 'er voice dronin' on outside. but. She's on a roll. an' is determine to carry right on. "it's real clear to me. Most. sit back an' watch other's bein' 'urt. Only a few. do sometin' to 'elp out. Only Wolves 'elp me."

even as I turn to run into da Forest. I still can ear 'er goin' on'n'on. Full of 'erself as usual. "All my 'ard work for others seems useless. We can't come Together. as One Community. Now. dis jis make it Worse. causes a big OpenWater between us. I'm really 'avin' a 'ard time." Mahê'kun whine. She is feelin' very very sorry for 'erself indeed. Me. I'm sick of it all. already. an' start to run faster.

I 'ad jis cut round BigSpruce. an' tink I am in a clear. den SnowyOwl. Ooo 'ad sat in silen' awe when Mahê'kun ketch on Fire. Swoop down. Wings wide. in a rush she begin to tell me 'er version. jis can't wait to get it off 'er puffy white Ches'. I guess. Funny. I never tought I'd see da Day dat Snowy would be tryin' to explain anythin' to me.

She 'oots. all fast like. like a Falcon chasin' a Rat. She's as determine to tell me. as I am to get away. "I jis sit dere. I like to tink dat. it's because dere were Wolves dere. dat jump right up. but. den when I say dat. I know. I'm tryin' to save face. Screeeeeech. to meself. let alone to youall." She says. I can see she's tought about nuttin else since it 'appen. She' bin hootin' round wit most of Others since Fire. I mean Circle. Owl gives a 'oot. Ararararar. an' I try to cut in. but. Owl wouldn't 'ave nona it. She jis carry right on.

"I don't know. If. it's a Split. wit 'er bein' Teacher. like she's Different. can't reach 'er. I'm very Uncomfortable. when it 'appen. I still don't know if dat is Fear. or what it is. Probably Not Fear. No. Not Fear. Owls are Not Afraid." She 'oots den. Real Loud. 'Er YellowEyes bulgin' out. real Wide an' Roun'.

"Hieee. why me? why do I getta listen to everybeing. ToDay?" I wonder. I yawn real wide. Show all my Teeth. I try to look real bored. hopin' dat Owl will get da hint. an' fly away. but. Nope. She goes on.

"I'm supposed to be Wise and Understand everything. an' I don't. I wonder if it's growin' up. where you're not really taught to feel. like when I grab Mouse to Eat. I don't stop to wonder 'ow he feels. I don't have to feel about 'im. like Mahê'kun. an' it make me look at my NestLife. an' in SlipperyHollow." Owl 'ardly take a Breath. an' carries right on. I start to slump down to da ground. fearin' I'll be 'ere All Night Long.

"LastNight. I fly over by Mahê'kun's Den. to drop her off a little sometin to eat. an' I 'ear Bear growlin' gruff like. tellin' Mahê'kun she 'as to come to Ceremony soon. Mahê'kun whine she feels a Alien.Ated. I am struck dumb by dis!" 'Oooots Owl.

"Struck Dumb." I tink to meself. "Owl's supposed Wise. what's a Alien.Ated?" I'm still wonderin'. but. I never gotta chance to ask. Cause. She's talkin' so fast'n'Furious like. "I couldn't believe dat Mahê'kun feels

Alien.Ated from Others in SlipperyHollow. den in almost da same instant I tink. Of Course she does! as a Teacher dere's a Separation. an' between. say WingedOnes and FourLeggeds. We 'ave different ideas of Belongin'. what a Surprise!! I 'ave no idea Mahê'kun is takin' it so 'ard."

Finally. Owl slow down. enough for me to stick me long Nose in. "Wellsireee." I growl. "why dontcha rush right over dere to see 'er. an' share yer Wisdom wit 'er. I'm sure she'll appreciate it. more dan I ever possibly could." I growl in my most sarcastic Voice. which of course is lost on Owl. She always takes tings literally.

Owl takes da bait. an' flies right over to hoot 'er tanks to Mahê'kun. swoopin' to catch another Rabbit on da way. I figure I'll sneak along an' overhear. jist in case she wants to share 'er Rabbit agin. Mahê'kun is surprise to ear what Owl 'as to 'oot. "Yer my teacher Owl." Mahê'kun 'owls. "You 'elp me to understand dis whole ting. I can see a big gap between me an' Other Bein's. mebbe. I've said an' done tings to make it dat way. I believe I belong wit ThePack. an' we should all 'elp each other. Not everyone is raised in Pack. No wonder I feel so bad about everytin'. and everybein'." Mahê'kun 'owl appreciatin' Owl.

I am kinda gettin' sick to me Belly. listenin' in on dem. I laugh when I tell Crow. "Mahê'kun sets 'erself apart tryin' to be a Teacher. tryin' to teach Others about what it's like to Live Right. as Wolf. If. she wants to fit in. mebbe she should learn to leave well enough alone." Of course. what I 'owl geta back to Mahê'kun. She is draggin' round for months after.

One Day. when I stop by. I ketch 'er nappin'. She jumps up like 'er Tail's on Fire. Jis Jokes. Ararararar. Mahê'kun starts in on me right away. "is dis Loss of Fur a Sign? a sign of some sort? should I give up strugglin' to bring Ceremony to SlipperyHollow?" She ast me like she really wants to know what I tink. can you believe it? So. I growl. "Yer askin' me. Coyote. You mus' be desperate or sometin'." I tell 'er. "Yer actin' jis like a 'uman. all worryin' about yer Fur. like its 'air or sometin'."

but. Dat didn't stop Mahê'kun. No. Not attall. Den. She tells me sometin' someother being might 'ave consider Strange. but. not me. Not L'il ol' Coyote. I'm use to stuff like dat. Dat's probly why she tell me. "I decide to stop burnin' Sweetgrass Smudge." Mahê'kun growls. droppin' 'er voice to a low growl.

I 'ad to listen up real close like. "Not that long after. Ol'LoneWolf wanders into Circle from nowhere. wonders out loud to no one in particular. as I burn some Lavender. "why would she burn a Smudge witout proper Medicines?" Ol'LoneWolf disappears. before I can get a

Word wit 'im." She whispers. "Now. I really don't know what to do".
I coulda felt all Proud. dat Mahê'kun is seekin' advice. from L'il ol'
Coyote me. I puff out me Furry Chest. takes a big Breath. an' growls in
me wises' Voice."Me neither. see ya later." I takes off outta dere real fast.
can ya believe it? askin' me. L'il ol' Coyote. for advice.

I 'ear later. She journeys far'n'wide to Camps of OldOnes. to find out
what It. means. "Dey talk of LongFurred ones." FyreMahê'kun tol' me.
"who believe dere magic Power is in der Fur. Only one Time. each Year.
Spring. do we shed Old. make way for New to come into our Lives. Some
lose der Fur for other reasons. mos'ly Illness. Imbalance. Grievin' for a loss.
or a Death of somebein' very significant. You can lose Fur in a Fight.
someBein' Countin' Coup."[6]

I guess. Mahê'kun learn sometin' tru 'er experience. She's like me.
We 'ave to learn to accept dat Fire likes Fur. as FireKeeper for Bear's
Lodge. Now. I see 'er offerin' a bit of Fur wit 'er Tobacco. each Fire.
Good thinkin'. Cause Fire will take some on 'er own.

Ya know. Names are very very Powerful. OurAncestors. teach us in
Unexpected ways. taught Mahê'kun 'ow to really Live her new Name.

but. Stories never end. dey go on an' on. changin' all along. a long
Time Later. Me an' Mahê'kun are visitin' a MedicineWolf. Mahê'kun's
in midst of a bunch a Trouble agin. She gets told. "You must still be
doin' pretty darn good. I see you still 'ave yer long Fur." I didn't know
'ow she's gonna take it. I'm Surprise. Mahê'kun 'owl in Glee. at 'is
comment.

She tells me. Later. She remember jis for a moment. long ago an' far
away. when 'er Fur burn off. Some lessons take a Lifetime to understan'.
dere are no easy answers. She may be a Teacher. but. FyreMahê'kun is
still learnin'. aren't we all. I 'ope yer ears are open. an' yer learnin'
sometin'.

Notes

1. Feminist researchers. like Raymond. Lather. Smith. Acker, Barry and
    Esseveld. Tomm. Harding. Brookes. are my Guides. to passionate. subjec-
    tive. grounded. Research.
2. Whiteness has been researched. by a few. like Hall. and Jay. (on recognizing
    Whiteness). Sleeter. (on racism). Said 1993. and Blaut. (on global coloniza-
    tion). Razak. (on "the Imperial Gaze").
3. Students' journal excerpts. and Circle Talk participants' words. are *italicized*.
    appeared in *Circle Works*.
4. Paradigms. are beliefs that Guide. our Research choices. see Guba.

5. Some. Nehiyâw'ak peoples. address contradictions in transforming oral to written. including Murray and Rice.
6. In early days of Tribal Warfare. rather than killing opponents. Coup was taken. a lock of Hair was removed. by successful Warrior. to signify Victory. Tragically. this relatively harmless custom. was brutally transformed. into Scalping of millions of Nehiyâw'ak men.women.children. see Dan Paul's (2000) discussion in EasternTribes. for one example.

COMPLETING THIS CIRCLE.
TRADITION HEALS. WOUNDEDHEARTS.

Healing me.
hopeful Vision. my Recovery. past Pains illuminated as Strengths.
Creator's image reflected. in calmness of SunSet on River.

I learn. I know. I desire. to surround myself with Nehiyâw'ak colleagues.
    in contexts designed for Nehiyâw'ak Teachers and learners.
                                                    They now exist.
    Now. I tell Stories of Building. Educational Spaces.
        where Teachers are Expected to be Traditional.
        where Colleagues and Administrators.
                        support Nehiyâw'ak Teachings.
        where Students are told.
            "if you don't want to Smudge. do Ceremony.
            or learn Traditional ways. go to another School."
Traditional Ways are Required.
        for Recovery of Cultural Pride.
        for Healing Wounded Hearts.
OurPeoples experience Theft of SacredLands
                early Childhood Separation through ResidentialSchools.
                Loss of Family members through violent early Deaths.
                daily denigration of Pride. and Dignity as Persons.
                appropriation of Language. and Cultural practices.
                Ongoing acts of Ethnocide. Genocide.
                        result in breakdown of Traditional Strengths.
        Recovery requires Healthy Individuals.
                    Supportive Extended Families.
                    Cohesive Communities.
                    Strong Proud Nations.
recent HealthTransferAgreements
        means Nehiyâw'ak Communities.
            are expected to take more and more Responsibility.
            for Care.WellBeing. of our own Members.
Teachers.Healers. those working within Nehiyâw'ak Communities.
        are facing serious multi-generational patterns of Distress.
        are having unrealistic Expectations placed on us.
            need more training. more backup.
            need Healing. for our own issues. in order to help others.
HealingWoundedHearts requires Daring thoughts.
                Challenging what we Know.
                what we Thought we Knew.
                what we Need to Know.
                        to face Dawning of a NewDay.
                requires Living. Working to revitalize Spirit.
                EveryDay. EveryPlace.
                requires Bridging OldWays. and New Challenges.
                requires Being Open to change. withIn and withOut.
                        a change of Heart.
                        a change of Form.

requires Heart. Courage. Commitment.
Belief. Intuitive Understanding.
Involves a total Person. in their Deepest sense.
to be a Healer. we SelfActualize ourselves.
Fulfil our human Potentials.
EnLiven our Creative spirits.
Find our personal Meaning. Power. Medicine.
Healing myself. is a prerequisite to Helping Others.
Be. a positive RoleModel.
Demonstrate. Commitment to ongoing SelfCare.
"Only by looking inward and Healing ourselves first can we ever
have the strength and understanding to slowly reach out to others
and share in their Healing and growth." says Ester Supernault.
Healers' openness to change. is necessary to Healing Others.
Valuing. Respecting Others. is vital.
Ask. what do I Feel in my Heart?
what is Right for me?
NoOne can decide what is Right for another being.
We each Experience. Learn. what we need to Know.
what we are Open to. depends on our Life path.
We reach Completeness. Trusting our Natural Instincts.
We Heal. Recognizing. Honouring. Teachings of Spirit with.in. of.
Natural Worlds.
how can we HealWoundedHearts?
Participate in Ceremony.
establish a Spiritual Connection.
establish a Connection with Nature.
anchor self in Tradition.
Establish healthy social Connections.
express Emotion.
obtain Support from others.
learn from a RoleModel.
be a RoleModel.
help others.
Self-Care.
Create. Art.
get involved in Challenging activities.
gain an understanding of our Patterns.
Healing individuals requires Supports.
Family. Community. Nation.
challenge Unhealthy systems.
create Positive environments.
on Healing.Journeys. We can find OurSelves.
Separate from an unhealthy Life.

when we recognize we are Hurting ourSelves. Others.
Obtain social Supports. Services. to sustain new Lives.
Begin to experience a Healthy Life. sometimes. seems harder than Old Life.
Grow to enjoy living a Healthy Life. on an everyDay basis.
Experience Success. reOccurring.
Emphasize Strengths.
re-Educate Self.
Story Survival. Growth. Change.
Life changing. is bigger than one Life. We Change our Lives Together.
We need Support to take these essential steps.
to heal Self and assist Others.
HealingWoundedHearts.
Planted like a Seed.
Nurtured.Cultivated. through Relationship.
until we bear Fruit.
We can Not build and grow Healthy Hearts. Healers.
Healthy Communities.
on our own.
Our Elders say. more Voices give same Messages. Repetition.
one MedicineStory will emPower. Somebody.
another MedicineStory will Inspire. Somebody else.
We can Heal through Story.
I Story. daily Lived experiences for others to learn.
Elders value Oral Tradition. to recreate situations.
to help someone Live through Life's challenges.
for others to benefit Directly. from my.our. experiences.
Sharing our Stories in Circle.
Intensifies our Connections to our Authentic selves.
to others who can Support us.
in Circle. We speak our Truths.
Words shoot like Flames. out of our Mouths.
Jump as if from their own will. out into Universe.
Deeply felt emotional declarations.
Vibrate as Drum Beats within.
Pierce complacency.
Create Openings. Doorways. Pathways. for change.
Tears shed. Laughter shared.
Powerful feelings are a Gift.
We need to Feel. Connect to others.
Friendship. Family. Community.
OurElders teach. We are all In-Relation. All of Creation.
Beings thrive. when there is a Web of Interrelatedness.
between Individual. Community. Mother Earth.
become ReEnchanted with EarthMother.

embrace Environmental Traditions in our Lives.[2]
through TraditionalTeachings. Ceremonies.
We learn.teach. about ReBuilding Relationships.
with All Beings.
within diverse Communities.
Lessons can be learned from past History. present Struggles. future Visions.
from Elders. MedicinePeople. CeremonialLeaders.
Ceremony teaches.heals. us.
Be. in Touch. with our Human Powers. our Senses.
our Gifts to See. Hear. Smell. Taste. Touch.
We Heal. with our entire Bodies.
Not only with our Minds. or Hearts.
Ceremony. Meditation. Dreaming.
Smudge. Circle. Feasting.
Crystals. Feathers. Herbs.
Drumming. Singing. Dancing.
Art. Drama. Poetry. Story.
Externalize inner Thoughts. reach for deeper Understandings.
HealingWoundedHearts requires.
revitalizing. Nehiyâw'ak holistic World.Views.
identifying.mediating. impacts of oppressive socio-political circumstances.
being open. to multiple ways of knowing within Aboriginal contexts.
Healing requires us to take up personal change.
and socio-cultural revitalization.
in any and all contexts.
EveryDay actions of Healthy Individuals.
will contribute to Socio-Political Strength.
Self-determination and Self-government.
Healing our Selves. Families. Communities.
requires welcoming our WarriorSpirits.
"A warrior is the fighting part of our spirit
and the connected part of our soul." says Ester Supernault.
Remember Eva. Mahê'kun. Fyre.
Living Traditional Life. Teaches us.
True learning. gaining significant knowledge.
does not come without Sacrifice. DeepWounds.
my Woundedness can symbolize something deeply important.
what I Know and Understand. Now.
my Tears.Scars. are a Powerful Doorway.
Open me to Renewal. Insight. Growth.
I Learn. from my Tears.Scars.
Lessons about Life. about who I am.
inRelation to Family. Communities. Students. Colleagues. Authorities.
Lessons about my professorial Authority.

my Nehiyâw'ak identity.
my Woman's responsibilities.
   for Personal. Community. Global. Healing.

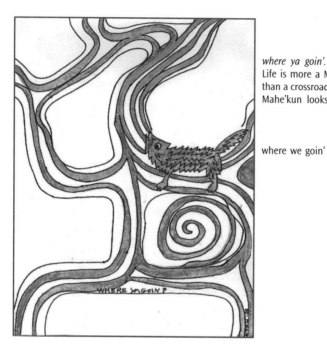

where ya goin'.
Life is more a Maze.
than a crossroads.
Mahe'kun looks Ahead.
          Behind.
          Side to Side.
          Round. and Round.
where we goin' to?

So. Whe're We Goin' to?

So. it's a New Millennium. So what?
   Time to reflect. "where're we goin' to?"
          OldOnes Know.
   I know. where I'm comin' from.
   MedicineStories Tell All. All I want to Tell.
          for Now that is.
   Now. I want to know. "where're we Goin' to?
      how can we Imagine. Equity Issues.
          Sexism. Racism. Classism. Heterosexism. Eurocentrism.
          looking Forward to another Thousand Years?
I Wonder.
      given rapid rates of Decline.
          conditions we Exist. Together. Today. on Earth Mother.
      given Hopi Prophesies. Earth Changes.[3] are currently unfolding.
      given pace of Technological Advancement.

especially "apocalyptic potential of technology."[4]
grinding machines of IndustrialCapitalism.
   consuming Forests. Oceans. Mountains.
            Birds. Animals. Humans.
            All Living Beings. reduced to Dollars.
I Wonder.
   do we have another Thousand years?
   do we have another Hundred?
       another Decade?
   can we establish Equitable Relations for Humans?
   what about Equity for All our Brothers and Sisters?
       TreeNations. Flyers. Swimmers. Crawlers.
       FourLeggeds. StonePeople. StarNations.
       GrandMotherMoon. GrandFatherSun.
       Other Relatives. Known. and Unknown. in Universe.
   how do we Respectfully Include. AllOurRelations.
       in our Visions for New Millenniums?
Our Journey is long. hard to recover from 500 years of Colonization.
   unabated forces of multinational Capitalism.
   fueled by Eurocentric ideologies. Rationalism. Materialism. Mechanism.
       wreak havoc upon. All Neeheyah'wak Peoples.
       All Beings of OurWorlds.
   We spiral towards Genocide. in most Indigenous Cultures.
               in Humanity as a whole.
       this deplorable state can only be remedied.
           by Peoples who are willing to Listen. and Hear.
               Diverse views of history.
               Visions of new realities.
   can we find Spaces. and Places.
   quiet Machines. and Minds.
       seek Visions of impossibly possible.
           Worlds in which all Beings.
           All Peoples are Respected.
               Valued for their contributions?
If. Human Existence is to continue.
       it will require all HumanBeings.
       to become more Attuned.
           Pay Attention.
           Be Aware.
           Notice our interRelationships.
               with each other. and EarthMother.
               can your Ears listen now?
               can you quiet your Mind.
                       and listen now?

We look to our Ancestors for Strength.
        for in our present. We see OurPeoples perishing.
        don't get Caught up. Bogged down. Beat up. by Day to Day.
We can look towards Futures. Vow to make it Better.
        for our Children. GrandChildren. GreatGreatGrandChildren.
how do we regain Power of Visioning?
    Vision is essential to Survival in these Systems.
    what is your Life.Work. Vision. Heart.Work.
        your connection to EarthMother?
    do you take Time to Vision?
        Go out on Earth. spend Time. maybe Days. wait to Hear.
        a Message will Guide you. lead you to your future Path.
        Gift you certain Knowingness. You are on TheRightPath. a GoodPath.
Vision. Transform.
    Actively create more potent Lives. for ourSelves.
                for All OurRelations.
through Visioning we can tap into Strengths.
    Traditions of our Ancestors. Energy of our Earth Mother.
are you ready. to seek Vision?
    Feel your straight Spine.
        like our Sister Tree.
        Roots growing down to Earth.
        Boughs reaching up to Sky.
    let Energy of all Dimensions. Flow through you.
        Ask to be Informed. Inspired. Connected. Moved.
        Ask what you might Do.
        Ask to be put to Good Use.
Visioning in Lodge.
    I listen. ThunderSpirit Voice. Feeds my Soul.
        "place your Struggles in context.
            EarthChanges are happening. Now!
            You are Awake. Aware. Alive.
                Healthy. Well fed.
      that is more than can be said.
        for most Brothers. Sisters.
                    Think again.
                    Think Gratitude."
Thank you Creator.
    for Gift of ThisDay.
    for Gift of Life.
    for Gift of Spirit.
        Spirit of Resistance.
Thank you Creator.
    for Nourishing me.

Nourishing Desire.
Desire to Revitalize Tradition.
in modern contexts.
Thank you Creator.
for Feeding me.
Body and Soul.
Feeding me what I need to Know.
what I need to Do.
to remain Strong.
Committed to Life.
Thank you for bringing Light. Love. Prosperity.
into my Life.
my Home.
on EarthMother.
let us Vision. Together.
what can we do?
to create a more Hopeful future. a Meaningful future.
where all Communities. Nations.
are able to participate. influence major decisions.
where Respect. Integrity for cultural belief systems.
are Promoted. Enhanced.
a revolutionized world will come in a Circular way.
Honouring. All Beings. All Dimensions. All Realities.
Ceremony Teaches. Personal Responsibility.
Gives. Strength required to be Warriors.
Helps us. to work with Others. to actualize Visions.
to change Oppressive Systems.
EveryBeing. must Contribute what they are Able. can make a Difference.
let us enVision
New Millenniums.
without Fear. without Cages.
Megwetch.

Notes

1. People like Supernault. Absolon. Morrisseau. McCormick. Hart. Wastasecoot. understand.write.teach. Nehiyâw'ak Counselling practices.
2. enjoy work of Gregory Cajete. on ecology. science. and Tradition.
3. global warming. greenhouse effect. and other global climate changes. all effect all life on Earth Mother. see Wyman.
4. like nuclear catastrophe. at Chernobyl. for example. see Kaiser.

If You Want to Know. Who I Read. Read This.

Absolon, Kathy. 1994. "Building Health from the Medicine Wheel: Aboriginal Program Development." Paper presented at Native Physicians Association Meeting, Winnipeg, Manitoba. March 6–8.

Acker, Joan, Kate Barry and Joke Esseveld. 1983. "Objectivity and Truth: Problems in Doing Feminist Research." *Women's Studies International Forum* 6(4): 423–35.

Acoose, Janice. 1995. *Iskwewak-Kah' Ki Yaw Ni Wahkomakanak: Neither Indian Princesses Nor Easy Squaws.* Toronto: Women's Press.

Adams, Howard. 1989. *Prison of Grass: Canada from a Native Point of View.* Saskatoon: Fifth House.

Aglukark, Susan. 1995. "Suffer in Silence." On *This Child* CD. EMI Music Canada.

Ahanekew, Freda. Brenda Gardipy and Barbara Lafond. 1995. *Voices of First Nations.* Toronto: McGraw-Hill Ryerson.

Alberta Report. Jan 11, 1988: (35).

Alladin, M. Ibrahim. 1996. *Racism in Canadian Schools.* Toronto: Harcourt Brace and Company.

Anderson, Kim. 2000. *A Recognition of Being: Reconstructing Native Womanhood.* Toronto: Second Story Press.

Armstrong, Jeannette. 1999. *Whispering Shadows.* Penticton, BC: Theytus.

_____. 1990. "The Disempowerment of First North American Native Peoples and Empowerment through Their Writing. *Gatherings:The En'owkin Journal of First North American People* 1(Fall): 141–46.

_____. 1990. "Real Power: Aboriginal Women—Past, Present and Future." *The Phoenix* (Summer): 4–7.

_____. 1988. *Slash.* Penticton, BC: Theytus.

_____. 1987. "Traditional Indigenous Education: A Natural Process." *Canadian Journal of Native Education* 14(3): 14–19.

Baker, Annharte. 1990. *Being on the Moon.* Winlaw, BC: Polestar Press.

Banks, James. 1997. *Multicultural Education.* Toronto: Allyn and Bacon.

Baptiste, Ian. 2000. Opening General Session: "Setting Agendas for the 21st Century: Regional Perspectives on Research Priorities." AERC 41st Annual Adult Education Research Conference, June 2–4, Vancouver, BC.

Barkwell, Lawrence. 2001. *Métis Legacy: A Métis Historiography and Annotated Bibliography.* Winnipeg: Pemmican Publications.

Barman, Jean, Yvonne Hebert and Don McCaskill, eds. 1986. *Indian Education in Canada, Volume 1: The Legacy.* Vancouver: University of British Columbia Press.

Barreiro, Jose. 1992. *Indian Roots of American Democracy.* Cornell University: Akwe:kon Press.

Battiste, Marie. 2000. *Reclaiming Indigenous Voice and Vision.* Vancouver: UBC Press.

Battiste, Marie, and Jean Barman. 1995. *First Nations Education in Canada: The Circle Unfolds.* Vancouver: University of British Columbia Press.

Beck, Peggy, and A.L. Walters. 1977. *The Sacred.* Tsaile, AZ: Navajo Community College.

Beckwith, Francis, and Todd Jones. 1997. *Affirmative Action: Social Justice or Reverse Discrimination?* Amherst, NY: Prometheus Books.

Begun, Patricia. 1994. *Child Sexual Abuse: The Recovered Memory/False Memory Debate.* Ottawa: Library of Parliament Research Branch.

Beider, Robert. 1996. "The Representation of Indian Bodies in Nineteenth-Century American Anthropology." *American Indian Quarterly.* 20(2): 165–179.

Blaut, James. 1993. *The Colonizers' Model of the World.* New York: Guilford.

Bouvier, Rita. 2001. *Resting Lightly on Mother Earth: The Aboriginal Experience in Urban Educational Settings.* Calgary: Detselig Enterprises.

Boyd, Loree. 1996. *Spirit Moves: The Story of Six Generations of Native Women.* Novato, CA: New World Library.

Brandon Sun, March 19, 2002: B5; December 17, 2002: A5; March 13, 2002: A2.

Brant, Beth. 1995. *Writing As Witness.* Toronto: Women's Press.

_____. 1994. *A Gathering of Spirit: A Collection by North American Indian Women.* Toronto: Women's Press.

Brecher, Jeremy, and Tim Costello. 1994. *Global Village or Global Pillage: Economic Reconstruction from the Bottom Up.* Boston, MA: South End Press.

Bright, William. 1993. *A Coyote Reader.* Berkley: University of California Press.

Broden, Adrienne, and Steve Coyote. 1991. "Sacred Herbs: The Smudging Ceremony." *Native Friendship Centre of Montreal Newsletter.* January.

Brookes, Anne Louise. 1992. *Feminist Pedagogy: An Autobiographical Approach.* Halifax: Fernwood.

Brown, Jennifer. 1983. "Women as Centre and Symbol in the Emergence of Métis Communities." *Canadian Journal of Native Studies.* 3(1): 39–46.

Bruchac, Joseph. 1993. *The Native American Sweat Lodge: History and Legends.* Freedom, CA: Crossing Press.

Bussidor, Ila, and Ustun Bilgen-Reinart. 1997. *Night Spirits: The Story of the Relocation of the Sayisi Dene.* Winnipeg: The University of Manitoba Press.

Callan, Dawn. 1995. *Awakening the Warrior Within.* Novato, CA: Nataraj.

Cajete, Gregory. 2000. *Native Science.* Santa Fe, NM: Clear Light.

_____. 1997. *Look to the Mountain: An Ecology of Indigenous Education.* Skyland, NC: Kivaki.

Campbell, Maria. 1995. *Stories of Road Allowance People.* Penticton, BC: Theytus.

_____. 1973. *Halfbreed.* Halifax: GoodRead Biographies.

Canada, Government of. 1996. *Looking Forward, Looking Back. Royal Commission on Aboriginal Peoples.* Ottawa: Minister of Supply & Service.

Canadian Race Relations Foundation 2001. Toronto: Canadian Race Relations

Foundation.

Cardinal, Harold. 1969. *Unjust Society: The Tragedy of Canada's Indians*. Edmonton: M.G. Hurtig.

Carniol, Ben. 1992. "Structural Social Work: Maurice Moreau's challenge to social work practice." *Journal of Progressive Human Services*. 3(1): 1–20.

_____. 1990. *Case Critical*. Toronto: Between the Lines.

Carnoy, Martin. 1974. *Education as Cultural Imperialism*. New York: David McKay.

Carpenter, Jock. 1977. *Fifty Dollar Bride: Marie Rose Smith, A Chronicle of Métis Life in the 19th Century*. Sidney, BC: Gray's Publishing.

Chaitow, Leon. 1987. *Vaccination and Immunization: Dangers, Delusions and Alternatives. (What every parent should know)*. Saffron Walden, England: C.W. Daniel Co.

Charnley, Kerrie. 1990. "Concepts of Anger, Identity and Power and the Visions in the Writings and Voices of First Nation's Women." *Gatherings: The En'owkin Journal of First North American People* 1(Fall): 10–22.

Chartier, Clem 1988. *In the Best Interests of the Métis Child*. Saskatoon: University of Saskatchewan, Native Law Centre.

Chesler, Phyllis. 1987. *Mothers on Trial: The Battle for Children and Custody*. Seattle, WA: Seal Press.

_____. 1979. *With Child: A Diary of Motherhood*. New York: Thomas Y. Crowell.

Christian Peacemaker Teams. 2001. *Gunboat Diplomacy: Canada's Abuse of Human Rights at Esgenoopetitj (Burnt Church, NB)*. Toronto: The Teams.

Collins, Patricia Hill. 1991. *Black Feminist Thought*. New York: Routledge.

Coltelli, Laura. 1990. *Winged Words: American Indian Writers Speak*. Lincoln, NB: University of Nebraska Press.

Connors, Edward. 1994. "The Role of Spirituality in Wellness or How Well We Can See the Whole Will Determine How Well We Are and How Well We Can Become." Paper presented at the Native Physicians Conference, Winnipeg, MB. March 6–8.

Chrystos. 1995. *Fire Power*. Vancouver: Press Gang.

_____. 1993. *In Her I Am*. Vancouver: Press Gang.

_____. 1991. *Dream On*. Vancouver: Press Gang.

_____. 1988 *Not Vanishing*. Vancouver: Press Gang.

Cruikshank, Julie. 1992. *Life Lived Like a Story*. Vancouver: University of British Columbia Press.

Culleton Moosionier, Beatrice. 2000. *In the Shadow of Evil*. Penticton, BC: Theytus.

Culleton, Beatrice. 1983 (1984. 1999). *In Search of April Raintree*. Winnipeg: Pemmican.

Cuthand, Stan. 1988. *Nehiyaw atayokewina: Cree Legends: Stories of Waisakecaahk*. Saskatoon: The Centre.

CASSW. 1998. *Canadian Association of Schools of Social Work Accreditation Guidelines*.

Deloria Jr., Vine. 1994. *God is Red: A Native View of Religion*. Golden, Co:

Fulcrum.

Dion Buffalo, Yvonne Rita. 1990. "Seeds of Thought, Arrows of Change: Native Storytelling as metaphor." In Toni Laidlaw, Cheryl Malmo and Associates. *Healing Voices: Feminist Approaches to Therapy With Women*. San Francisco: Jossey-Bass.

Dumont, Gabriel. 1993. *Gabriel Dumont Speaks (1838–1906)*. Michael Barnholder (trans.) Vancouver: Talonbooks.

Employment and Immigration Canada. 1994. *Employment Equity: Federal Contractors Program, questions and answers*. Ottawa.

English-Currie, Vicki. 1990. "The Need for Re-Evaluation in Native Education." In Jeanne Pereault and Sylvia Vance (eds.) *Writing the Circle: Native Women of Western Canada*. Edmonton: NeWest.

Eramus, George. 1989. "Twenty Years of Disappointed Hopes." In Boyce Richardson (ed.) *Drumbeat: Anger and renewal in Indian Country*. Toronto: Summerhill.

Erdrich, Louise.1998. *Beet Queen*. New York: Harper Flamingo.

_____. 1995. *The Blue Jay's Dance*. New York: Harper Collins.

_____. 1993. *Love Medicine*. New York: Henry Holt.

_____. 1988. *Tracks*. New York: Henry Holt and Company.

Estes, Clarissa Pinkola. 1992. *Women Who Run with the Wolves*. Toronto: Random House.

Fife, Connie. 1993. *The Colour of Resistance: A Contemporary Collection of Writing by Aboriginal Women*. Toronto: Sister Vision.

Fineman, Martha, and Isabel Karpin. 1995. *Mothers in Law: Feminist Theory and the Legal Regulation of Motherhood*. New York: Columbia University Press.

Fiske, Jo-Anne. 1991. "Gender and the Paradox of Residential Education in Carrier Society." In Jane Gaskell and Arlene McLaren (eds.) *Women and Education*. Calgary: Detselig.

Fleury, Norman. 2000. *LaLawng: Michif Peekishkwewin (or the Canadian Michif Language Dictionary): Introduction level*. Winnipeg: MMF Mitchif Language Program.

Fournier, Suzanne, and Ernie Crey. 1997. *Stolen from Our Embrace: The Abduction of First Nations Children and the Restoration of Aboriginal Communities*. Vancouver: Douglas and McIntyre.

Fox-Genovese, Elizabeth. 1991. *Feminism without Illusions: A critique of Individualism*. Chapel Hill: University of North Carolina Press.

Freedman, Jill, and Gene Combs. 1996. *Narrative Therapy: The Social Construction of Preferred Realities*. New York: WW Norton and Company.

Freire, Paulo. 2000. *Pedagogy of the Oppressed*. New York: Continuum International Publishing Group.

_____. 1985. "Rethinking Critical Pedagogy: A dialogue with Paulo Freire." In *The Politics of Education: Culture, Power and Liberation*. South Hadley, MA: Bergin and Garvey.

_____. 1972. *Cultural Action for Freedom*. Harmondsworth: Penguin.

Frye, Marilyn. 1983. *The Politics of Reality: Essays in Feminist Theory*. Trumansburg, NY: Crossing.

Fulani, Lenora. 1988. *The Psychopathology of Everyday Racism and Sexism*. New York: Harrington Park Press.

Gitlin, Todd. 1980. *The Whole World is Watching: Mass Media in the Making and Unmaking of the New Left*. Berkeley, CA: University of California Press.

Gladding, Samuel. 1995. *Group Work: A Counselling Specialty*. Englewood Cliffs, NJ: Prentice Hall.

Godard, Barbara. 1992. "The Politics of Representation: Some Native women writers." In W.H. New (ed.) *Native Writers and Canadian Writing*. Vancouver: University of British Columbia Press.

Goehring, Brian. 1993. *Indigenous Peoples of the World: An Introduction to their Past, Present and Future*. Saskatoon: Purich Publishing.

Grant, Agnes. 1996. *No End of Grief: Indian Residential Schools in Canada*. Winnipeg: Pemmican.

Graveline, Fyre Jean. 2004 (forthcoming). "Caged-In Eurocentrism: Aboriginal Un-Clusion in the Canadian Nation State." In Joy Mannette (ed.) *The Presence of Absence: Reconceptualizing Nation in the Neo-colonial Canadian Context*. Halifax: Fernwood.

_____. 2004. "What Part of No Don't You Understand?" *American Indian Quarterly* 27, 1 and 2 (edited by Devon A. Mihesuah).

_____. 2002. "I know how and when but never why." In Elana Hannah, Linda Paul and Swani Vethamany-Globus (eds.) *Women in the Canadian Academic Tundra: Challenging the Chill*. McGill-Queen's University Press.

_____. 2000a. "Lived experiences of an Aboriginal Feminist Transforming the Curriculum." In Carl James (ed.) *Experiencing Difference*. Halifax: Fernwood.

_____. 2001. "Imagine My Surprise: Smudge Teaches Holistic Lessons." *Canadian Journal of Native Education*, Special Issue: *Sharing Aboriginal Knowledge and Aboriginal Ways of Knowing*. 25(1): 6–17.

_____. 2000b. "Circle as Methodology: Enacting an Aboriginal paradigm." *International Journal of Qualitative Studies in Education*. Special Issue: Through our Own Eyes & In Our Own Words. 13(4): 361–370

_____. 1999. "Trickster Teaches: Doing Means Being Done To." *Atlantis*. 24(1) (Fall): 4–14.

_____. 1998. *Circle Works: Transforming Eurocentric Consciousness*. Halifax: Fernwood.

_____. 1994. "Lived Experiences of an Aboriginal Feminist Transforming the Curriculum." *Canadian Women's Studies*. 14(2) (Spring): 52–55.

Graveline, Madeline Jean. 1996. *Circle as Pedagogy: Aboriginal Tradition Enacted in a University Classroom*. Unpublished Thesis. Halifax: Dalhousie University.

Guba, E. 1990. *The Paradigm Dialogue*. Newbury Park: Sage.

Gunn, Rita, and Candice Minch. 1988. *Sexual Assault: The Dilemma of Disclosure, the Question of Conviction*. Winnipeg: University of Manitoba Press.

Gunn Allen, Paula. 1998. *Off the Reservation: Reflections of Boundary Busting, Border*

Crossing. *Loose Canons*. Boston: Beacon.

_____. 1991. *Grandmothers of the Light: A Medicine Woman's Sourcebook*. Boston: Beacon.

_____. 1986. *The Sacred Hoop: Recovering the Feminine in American Indian Traditions*. Boston: Beacon.

Haig-Brown, Celia. 1988. *Resistance and Renewal: Surviving the Indian Residential School*. Vancouver: Tillicum.

Hall, Kira, and Mary Bucholtz. 1995. *Gender Articulated: Language and the Socially Constructed Self*. New York: Routledge.

Hall, Stuart. 1991. "Ethnicity: Identity and Difference." *Radical America* 24(4): 9–20.

Hamilton, A.C., and C.M. Sinclair. 1991. *Report on the Public Inquiry into the Administration of Justice and Aboriginal People (Manitoba) Vol. I & II*. Winnipeg: Queen's Printer.

Harding, Sandra. 1991. *Whose Science? Whose Knowledge?* Ithaca, NY: Cornell University Press.

_____. 1987. *Feminism and Methodology*. Milton Keyes: Open University Press.

Harjo, Joy, and Gloria Bird. 1997. *Reinventing the Enemy's Language*. New York: W.W. Norton.

Harrison, Julia. 1985. *Métis: People between the Two Worlds*. Vancouver: Douglas and McIntyre.

Hart, Mechtild. 1991. "Liberation Through Consciousness-Raising." In Jack Mezirow (ed.) *Fostering Critical Reflection in Adulthood*. San Francisco: Jossey-Bass.

Hart, Mechtild, and Deborah Wood Holton. 1993. "Beyond God the Father and the Mother: Adult Education and Spirituality." In Peter Jarvis and Nicholas Walters (eds.) *Adult Education and Theological Interpretations*. Melbourne, FL: Krieger.

Helms, J. 1990. *Black and White Racial Iidentity: Theory, Research and Practices*. Westport, CT: Greenwood.

Hepworth, Dean, and Jo Ann Larsen. 1986. *Direct Social Work Practice: Theory and Skills*. New York: Dorsey Press.

Hogan, Linda. 2001. *The Woman Who Watches over the World*. New York: W.W. Norton.

_____. 1998. *Power*. New York: W.W. Norton.

_____. 1995. *Dwellings: A Spiritual History of the Living World*. New York: W.W. Norton.

hooks, bell. 2000. *All About Love*. New York: Harper Collins.

_____. 2000. *Feminist Theory: From Margin to Centre*. Cambridge, MA: South End Press.

_____. 1994. *Teaching to Transgress*. New York: Routledge.

_____. 1990. *Yearning*. Toronto: Between the Lines.

_____. 1989. *Talking Back*. Toronto: Between the Lines.

_____. 1981. *Ain't I a Woman*. Boston, MA: South End Press,

Howse, Yvonne, and Harvey Stalwick. 1990. "Social Work and the First Nations Movement: Our Children, our Culture." In Brian Wharf (ed.) *Social Work and Social Change in Canada*. Toronto: McClelland and Stewart.

Hudnall Stamm, B. 1999. *Secondary Traumatic Stress*. Lutherville, ML: Sidran Press.

Hylton, John. 1994. *Aboriginal Self-Government in Canada: Current Trends and Issues*. Saskatoon: Purich.

Irwin, Lee. 1997. "Freedom, Law, and Prophecy: A brief history of Native American religious resistance." *American Indian Quarterly* 21(1): 35–55.

James, Carl. 2000. *Experiencing Difference*. Halifax: Fernwood.

James, Carl, and Adrienne Shadd. 1996. *Talking About Identity*. Toronto: Between the Lines.

Jay, Gregory. 1995. "Taking Multiculturalism Personally: Ethnos and ethos in the classroom." In Jane Gallop (ed.) *Pedagogy: The Question of Impersonation*. Bloomington: Indiana University Press.

Jevne, Ronna Fay. 1998. *When Dreams Don't Work: Professional Caregivers and Burnout*. Amityville, NY: Baywood.

Kaiser, Rudolf. 1991. *The Voice of the Great Spirit: Prophecies of the Hopi Indians*. Boston: Shambhala.

Kalia, Seema. 1991. "Addressing Race in the Feminist Classroom." In Jane Gaskell and Arlene McLaren (eds.) *Women and Education*. Calgary: Detselig.

Kasl, Charlotte Davis. 1992. *Many Roads, One Journey: Moving beyond the 12 Steps*. New York: Harper Collins.

Katz, Judith. 1985. "The Sociopolitical Nature of Counselling." *The Counselling Psychologist* 13(4): 615–24.

Katz, R., and V. St. Denis. 1991. "Teacher as Healer." *Journal of Indigenous Studies* 2(2): 24–36.

Kearney, Michael. 1984. *Worldview*. Novato, CA: Chandler and Sharp.

Keeshig-Tobias, Lenore. 1996. *Into the Moon: Heart, Mind, Body, Soul*. Toronto: Sister Vision.

_____. 1992. "Trickster Beyond 1992: Our relationship." In Gerald McMaster and Lee-Ann Martin (eds.) *Indigena*. Vancouver: Douglas and McIntyre.

Kelly, Jennifer. 1998. *Under the Gaze*. Halifax: Fernwood.

Kelusultiek: Original Women's Voices of Atlantic Canada. 1994. Halifax: Mount St. Vincent University.

King, Thomas. 1990. *All My Relations*. Toronto: McClelland and Stewart.

Kline, Marlee. 1992. "Child Welfare Law, 'Best Interests of the Child' Ideology, and First Nations." *Osgood Hall Law Journal* 30(2): 376–425.

Knockwood, Isabelle. 1992. *Out of the Depths: The Experiences of Mi'Kmaw Children at the Indian Residential School at Shubenacadie*. Lockeport, NS: Roseway.

Kulchyski, Peter, Don McCaskill and David Newhouse. 1999. *In the Words of Elders: Aboriginal Cultures in Transition*. Toronto: University of Toronto Press.

Ladd-Taylor, Molly, and Lauri Umansky. 1998. *"Bad" Mothers: The Politics of Blame in Twentieth Century America*. New York: New York University Press.

LaRocque, Emma. 1991. "Racism Runs through Canadian Society." In Ormond McKague (ed.) *Racism in Canada*. Saskatoon: Fifth House.

Lather, Patricia. 1991. *Getting Smart*. London: Routledge.

Laub, Dori. 1995. "Truth and Testimony: The process and the struggle." In Cathy Caruth (ed.) *Trauma: Explorations in Memory*. Baltimore, MD: Johns Hopkins University Press.

Leonard, Peter. 1990. "Fatalism and the Discourse on Power: An introductory essay." In Linda Davies and Eric Shragge (eds.) *Bureaucracy and Community*. Montreal: Black Rose.

Lewis, Tanya. 1999. *Living Beside: Performing normal after incest memories return*. Toronto: McGilligan Books.

Longfish, George. 1992. "Portfolio." In Gerald McMaster and Lee-Ann Martin (eds.) *Indigena*. Vancouver: Douglas and McIntyre.

Lutz, Harmut. 1991. *Contemporary Challenges: Conversations with Canadian Native Authors*. Saskatoon: Fifth House.

MacEwan, Grant. 1984. *Marie Anne: The Frontier Adventures of Marie Anne Lagimodiere*. Saskatoon: Western Producer Prairie Books.

Manitoba Indian Brotherhood. 1977. *The Shocking Truth about Indians in Textbooks*. Winnipeg.

Manuel, George. 1974. *The Fourth World: An Indian Reality*. Don Mills, ON: Collier-MacMillan.

Maracle, Brian. 1994. *Crazy Water: Native Voices on Addiction and Recovery*. Toronto: Penguin.

Maracle, Lee. 2002. *Daughters are Forever*. Vancouver: Raincoast Books.

_____. 1996. (1988) *I Am Woman*. North Vancouver: Press Gang.

_____. 1990. *Bobbi Lee: Indian Rebel*. Toronto: Women's Press.

marino, dian. 1997. *Wild Garden: Art, Education and the Culture of Resistance*. Toronto: Between the Lines

Marsden, Rasunah. 2000. *Crisp Blue Edges: Indigenous Creative Non-fiction*. Penticton, BC: Theytus Books.

Maslach, Christina. 1982. *Burnout: The Cost of Caring*. Englewood Cliffs, NJ: Prentice-Hall.

McCormick, Rod. 1994. *The Facilitation of Healing for First Nations People of British Columbia*. Unpublished Dissertation. University of British Columbia, Vancouver, BC.

McGillivray, Anne, and Brenda Comaskey. 1999. *Black Eyes All of the Time: Intimate Violence, Aboriginal Women and the Justice System*. Toronto: University of Toronto Press.

McIntosh, Peggy. 1990. "White Privilege: Unpacking the invisible knapsack." *Independent School* (Winter): 31–36.

McMahon, Anthony, and Paula Allen-Meares. 1992. "Is Social Work Racist? A content analysis of recent literature." *Social Work* 37(6): 533–539.

McMaster, Gerald, and Lee-Ann Martin. 1992. *Indigena.* Vancouver: Douglas and McIntyre.

McLeans. 1986. "A Canadian Tragedy" (14 July).

McTaggart, Lynne. 1991. *The wddty Vaccination Handbook: A Guide to the Dangers of Childhood Immuizations.* London: Wallace Press.

Means, Russell. 1995. *Where White Men Fear to Tread.* New York: St. Martin's Press.

_____. 1980. "Fighting Words on the Future of the Earth." *Mother Jones* (December): 22–28.

Medicine, Beatrice. 1987. "My Elders Tell Me." In Jean Barman, Yvonne Hebert and Don McCaskill (eds.) *Indian Education in Canada, Volume 2: The challenge.* Vancouver: University of British Columbia Press.

Meili, Dianne. 1992. *Those Who Know: Profile of Alberta's Native Elders.* Edmonton: NeWest Press.

Merchant, Carolyn. 1989. *Ecological Revolutions.* Chapel Hill: University of North Carolina Press.

Mihesuah, Devon A. 1996. "American Indians, Anthropologists, Pothunters, and Repatriation: Ethical, religious and political differences." *American Indian Quarterly* 20(2): 229–237.

Miller, J.R. 1996. *Shingwauk's Vision: A History of Native Residential Schools.* Toronto: University of Toronto Press.

_____. 1991. *Skyscrapers Hide the Heavens: A History of Indian-White Relations in Canada.* Toronto: University of Toronto Press.

Milloy, John. 1999. *A National Crime: The Canadian Government and Residential School System 1879–1986.* Winnipeg: University of Manitoba Press.

Minh-ha, Trinh. 1989. *Woman, Native, Other.* Bloomington: Indiana University Press.

Mohanty, Chandra. 1994. "On Race and Voice: Challenges for liberal education in the 1990's." In Henry Giroux and Peter McLaren (eds.) *Between Borders: Pedagogy and the Politics of Cultural Studies.* New York: Routledge.

Monture-Angus, Patricia. 1999. *Journeying Forward: Dreaming First Nations' Independence.* Halifax: Fernwood.

_____. 1995. *Thunder in My Soul: A Mohawk Woman Speaks.* Halifax: Fernwood.

Morrisseau, Calvin. 1998. *Into the Daylight: A Wholistic Approach to Healing.* Toronto: University of Toronto Press.

Murray, Laura, and Keren Rice. 1999. *Talking on the Page.* Toronto: University of Toronto Press.

Medical Services Branch (MSB). 1991. *Agenda for First Nations and Inuit Mental Health.* Ministry of Health, Government of Canada.

New, W.H. 1992. *Native Writing and Canadian Writing.* Vancouver: UBC Press.

Niezen, Ronald. 2003. *The Origins of Indigenism.* Berkeley: University of California Press.

Ng, Roxanna. 1991. "Teaching Against the Grain: Contradictions for minority teachers." In Jane Gaskell and Arlene McLaren (eds.) *Women and Education.*

Calgary: Detselig.

Obomsawin, Alanis. 1986. *Richard Cardinal: Cry from a Diary of a Métis Child.* Montreal: NFB.

O'Brien, Sharon. 1989. *American Indian Tribal Governments.* Norman: University of Oklahoma Press.

O'Hallarn, B. 1999. "Natives Burn Over Smudge Incident." *Winnipeg Sun,* March 11.

Opasquia Times. 1987. 10(73). Nov. 27 (8).

Opasquia Times. 1987. 10(74). Dec. 2 (1).

O'Reilly, Edmund. 1997. *Sobering Tales: Narratives on Alcoholism and Recovery.* Amherst: University of Massachusetts Press.

Paul, Daniel. 2000. *We Were Not the Savages: A Mi'kmaq Perspective on the Collision between European and Native American Civilizations.* Halifax: Fernwood.

Perreault, Jeanne, and Sylvia Vance. 1990. *Writing the Circle: Native Women of Western Canada.* Edmonton: NeWest.

Pettipas, Katherine. 1994. *Severing the Ties that Bind: Government Repression of Indigenous Religious Ceremonies on the Prairies.* Winnipeg: University of Manitoba Press.

Priest, Lisa. 1989. *Conspiracy of Silence.* Toronto: McClelland and Stewart.

Raymond, Janice. 1985. "Women's Studies: A knowledge of one's own." In Margo Culley and Catherine Portugese (eds.) *Gendered Subjects: The Dynamics of Feminist Teaching.* Boston: Routledge and Kegan Paul.

Razak, Sherene. 1998. *Looking White People In the Eye: Gender Race and Culture in Courtrooms and Classrooms.* Toronto: University of Toronto Press.

Richardson, Boyce. 1991. *Strangers Devour the Land.* Vancouver: Douglas and McIntyre.

_____. (ed.). 1989. *Drumbeat: Anger and renewal in Indian Country.* Toronto: Summerhill Press/Assembly of First Nations.

Robertson, Robbie. 1994 "Words of Fire, Deeds of Blood." On Robbie Robertson and the Red Road Ensemble. *Music for The Native Americans.* Capitol Records.

Rosco, Will. 1988. *Living the Spirit.* New York: St. Martin's Press.

Rossiter, Amy. 1995. "Teaching Social Work Skills from a Critical Perspective." *Canadian Social Work Review* 12(1): 2–25.

Russell, Edmund. 2001. *War and Nature: Fighting Humans and Insects with Chemicals from WWI to Silent Spring.* Cambridge, MA: Cambridge University Press.

Said, Edward. 1993. *Culture and Imperialism.* New York: Knopf.

Schniedewind, Nancy. 1978. *Confronting Racism and Sexism: A Practical Handbook for Educators.* New Paltz, NY: Commonground Press.

Sealey, Bruce (ed.). 1975. *Stories of the Métis.* Winnipeg: Manitoba Métis Federation.

Siggins, Maggie. 1994. *Riel: A Life of Revolution.* Toronto: Harper Collins.

Silko, Leslie. 1981. *Storyteller.* New York: Seaver.

Singleton, Sharon. 1994. "Faculty Personal Comfort and the Teaching of Content on Racial Oppression." *Journal of Multicultural Social Work* 3(1): 5–16.

Sleeter, Christine. 1994. "White Racism." *Multicultural Education* (Spring): 5–8.

_____. 1993. "How White Teachers Construct Race." In Cameron McCarthy and Warren Crichlow (eds.) *Race, Identity and Representation in Education.* New York: Routledge.

Slipperjack, Ruby. 2000. *Weesaquachak and the Lost Ones.* Penticton, BC: Theytus.

_____. 1992. *Silent Words.* Saskatoon: Fifth House.

_____. 1987. *Honour the Sun.* Winnipeg: Pemmican.

Smith, Dorothy. 1987. *The Everyday World as Problematic.* Boston: Northeastern University Press.

_____. 1973. "The Social Construction of Documentary Reality." *Sociological Inquiry* 44(4): 257–268.

Spelman, Elizabeth. 1988. *Inessential Woman: Problems of Exclusion in Feminist Thought.* Boston: Beacon.

St. Marie, Buffy. 1992. "Priests of the Golden Bull." On *Coincidence and Likely Stories.* CD. Chrysalis Records.

St. Pierre, Mark, and Tilda Long Soldier. 1995. *Walking in the Sacred Manner.* New York: Touchstone.

Starhawk. 1987. *Truth or Dare.* San Francisco: Harper and Row.

Supernault, Ester. 1995. *A Warrior's Heart.* Edmonton: Native Counselling Services of Alberta.

Swan, Margaret. 1999. *Windspeaker* 16(11): 1.

Tal, Kali. 1996. *Worlds of Hurt.* Cambridge, MA: Cambridge University Press.

Tedlock, Barbara, and Dennis Tedlock. 1975. *Teachings from the American Earth.* New York: Liveright Press.

Teichroeb, Ruth. 1997. *Flowers on My Grave: How an Ojibwa Boy's Death Helped Break the Silence on Child Abuse.* Toronto: HarperCollins.

Thomm, Winnie. 1989. *The Effects of Feminist Approaches on Research Methodology.* Waterloo: Wilfred Laurier Press.

Thompson, Edward Palmer. 1991. *Customs in Common.* London: Merlin.

Todd, Loretta. 1992. "What More Do They Want?" In Gerald McMaster and Lee-Ann Martin (eds.) *Indigena.* Vancouver: Douglas and McIntyre.

Warry, Wayne 1998. *Unfinished Dreams: Community Healing and the Reality of Aboriginal Self Government.* Toronto: University of Toronto Press.

Wassil-Grimm, Claudette. 1995. *Diagnosis for Disaster: The Devastating Truth about False Memory Syndrome and its Impact on Accusers and Families.* Woodstock, NY: Overlook.

Wastasecoot, Brenda. 2000. *A Study of Aboriginal Healing/Counselling Experiences: In Search of Culturally Effective Counselling for Aboriginal People.* Unpublished Thesis. Brandon University, Brandon, MB.

Weatherford, Jack. 1988. *Indian Givers: How the Indians of the Americas Transformed the World.* New York: Fawcett Columbine.

West, Cornel. 1993. "The New Cultural Politics of Difference." In Simon During (ed.) *The Cultural Studies Reader.* New York: Routledge.

Whitehead, Paul C., and Michael J. Hayes. 1998. *The Insanity of Alcohol: Social Problems in Canadian First Nations Communities.* Toronto: Canadian Scholars' Press.

Woodcock, George. 1976. *Gabriel Dumont: The Métis Chief and His Lost World.* Edmonton: Hurtig.

Wyman, Richard (ed.). 1991. *Global Climate Change and Life on Earth.* New York: Routledge, Chapman and Hall.

ACKNOWLEDGEMENTS

I gotta say.
  someTimes. I need Help. ask for It. get It. get more than I ask for.
                    in my Life. on ThisBook.
I gotta say. *Thanks.*
  Ki'nunas'komítin.
    to Ancestors.GrandMothers. for Inspiration. StoryTelling.
  Ki'nunas'komítin.
    to MaryAnn Whitefish. my Partner.
      Traditional Cree. Beadwork Artist. StoryTeller.
      for generously Giving. Collaborating. on Cover design.
                          Mahe'kun Stories.
                          Cree translation.
  Ki'nunas'komítin.
    to Aldin Foy. AnishnabeArtist.Academic.
      for Reading.Rereading. Commenting.Critiquing.
      for Transforming Art. from technicolor. to monochrome.
  Ki'nunas'komítin.
    to informal.formal. friendly.critical. Reviewers.
      some Anonymous. who know who you are.
      some Known. Zabet. Bev. Kim. Glenda.
  Ki'nunas'komítin.
    to my Daughter.
      for last line of WARNING!!!
      and reminders to add funny parts.
        "who wants all mad and sad? mom?"
  Ki'nunas'komítin.
    to Manitoba Arts Council. for buying me some writing Time.
    to Fernwood staff. Wayne. Bev. Brenda. Debbie.
  Ki'nunas'komítin.
    to those who discover.uncover. themSelves. in Stories.
      you make Telling worthwhile.
So. I gotta say. *Ki'nunas'komítin.*
      to All. I Story about. Story with.
      for helping Birth. ThisBook. Together.